CW00552464

BLAISDON

MEMORIES OF A COUNTRY PARISH

Blaisdon: A quiet country village c1950,
Mrs Oscar Jones with nieces, Vera & Doreen Jones
& Joe, the dog.

BLAISDON

VOL 2

MEMORIES OF A COUNTRY PARISH
1935-1964.

ELIZABETH ETHERINGTON
MARGARET HOGG
STEPHEN WATERS

BLAISDON PLUMLICATIONS

First Published 2010
Reprinted 2011

Blaisdon Plumlications
The Temple
Longhope
Gloucestershire
GL17 0NZ
Email: blaisdon@hotmail.co.uk

© E Perry, M Hogg, S Waters 2010

All rights reserved. No part of this book may be reprinted or reproduced or utilised in any form
or by any electronic, mechanical or other means, now known or hereafter invented, including
photocopying and recording, or in any information storage or retrieval system, without the
permission in writing from the Publishers.

The right of E Perry, M Hogg and S Waters to be identified as the Authors of this work has been
asserted in accordance with the Copyrights, Designs and Patents Act 1988.

British Library Cataloguing in Publication Data.
A catalogue record for this book is available from the British Library.

ISBN: 978-0-9543775-1-9

Printed by Gomer Press, Llandysul, Ceredigion, SA44 4JL.

Dedicated
To the memory of

Cedric & Dinah Etherington
Frank & Elsie Hogg

And all who have loved Blaisdon

24 October 2010

Like most people I have a fascination with the past, not only the great national and international events that shaped our country and our world, but a curiosity about the people and places that directly influenced my life. This is one of the many reasons that I warmly welcome this book about Blaisdon, the plum village that has been my home since 1966.

In many ways this is an oral history, skillfully woven together by the authors, a collection of living memories about families and the homes in which they lived. It is a rural history that provides us with a picture of the reality of village life, the daily challenges and experiences, the joys and sorrows of people living in a small community, my community, on the edge of the Forest of Dean.

This is a fascinating story for anyone who lives, or used to live, in Blaisdon, but it is also an important piece of social history that helps us to better understand our past and therefore our present. When I look out of my window it seems as if little has changed over the last hundred years or so, but this book tells me that looks can be deceptive. There have been huge changes in our village life, but I celebrate the fact that we still live in a beautiful village, a community.

Elizabeth Etherington, Stephen Waters and others have done a magnificent job putting together this wonderful patchwork of memories. Thank you.

Baroness Royall of Blaisdon

I came to live in Blaisdon in 1977 some thirteen years after the

closure of the school and railway and although so much of what is

recorded here was before my time I knew the parents of Elizabeth

Etherington and Margaret Hogg.

Liz has enjoyed continuing her father Cedric's research into the

history of this tiny community while Elsie and Frank Hogg were

still running the Red Hart.

The changes in village life within the span of this book were some of

the biggest in its history and this is a wonderful record of how it has

evolved. In only a few years so much of the knowledge and stories could

have been lost forever but it is now in print to inspire and encourage those

who are lucky enough to live in Blaisdon to preserve its traditions of

community spirit and care for all aspects of village life.

Rosemary Wagstaff for her delightful letter artwork throughout the book. Her beautiful work can be seen in full colour on her 'Words of Art' website (www.words-of-art.com).

Brian Jones for painstakingly creating period maps to guide readers through the Parish.

Nigel Hogg for his tireless work and many hours spent in proofreading the entire book.

Tony Brady for his support during the last year and also for encouraging his fellow 'Old Blaisdon Hall Boys,' to provide insights and photographs of their days in Blaisdon.

Jean Waters and Tony Budden for lending Steve and Margaret to the project.

Joey Vick for her help and support.

Last, but not least, a huge 'thank you' to all the contributors who have made this book possible. This book is a lovely record of our time growing up in Blaisdon village, Woodgreen and Nottwood Hill, which can be treasured and passed down to the future generations.

Except where indicated, photographs have been provided by the families concerned, who retain the originals. Every effort has been made to locate copyright holders and obtain permission. Any omission or error brought to our attention will be remedied in future editions.

The idea for this book was conceived one beautiful Sunday afternoon following a good lunch at the Bistro Restaurant, at the end of Frampton on Severn's village green. Elizabeth, Josephine and myself, Margaret, had gone to revisit the village where Josephine, my sister, Iris, and I were born and, specifically, to visit the church where we were all christened more than 60 years before. It was outside the church that Elizabeth produced a scrapbook from the boot of her car, which she had put together detailing her family history, using old letters and photographs that had recently come into her possession. It was so good. We talked about it and decided that we ought to do something similar, capturing village life as we knew it, growing up in Blaisdon. From these first musings, the beginnings of this book were born. We decided we would take each house in turn, starting at the bottom of the village at Blaisdon Halt. We would write a short note about each of the families who occupied the houses from the mid 1930s to 1964 when the railway and village school closed. Once we started, the enthusiasm of the people we approached was overwhelming and the project grew and grew, until a small project became a big one that has taken about 4 years work from start to finish.

It has been, for us, a journey of discovery and a rekindling of old friendships. We hope you enjoy reading these stories, told by the people themselves, and seeing the old photographs that go with the tales as much as we have enjoyed collecting them. Memories may be happy, sad or amusing. One person's memory of a certain event may differ from another's, but after all these years, who can say with certainty, which account is the most accurate? One thing is certain; village life will never again be quite like it was back then.

Elizabeth Perry (nee Etherington) and Margaret Hogg.

St Michael & All Angels.

The production of this book is to support our Parish Church, which remains central to the village community. Village people are remembered on the War Memorial and on memorials in the church and the many gravestones around it. Many will have worshipped here and it has been the scene of christenings, marriages and funerals, thanksgiving in good times and intercessions in bad. Many whose pictures grace the pages of this book now rest in the tranquil churchyard that surrounds the church.

People come and go but St Michael's has remained as a constant cornerstone of the community and, hopefully, will remain so for future generations. The authors are grateful to the numerous people who have made this book possible, so that it can contribute, albeit in a small way, to enable the church to go forward into the future to benefit and be enjoyed by many future generations of Blaisdon Parishioners.

CONTRIBUTORS

Our thanks go to the following people and where relevant, their families, who have contributed to this book and without whom its production would not have been possible.

Peter & Jean Adams
Jack Alcock & Jennifer Griffiths
Doug Allen
Jim Allum
Pam Allum
Andrew Ashcroft
Elizabeth Ashcroft
Ben Ashworth
George & Beryl Austin
Michael Ayland
Sue Baber (nee Harvey)
Judith Badminton (nee Pickering)
Kevin & Angela Baker
Margaret & Claude Barnard
Christine Barnard
Ken & Glenys Barnard
Heather Boakes
Jenny Bomberg
Sue & Peter Booth
Alastair C Bourne
Tony Brady
Shirley Brickel
Lewis Brooks
Colin Brown
David & Pauline Brown
Gill Brown
Travers, Joan & Paul Buckley

Madelaine Burns.
Margaret Cale (nee Dowding)
The late Janet Coldrick (nee Brown)
Arthur Carpenter
Ron & Jackie Carpenter
Helen Clare (nee MacIver)
Clive Clayson
Mary Cole
Margaret Cookson (nee Ashcroft)
Mrs Crompton
Bert and Sheila Daniell
Arthur Davies
Ursula Davis (nee Howells)
Barry & Doreen Davis
Elena Dickinson
John Dunbar
David East
David Eggleton
Roger Etherington
Michael Etherington
Sheila & Ceri Evans
Iris Faulkner (nee Hogg)
Susan Gobbin (nee Young)
Jackie Goode (nee Smith)
Mary Goulding (nee Jones)
Anita Grace (nee Martin)
Freddie & Valerie Grace

Ashley Green
Phillip & Susan Green
Carlton Green
Peggy Wellington (nee Gregson)
Doris Hadley (nee Bowkett)
Brenda Hales (nee Brain)
Penny Harris
Geoff Hart
Bryan & Barbara Hayward
Peter & Eunice Hayward
Russell Hayward
Hilary Hawker
Maureen Hending (nee Blake)
John & Pat Higgins
The late Elsie Hogg
Nigel Hogg
Ann & Mark Hopkins
The late Molly Hopkins
David Hudson
Alice Hyett (nee Rickett)
Hilary Jayne
Anthony Jones
Betty Jones (nee Pugh)
Brian Jones
Michael Jones
Roger Jones
Sandra Jones

Gerald & Megan Kear

Kevin Keating

Michael Keating

The late Ada Keyse

Roger & Aubrey Keyse

David Kibble

Tony Kibble

Elaine Lanciano (nee Smith)

Beryl Little (nee Walker)

Tessa Lysaght (nee Back)

Michael McKenna

Mrs Maddock

The late Ruth Magee

Christopher & Patricia Manners

David & Sharon Marshall

John & Daphne Martin

The late Fred Matthews

Catherine Millin (nee Jones)

Rosa Millin (nee Bowkett)

David & Janet Morris

Will Nicol

Eric Nutcher

Sue Oldham

Chris O'Carroll

The late John O'Reilly

Neville & Margaret Pailing

Dr Ken Parsons

Brian Pearce

Gerald Pedley

Norman Penny

Humphrey Phelps

Rachel Price (nee Hayward)

Elizabeth Pymont

Joan Reid (nee Wyman)

Don & Ann Rich

Jill Rodgett

Janet Royall

Gerald Savage

Colin Shannon

Fiona Shaw

Rosemary Skivington (nee Keating)

Ann Smith

John Smith

Lawrence Stanton

Jean Stone (nee Allum)

Geoff & Sue Sterry

Barbara Taylor

Dennis Tobin

Betty Toombs (nee Howells)

Josephine Vick (nee Warlow)

Rosemary Wagstaff

Susan Waldron (nee Evans)

Richard Walton

Leslie & Rose Warren

Wendy Warner (nee Brain)

Jean Waters

Lynn Watkins

Nancy Watkins (nee Bate)

Pam Weaver (nee Pensom)

Gilly Wells

Guy Wilkins

Sally Wynn

The Forest Review

British Library

Jamaican High Commissioner

Imperial War Museum

Haresfield Parish Church

David Read, Soldiers of Gloucester Museum

SUBSCRIBERS

Our thanks to the following, whose generous subscriptions
have contributed towards the production of this book.

Peter & Jean Adams

Margaret Allen

Stephen Allum

Christine Pimm

Jean Stone

Pam Allum

Kevin and Angela Baker

Ken Barnard

Margaret, Claude and
        Christine Barnard

Peter and Sue Booth

Richard Boyles

Tony Brady

Colin Brown

Joyce Deakins

Shirley Barnard

Sally Syed

Eric & Angela Brown

Peter & Chris Brown

David and Pauline Brown

Gill, Mandy & Kenny Brown

Travers and Joan Buckley

Tony Budden

Richard & Andrea Butland

Margaret Cale

Muriel and David Tyas

Arthur Carpenter

Ron and Jackie Carpenter

P.H. & E. Clarke

Clive Clayson

Bert and Sheila Daniell

M. Daunter

Geoff Davis

Ursula Davis

Peter, Katherine, Ewan and
        Lewis Davis

Brian & Pam Denton

Dennis and Jo Dormer

Descendants of John Dowding

Jean and Ken East

Rev. Clive and Linda Edmonds

Angela Etherington

Roger Etherington

Ceri and Sheila Evans

Michael Gander

Lyn Garside

Stuart Gent

Rev. Ian Gobey

Freddie and Valerie Grace

Susan Green

Jennifer Griffiths & Jack Alcock

Gordon and Doris Hadley

Brenda and Peter Hales

Heather Harrington

Beryl and David Hart

Pauline Hart

Hilary Hawker

Peter and Eunice Hayward

Joy Henbest

John & Pat Higgins

Quincey Hobbs

Margaret Hogg

Nigel and Lynne Hogg

Andrew Hogg

Ann Hopkins

Mandy Howell

Freda Hunt

Brian Jones

Roger Jones

Gerald & Megan Kear

Bridgett Kerton

Roger Keyse

Aubrey Keyse

David Kibble

Bernard and Miriam Knight

Elaine Lanciano

David and Joyce Lilley

Christopher and Patricia Manners

The Martin Family

Ted and Rosa Millin

Cath and Bernard Millin

Don and Ruth Morgan

Pauline Morgan

Mrs M. Mould

Father Aiden Murray
Kevin Nash
Fred Parslow
Jeanne Parsons
Brian Pearce
Liz Perry
David and Jo Phillips
Pauline Price
Rachel Price
Gerald and Sue Pedley
Joan Reid
Don and Ann Rich
Jill Rodgett
Janet Royall
Charlie Royall
Ned Hercock
Harry Hercock
Janine and Greg Bonn
House of Lords Library
John Saunders
Elizabeth Savage
Lawrence and Rita Stanton
Sue and Geoff Sterry
Louise and Nick Stoddard
Barbara Taylor
Cathy Thomas
Luke & Florence Toft
Betty Toombs
Kate Venn
Josephine Vick
Rosemary Wagstaff
Brian & Sue Waldron
Keith Walker (FoD Hist. Soc.)
Keith Walker

Eleanor Waters
Ian Waters
Jean Waters
Stephen Waters
Tom & Eileen Waters

Steve and Wendy Warner
Rose Warren
Jan Weeks
Guy & Louise Wilkins
Sally Wynn

IN MEMORIAM SUBSCRIBERS

Gill, Mandy & Kenny Brown in memory of Janet & Alan
Arthur Carpenter in memory of Audrey Carpenter
Sandra Jones in loving memory of Oscar and Joyce Jones
Roger and Aubrey Keyse and Josephine in memory of Ada Keyse and Charlotte
Elaine Lanciano in memory of Ron and Cynthia Smith, and Bro Joe Carter
Anita Grace(nee Martin) in memory of the Martin Family, 'To my loving family, may angels always hold their hands.'
John & Daphne Martin In memory of my father, Dennis Joseph (Joe) Martin, & Grandparents, Charles & Alice Martin.
Janet Royall, Charlie, Ned & Harry in memory of Stuart Hercock
Brian Pearce in memory of Rita Pearce
Margaret Cale, Muriel and David Tyas in memory of their brother, John Dowding
Rosemary Wagstaff in memory of Mike Wagstaff

Due to printing deadlines, it was not possible to include Subscribers whose orders were received after 15th November 2010.

BLAISDON

Blaisdon is a small village on the edge of the Forest of Dean in Gloucestershire. Together with the hamlets of Nottwood Hill to the north and Woodgreen to the west, it forms the Parish of Blaisdon. This is centred on the Church of St Michael and All Angels, which lies on rising ground to the north end of the village. Its history dates back to the mid 12th century but this book focuses on the years in the middle of the 20th century. This was a period when the way of life in the countryside began to change dramatically. It is also the period that is just beginning to move out of living memory.

In an age of instant communication with travelling to distant places within the grasp of the majority of people, it is already difficult to appreciate how isolated rural communities like Blaisdon were, even in the middle of the last century. In the period covered by this book, tales are told of the villagers only having 2 cars between them. For most, the only mode of transport was the occasional but regular train service or a long walk to the main roads for the bus. As a consequence, many villagers would travel only occasionally. It is not surprising that organised charabancs were very popular and feature strongly in the memories.

Blaisdon is just one of many villages in Gloucestershire and each has its own story, but to those of us who live here, Blaisdon is very special. Indeed, it has won the Bledisloe Cup for best-kept small village on several occasions, something that was awarded not only for the appearance but also for the public spirit shown within the community. It is the people that have made Blaisdon special and this book seeks to celebrate the village of Blaisdon by enjoying memories of those who have made Blaisdon what it is.

Stephen Waters

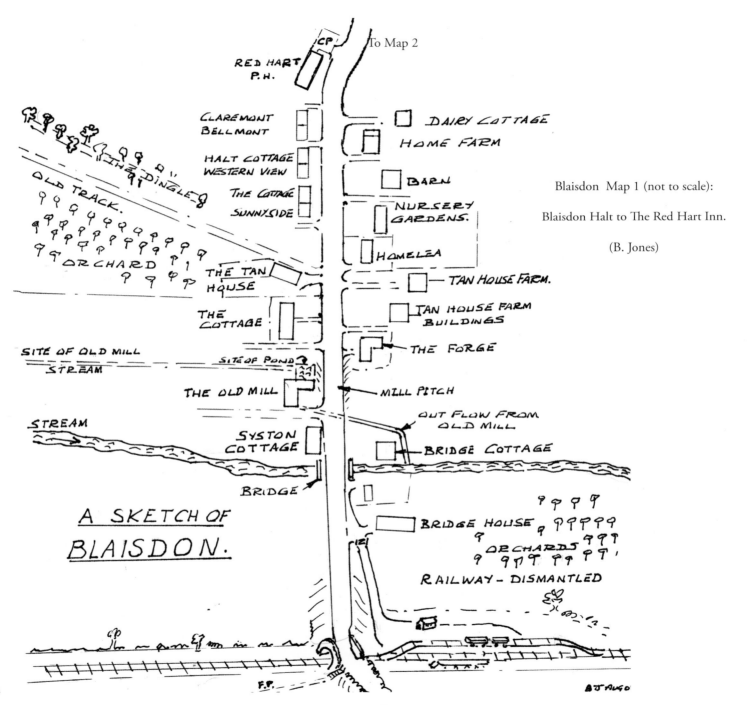

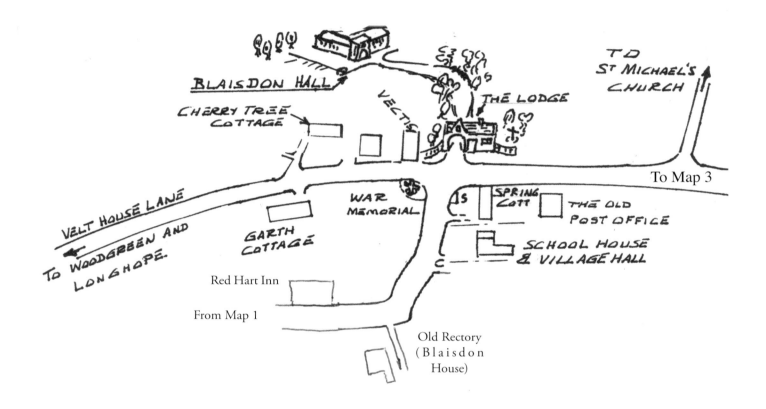

Blaisdon Map 2 (not to scale):

Red Hart Inn to Velthouse Lane & The Old Post Office.

(B. Jones)

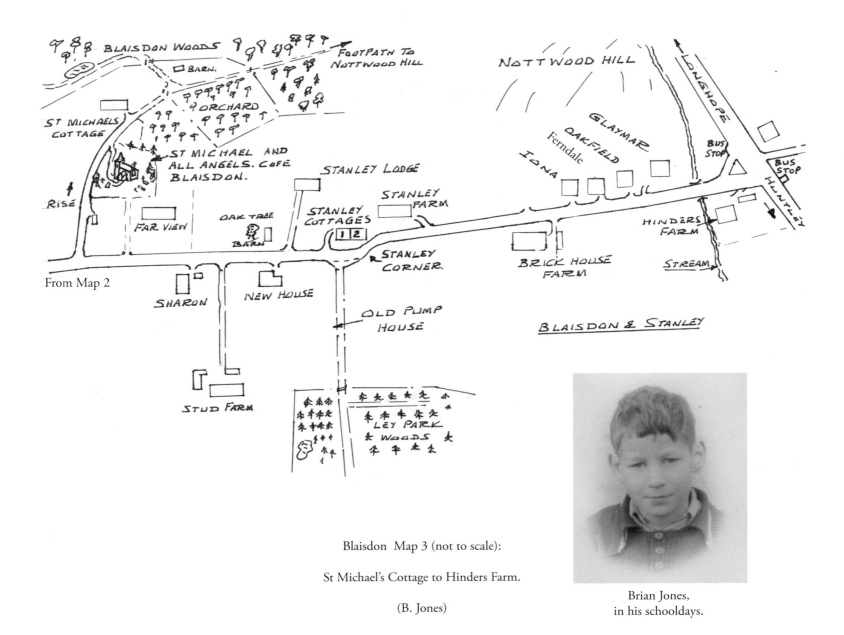

Blaisdon Map 3 (not to scale):

St Michael's Cottage to Hinders Farm.

(B. Jones)

Brian Jones,
in his schooldays.

LAISDON HALT

For the generation living in Blaisdon immediately after the 2nd world war, Blaisdon Halt meant easy and quick access to the city of Gloucester as well as the neighbouring villages of Longhope and Mitcheldean. The Halt was on the Gloucester to Hereford line, run by Great Western Railways. Leaving the main South Wales line at Grange Court, the line ran through these villages to Ross on Wye and on to Hereford. Although the line had been opened in June 1885 and goods' sidings opened at Blaisdon in November 1906, it wasn't until 4th November 1926 that the Halt opened to passengers. The siding served as a cattle dock and coal yard. The line was single track with a token being passed between train and station staff to ensure only one train was on the track at any time; a simple but secure safety system. Crossing points for trains were placed at some stations, such as Longhope. Sadly, the line felt Beeching's

Blaisdon Halt on a quiet day, 20-11-1963.
(B. J. Ashworth)

axe and was closed to passenger services on October 31st 1964 and goods services ceased on November 1st 1965.

Brian Jones remembers:

"Blaisdon Halt consisted of a standard single wooden platform with a corrugated iron shelter containing a bench for waiting passengers. There was a flight of stairs from the adjacent road to the platform though most people used the service road that ran to the siding and the footway across the track to the platform. The siding had a cattle loading dock, a secure parcel shed and a weighbridge with its balance mechanism housed in a brick building. Of the personnel who staffed the Halt, I remember Mrs Sharkey and, later, Mr Middlecote. It must have been a pleasant place to work.

Single Line
Token:
Grange Court
To
Longhope.
(S. Waters)

1

The Halt was served by 6 trains a day in each direction on weekdays, a restricted service on Saturdays and nothing on Sundays. Generally, the passengers were few, except for the 8.10am train to Gloucester, which had at least 10 regular commuters.

It was a blow in the early 1960s when this train ceased to call at Blaisdon Halt as it necessitated catching an earlier train up to Longhope, dashing across the line to catch the about to depart Gloucester train, only to pass back through Blaisdon a few minutes later. Soon, all the Blaisdon commuters had transferred to alternative methods of transport."

Blaisdon Halt showing the steep wooden steps leading from the road to the left of the bridge.

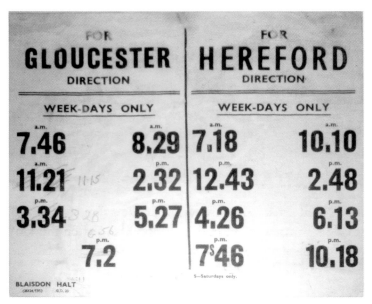

Timetable Poster from Blaisdon Halt
(with pencilled alterations).
(P Booth)

GLOUCESTER
DIRECTION

WEEK-DAYS ONLY

a.m.	a.m.
7.46	8.29
11.21	2.32
3.34	5.27
	7.2

HEREFORD
DIRECTION

WEEK-DAYS ONLY

a.m.	a.m.
7.18	10.10
12.43	2.48
4.26	6.13
7ˢ46	10.18

S—Saturdays only.

BLAISDON HALT

Elizabeth Etherington recalls the fun to be had as a child watching the trains from the road bridge that passes over the line just above the Halt.

"Darting from one side to the other as the train passed underneath, we would be covered in clouds of steam. We would also put pennies on the line so that they would be squashed flat by the train wheels. When we were teenagers, it was quite tricky coming down the steps in our stiletto heels as it was so steep, so we preferred to use the service road. However, the five bar gate across this always seemed to be chained and locked. This meant either climbing over it or squeezing through the narrow gap between the fence

A Pause at the railway bridge on a Sunday morning walk for the Salesian Boys.
Sitting on the bridge, left to right:
Mark Heckman, Alan Kelly, Martin Jay, Dennis O'Leary, John McAteer, Chris Little.
Standing:
Stephen Lees
Sitting on the ground, Left to right:
Peter Church, Robert Griffiths, David Clough.
(D. Hudson)

post and Mr Martin's hedge, though the latter could only be done by the thinnest of us. Shopping had to be passed over the gate and bikes were left in Mr Martin's yard to be collected on returning to Blaisdon. Once at the Halt, the train would almost certainly have been in sight and we had to decide whether to risk running in front of it or wait and cross after it had arrived. We would then have to face the wrath of Mrs Sharkey in her ticket office who would be none too pleased at our late arrival."

For some, Blaisdon Halt was their point of arrival in the Village. Perhaps those to whom this arrival had the most impact were the boys who were to live at Blaisdon hall under the care of the Salesian Order who ran a school for orphans and later, socially deprived children. **Norman Taylor** was a pupil at Blaisdon Hall during the 1940s and has written about his arrival in the book: 'Blaisdon Old Boys' Recollections Of Blaisdon Hall.' Leaving St Joseph's orphanage in Enfield, he describes the trepidation he felt at the time and continues:

"Paddington Station was crowded with Service Personnel but Sister Josephine found the platform from which our train would be leaving. She put us into a carriage and watched as we took our seats. Sister Josephine handed me the tickets and left.

Our journey into the unknown had begun. The journey to Gloucester was very exciting. I had never travelled on an express train before. We arrived in Gloucester station and a friendly Sergeant directed us onto the train to Blaisdon.

The guard cried ' Blaisdon Halt' as the train stopped at a small platform way out in the countryside. I often think of my arrival in Blaisdon. There was no one to meet us; the silence was eerie, broken only by the bleating of sheep and lowing of cattle. There we stood, four boys, lost in a sea of rural tranquillity, clutching the only possessions we had in the world wrapped in brown paper and tied with string. We made our way up some steps to the road and we saw Blaisdon Hall, on high ground about a mile away.

Sunday 4th March 1962
The Liverpool to Plymouth Train passes through Blaisdon Halt,
passing this way on Sundays, as there were no local services.
The coal wagon shows the siding used for unloading.
In the foreground is the Ticket Office & weighbridge.
(B. J. Ashworth)

The Longhope bound train stops at Blaisdon.
c1964.

We walked through the village and in a farm yard, two men were working. 'Would you tell us the way to Blaisdon Hall' I asked. ' It be that way through the village,' said the older man in a pure Gloucestershire accent."

In the 1950s, when **Tony Brady** and friends were sent from St Joseph's, little had changed. Tony recalls:

"On reaching Gloucester, the train came to a stop. We waited in the carriage until a man in black clothes came to the window and said ' I'm Brother Edward Baron and I'm here to take you to Blaisdon.'

Very soon we were approaching Blaisdon Halt. Brother Edward pointed out Blaisdon Hall, standing on a hill in the distance. It was a prominent house set high on a slope

Blaisdon Halt from the road bridge.
The siding can be seen with a series of wagons though the days of coal deliveries had passed.
Vehicle access was via a track running between the 2 buildings on the left.
(S. Waters)

in a great park with massive tall fir trees that framed what was a magnificent mansion with a high tower.

I will never forget the walk to the school. Every hedge was a wild extravagance of leafy growth thronged with birds. Behind hedges, fences and walls were cottages and houses. Their facades were like faces with doors like mouths and windows eyes. Paths, some crooked, some straight, led up to each, from different sorts of gate.

Brother Baron named some of the houses, the Old Forge, The Mill, The Tan House. I stared at each one as we filed along each side of a road that had no pavements. Sometimes we came to a gateway from where we could see long fields that stretched into what seemed like an endless distance. We passed a barn from which came a smell that was warm and pungent. We stopped to look through the thick wooden bars that faced the road. Standing on a floor of straw, I saw a group of cattle with curly hair: as they breathed, steam seemed to come out of their noses. One of them had a large head and it ran at the bars and butted them. I was scared. Brother Edward told us that it was the bull and the others were bullocks and that they belonged to the school farm. He told us that the school owned over 100 acres of farm and woodland. It was magical to a 12 year old boy who had been plunged into the country from the fastness of a city existence."

A little further on they passed the Red Hart pub and Brother Edward introduced them to the landlord, Gideon Price.

"The sight of Gideon Price was unforgettable. He stood in the doorway under a sign saying 'The Red Hart' which

20th November 1963
2.45pm Hereford to Gloucester.
Mr Middlecote, the Station Attendant, has
just lit the lamps.
The lady is thought to be Iris Hogg.
(B. J. Ashworth)

Lawrence Stanton and Roger Allen
outside the ticket office.

John Keating and sister-in-law Maureen Keating
awaiting the arrival of the Gloucester bound train.

swayed in the breeze above him. He was ten times more frightening than the bull. His eyes were black and bright. His hair was white and thick and his chest was covered with a beard that was square and reached his trouser belt. In his mouth was a long clay pie and from his nose was pouring not steam but thick smoke."

In the days before cars became the universal mode of transport, the Halt was also a point of departure where many left the village. For some, it was the exciting prospect of a new life together as they left Blaisdon for their honeymoon, or just a day out visiting friends or family. For others, there was the more scary prospect of time to be spent in the Armed Forces. As the war memorial testifies, not all of these men returned, their service to their country resulting in the ultimate sacrifice. Whatever the reason for their departure, all would be guaranteed a fond farewell from their families, neighbours and friends.

Alice Brewer with her son, William, in uniform, together with a friend.

Right:
Salesian Priests from Blaisdon Hall take a trip by train from Blaisdon Halt.
(R. Keating)
Above:
A Blaisdon Halt Train Ticket.

8

Well wishers watch a departing train carrying newly weds, Roger
and Hilary Etherington, on their honeymoon,
18th July 1964.

Above:
Lawrence Stanton returning
to his army base after leave.
Roger Allen is seeing him off.

Right:
Mrs Sharkey,
Blaisdon Halt Ticket
Attendant.

An early picture of Blaisdon Halt platform showing the original
doors on the platform shelter.

This smartly dressed couple waiting for the train at Blaisdon Halt were unknown until this photograph was printed in the Forest Review Newspaper.

Brian Jones recognised them:

" I had seen the photograph before. They were my aunt and uncle, Ruby and John Bushrod, who had just got married in Flaxley Church. Ruby was a daughter of Emma and Sydney Young of Garden Cottage, Flaxley and the sister of Evelyn Jones (Brian's mother). She had four sisters and many relatives living around Flaxley and Popes Hill.

Ruby and John had met while in service at Flaxley Abbey, John as a gardener and Ruby as indoor help. John was a native of Devon and it was there, near Ivybridge, that they retired from their employment. John died in 1995 and Ruby in 2004."

John & Ruby Bushrod.

The Blaisdon Halt mile stone was situated in front of the bridge. It depicted the number of miles from the end of the buffer stop on platform 1 at Paddington, London, to the platform at Blaisdon Halt - 123 miles.
(M. Ayland)

St Mary the Virgin Church, Flaxley
with Flaxley Abbey in the background
from an old postcard, posted 1936.
(S. Waters)

John & Ruby Bushrod
At Flaxley Church
on the occasion of their wedding.
(Mrs M. Cole)

A train approaching Blaisdon Halt on a misty day.
(Allum)

BRIDGE HOUSE

An early drawing by Joe Martin of Bridge House showing it before any of the modern alterations were undertaken.

The nearest house to Blaisdon Halt is Bridge House, situated just above the site of the station on the right hand side of the road. This has been extensively modernised in recent times but had been home for generations of the Martin family.

John Martin, whose grandparents lived at Bridge House says that the earliest mention of his family being in the area dates back to 1539 though reliable evidence starts in 1785 with the birth of John Martin. He became an Innkeeper marrying Hester. They had 2 sons and 7 daughters. One son Samuel was deported to Australia for horse stealing while the other, Charles, married Jane Eleanor Parry, having 10 children. The Blaisdon line continued with their son, George, marrying Emma Jane Harding and having 11 children. At least 4 sons went to Canada, working on the construction of the Canadian Pacific Railway. Some, including Charles, returned in the early 1900s and on the death of his father, George, in 1926, Charles Martin inherited Bridge House, together with a small farm to the west of Longhope Brook. He lived there with his wife, Alice (nee Higgins) who had been a teacher at Blaisdon School and children Joe and Ronald.

The Martin family Left to Right:
Charles, Ronald, Alice, Emma Higgins (Alice's sister),
Elma (wife of Joe), Ernie Higgins (brother to Alice).

Bridge House from Blaisdon Lane.

Joey, the Martins' horse in his stable.

The Martin Family, Haymaking.
August Bank Holiday
1927.

Left to right:
Ronald,
Charles,
Dennis (on wagon),
Edgar (brother of Charles),
Nellie (nee Higgins),
Fred (cousin to Ronald),
Alice (nee Higgins).

Charles' grandson, **John Martin** remembers visiting his grand parents in the 1940s:

"My first recollection of Blaisdon was visiting my grandparents in Bridge House in the 1940s. At the time we lived in Boulsdon near Newent, where I was born. The trip to Blaisdon was by bike, through Clifford's Mesne, around May Hill, up the Glasshouse then down Deep Filling to Hinder's Corner and hence to Blaisdon. My grandmother, being very Victorian, kept very strict mealtimes and, if we were late, we missed the meal! There were no drinks on arrival either.

Our visits to Blaisdon were centred on harvest times. My father, together with all the male members of the family worked in the fields, gathering stooks of wheat to feed a hired threshing machine, or picking plums. A real treat was collecting apples and pears to make cider and perry. Granddad climbed the tall Blakeney pear trees and shook the pears down, while we kids scrambled about underneath collecting the fruit, a dangerous task as the trees were up to 40 feet high. We should have been issued with crash helmets.

The Cider was made at Bridge House, next door to the stables. There was a big circular stone cider mill. Joey, our Clydesdale horse, walked around the trough turning a large stone wheel and apples were thrown into the trough. When they had been crushed, the apples were shovelled into large hessian sacks that had become bright orange

Above: Circular stone mill. Joey, the horse, walked around the trough turning the large stone wheel, crushing the apples.
Left: The apples were then placed in the cider press and the juice extracted.
(Long Ashton Research Centre)

over the years and placed in a press.

Joey was then used to turn the screw of the press via an ingenious connection between it and the central spindle of the mill. The old mill and press have been preserved and now stand as a feature in the house. We children used to sneak in and drink the sweet apple juice straight from the press, with disastrous effects on our digestive system. It never ceased to amaze me how such sour apples and pears

could produce such sweet juice. Mother forbad us to go near the place!

Another plus was sampling the finished product. Granddad had 4 very large barrels, 3 for consecutive years of cider and 1 for perry. We sampled them using an old white, chipped, enamel mug kept nearby. Also caged nearby were granddad's ferrets, which we avoided as they were particularly mean. They were used for catching rabbits, a staple meat for country folk in those days, as was game and pigeon.

The Martins were a large clan and intermarried with the Higgins, Irish farmers, who came to farm at Clevedon in Somerset during the potato famine in the 1800s. This motley group, all of whom were natural musicians, came up from Newport, to help with the plum picking. They worked hard from the time the plum tree leaves dried from the morning dew until almost sunset. After work, a large tarpaulin would be laid out and plum boxes used as tables and chairs. Meals, prepared by those ladies too delicate to help with the fruit picking, were served in the orchard. A small campfire was lit to heat water for tea but the main drink was granddad's cider, or perry for the ladies. Out came musical instruments and the sound of Irish jigs filled the Upper Mill Meadows. Joey, pulled the 56lb boxes of plums from the orchards to Bridge House, returning with the empty boxes and food for the workers. Blaisdon plums make excellent jam and in the early days were transported to Liverpool from Blaisdon Halt. By the late 1940s my Grandparents' siblings had become too old to work and only visited on rare occasions but musical evenings were still held in the house.

We loved going fishing in the Mill Pond attended by Granddad's ginger tom called Marmalade who sat by patiently waiting for his dinner; he was never disappointed! This cat ate marmalade and cornflakes off my Grandfather's spoon! Also at this time, trout were to be found in Longhope Brook though a discharge of toxic chemicals into the water around Mitcheldean in the early 1950s killed all the aquatic life. Thankfully, the stream recovered and fish are to be seen in the brook today.

Charles Martin & Joey.

My grandfather also started a coal business during the 1940s, supplying the village and surrounding farms with coal with Joey pulling the coal wagon. Another of my childhood jobs was to unload coal from the 20 ton wagons in the railway sidings. As I grew older, I was expected to help my Grandparents and this usually involved fruit picking and haymaking. I progressed from turning the hay to scything the grass by hand. I was also sent on errands by train to get vegetable seeds from Winfields in Westgate Street, as it was cheaper to send a child. When I was 15, I carried a 40 rung ladder that my grandfather had bought, all the way from Longhope to Blaisdon.

Charles and Alice Martin died in 1963 within weeks of each other. Charles was 84 and Alice 91. Their son Ronald is buried with them having died in 1991 at the age of 79.

2 watercolours by D. J. Martin (c1938).

Above:
The yard at Bridge House.
Joey is the horse in the stable.

Right:
The Kitchen at Bridge House.
The open range was used for cooking.
The calendar on the wall is dated March 1937.

(By kind permission of the present owners,
J. Alcock & J. Griffiths).

RIDGE COTTAGE

Mr & Mrs Annis outside Bridge Cottage
in the mid to late 1930s.
(Booth Family)

After Bridge House, the road crosses the Longhope Brook. On the right hand side is Bridge Cottage, though it is now known as Brook Cottage. It has the brook passing beneath its walls on one side and the Mill Race a few feet away on the other side. Luckily, it has been built high above both, as the brook can rise many feet when it rains.

This was the home of Mr Albert and Mrs Eliza Annis. Mr Annis, a retired Policeman from London, died in 1938. His wife continued to live at Bridge Cottage and is remembered as a lovely old lady who always gave us children sweets in a paper bag whenever we called or passed by.

During the Second World War Bridge Cottage was struck by a German bomb. There are two versions of exactly what part of the house was damaged. One version is told by *John Martin* a neighbour from The Old Mill:

During the war the German bombers used the U bend in the Severn at Westbury to get their bearings for raids on the Midlands. One night a bomb fell on the bridge over Blaisdon brook and took the side off the cottage. Mrs Annis was found uninjured half way up the stairs that were now exposed to the elements. Her hearing was affected and it never fully recovered. The bridge was rebuilt and her house repaired.

The other version is from the present owners *Peter and Sue Booth*:

"Soon after we moved to Blaisdon, forty years ago, we began to hear talk of the bomb that fell on our home.

George Keyse of Blaisdon Nurseries, told of how he was sat enjoying a drink outside the Red Hart one summer evening in 1943 when a German bomber dropped bombs close to the Gloucester – Hereford railway line. One of which landed in the front garden of the cottage then occupied by Mrs Annis and some evacuees. George and other villagers hurried down from the pub to find part of the front wall and roof blown away as well as damage to the road bridge.

Above:
Nancy Bate was on the spot to take this photograph of the damaged bridge.

Below:
Another view of the damaged bridge showing the hump in the lane that has since been flattened.

The bridge over Longhope Brook, taken after the bomb fell.

A good size crater was left in the front garden into which had fallen a ladened gooseberry bush. Thankfully, although very scared, Mrs Annis and her evacuees were safe and well. George never said if the gooseberry bush was retrieved and the fruit used, but with rationing taking hold it probably was!

After a few years living here we started to renovate our home. One particular dismal late summer afternoon, we were sat in the midst of our building work when an unknown visitor arrived. This lady, a Mrs P. Ditchburn, had been one of the evacuees hiding under the stairs when the bomb had dropped. She told us how frightened they had been on that summer's evening and the relief when they heard other people arriving to help them. We had a good chat with her and she spoke warmly of Mrs Annis and her time in Blaisdon. As she was leaving she remarked that we had made more mess than the bomb!"

Mrs Annis and her granddaughter, who was also staying with her at the time, went to live at the Tan House – home of Mr Joyce – whilst the repairs were carried out. Mrs Annis cooked and cleaned for Mr Joyce whilst she was there.

Mrs Annis died on the 24th December 1954 and is buried with her husband, Albert, in Blaisdon Churchyard.

The Gravestone of Mr & Mrs Annis, situated in Blaisdon Churchyard. The inscription reads:

In Loving Memory of
Albert Frank
The beloved husband of
Eliza E. M. Annis
Who died July 25 1938
Good-night, Sweet-heart, Good-night
Also of Eliza Maria, his wife
who passed away Dec. 24 1954
Aged 80 years.
Re-united

SYSTON COTTAGE

Situated across the road from Bridge Cottage, Syston Cottage is one of the oldest buildings in the village. The original part of the cottage is timber framed. Its construction and carpenters' marks suggest it was built in the mid 17th century.

Mrs Alice Lane (known to us all as 'Chuggy Lane') lived at Syston Cottage with her husband Mr Walter Gilbert Lane. He was a watch maker with premises in St John's Lane in Gloucester and we remember him cycling to work even though he had a stiff (or wooden) leg – a pedal had been removed from his bike to enable him to have a somewhat easier journey into work. Mr Lane died on the 5th February 1948 at the age of 48.

Syston Cottage 1950,
showing the original position of the front door.
Anita Martin, Susan Warlock, and Heather Martin.

Mrs Lane acquired the name of Chuggy because she used to call to her pig at feeding time, "Chuggy – Chuggy – Chuggy" and it stuck!!

She had many animals at Syston Cottage including two dogs, chickens, goats etc. She had the little plot of land opposite the Old Mill on which she kept the chickens and where there are chickens there are rats! She enlisted the help of a Dachshund whose owner lived in the village to sort them out which the dog did with great gusto. The men lifted the chicken hutch using crowbars and the rats ran out only to be killed by the dog!

Chuggy also had a couple of lambs at one point but they kept escaping into the Mill Meadows and she would spend several hours trying to catch them.

The small plot of land opposite Syston Cottage showing the hen house. At one time there was a building on this land.

Syston Cottage,
c1975.

One of her lodgers was a very good shot with a gun and John Martin from the Old Mill next door remembers one day the lodger came home by train from Ross and saw a fox in the Mill Meadows. He asked if he could go and shoot it. Mrs Martin agreed, having lost her own chickens to a fox. 10 minutes later he came back with a dead fox! There was no sentimentality when the lives of livestock were threatened.

Mrs Lane also took on the job of 'laying out the dead.' This was a tradition that extended into the 20th century especially among the poorer sections of society or where the services of an undertaker were not available. The deceased was prepared for burial by the family or friends.

The corpse was washed, the eyes kept closed with coins, limbs straightened and the body dressed or placed in a shroud.

Most of us children were rather nervous of Mrs Lane, but I think her bark was worse than her bite! But her dogs, one an Alsatian, really did bark and frighten us to death.

It seemed that we only ever saw Mrs Lane in her wellies and she was often to be seen riding her old bike through the village.

Mrs Lane left Blaisdon to live at Swiss Cottage in Chalford Nr Stroud, where she died aged 85, in January 1983.

Above: Mrs Lane (2nd on the left) at a friend's wedding, Blaisdon Church 1958.

Below: Outside Syston Cottage c 1958, left to right:
Jean Godwin, Jane Martin, Mrs Lane with Andrew Martin, Anita Martin, Mrs Martin, Heather Martin.

The Martin children (Old Mill): Anita, Heather, Jane and Andrew in the meadow opposite Syston Cottage with Rabbit Hill in the background. Also in the picture is Pat, one of Mrs Lane's dogs. (1958) Other animals of hers can be seen below.

LD MILL

When, in 1935, Charles Martin (Bridge House) bought The Old Mill, it had long ceased to be a working mill. He also acquired a small parcel of land with a small orchard of Blakeney Red pear trees and to these he added an orchard of Blaisdon Red Plums. There was a proviso that Blaisdon Hall could continue to take water from the Mill Pond. This involved keeping the millrace open from Woodgreen. Water was pumped up to a reservoir behind Blaisdon Hall and used to irrigate its large nursery garden. The Old Mill was not converted into Housing until 1946-7 when Charles' son Joe, his wife, Elma and their children moved into the Granary side.

Joe's son, **John Martin**, remembers working with his father on the alterations:

"By the mid 1940s, 'Woodlands View,' our house at Boulsdon, Newent, was bursting at the seams with 3 families sharing it. Granddad Charles suggested converting the Old Mill into a house. The Granary side was to be converted as the Mill side was always damp because of the millpond at the rear of it. Work began in the summer of 1946. Dad worked a long day at the Priestley Studios in Gloucester, his day starting at 5.30am and not getting back to Newent till 6pm. He would then have a bite to

The Old Mill as it was up till the Martin family leaving in 1967.
Only the end wall next to the path up to the meadows was painted because it was always damp facing the prevailing weather from the south west.

eat and cycle, sometimes with me on the crossbar, to Blaisdon. Most of the work was done during the weekends. The night-time journey was sometimes frightening. As we cycled through the dark woods strange sounds could be heard and I still remember seeing the shades of pink purplish aurora borealis and the brilliant stars, something today's children never see, unless they travel to somewhere that doesn't suffer from light pollution.

The floors of the new house were made with gravel from Blaisdon Brook and cement. I had the task of washing the gravel and picking out pieces of vegetable matter. The partitioning was made from timber taken from a floor in the Mill side of the building and clad with white hard asbestos sheeting, the only building material available just

Andrew Martin
1960.

The wedding of Joe & Elma Martin at Blaisdon Church 1939.
The Hand Bell Ringers formed a guard of honour. Oscar Jones senior is first on the right.

Below:
John, Anita & Heather Martin 1951.

Right:
Jane Martin
1961.

25

The Old Mill 1949.
Elma Martin watching Anita & Heather as they help wih the building work.

My mother kept chickens, ducks and geese in the orchard before the Mill but, although they were penned in, foxes took them at regular intervals. When we did get eggs, they usually tasted of garlic from the wild garlic plants growing in the orchard."

John also has vivid memories of growing up in Blaisdon, especially the animals:

"There were several notable dogs that were 'free range'. One, a big, Old English sheepdog, called Teddy Hawkins used to walk up from Boseley Farm to visit us kids at school. My dog, Mick, was an Irish terrier and arch-enemy of Nipper Davis a black and white mongrel. They fought at every occasion and my mother kept a broom at the front and back doors of the house to sort them out! The only problem for me was I had to walk past Nipper's house on my way to school and Nipper couldn't tell the difference between me and Mick, consequently I occasionally got bitten and have the scars to this day to prove it!

after the war. The dreadful winter of 1947 delayed work and it was not until May 1947 that we were able to move. We moved and settled into our new spacious house although it only had 3 bedrooms and a stove in the space that was to become the living room. It was not completed until several years later after we had added the living room and kitchen. We still had room upstairs and a fourth bedroom and a bathroom were added.

The Mill had pigsties at the back that, for the first few years, was occupied by a pig for home consumption. Percy, one of the large white Landrace pigs, was a truly terrifying beast who made a lot of noise and ferociously bashed the corrugated tin of his sty. One night, our pet chickens, Charlie, the cockerel, and Henrietta, the hen, made the mistake of trying to roost in his sty and he ate them. All that was left was a pile of feathers.

Heather Martin with family dog, Mick.

The Old Mill.

Village life was cyclical and followed the church calendar; Christmas, Lent, Easter, Harvest Festival and village fetes. Bell ringers and choir outings took us to exotic places like Barry, Porthcawl, and Weston-Super-Mare and once we even got to Aberystwyth. There was haymaking, plum picking and cider making. In the long winter evenings, there were Whist Drives, Advent and so back to Christmas. At Christmas the choir sang carols around the village and the hand bells were brought out and did a similar circuit. These calendar events were interspersed with National events such as the funeral of George VI and coronation of Queen Elizabeth and a visit of the Queen to Gloucester.

We were quite a religious family and attended Sunday School and church regularly every Sunday without fail. The Reverend McNamara had just died and a new vicar the Reverend Dennis Lane was installed. He was an enthusiastic chap who got the church choir going and the bells ringing again. We were active participants with the likes of Tom Board, Cedric Etherington, Oscar Jones senior and junior, Bertie Buckett, Ursula Howells, Honor Larner, Ivor Jones's girls from Woodgreen, Mary, Marjorie, Doreen, to name but a few.

I attended Blaisdon primary school with Mrs Smith as teacher; knuckle rapping with a ruler was her way of keeping us under control. However she still managed to get me to East Dean Grammar School. I started there in 1951, so the school cycle was imposed on the village one.

Also in that year I met my future wife, Daphne Dawn Evans, who had moved from Stourport-on-Severn into Vectis. When the Evans's moved into Vectis they had all the electrical gear but no electricity. Shortly after, Blaisdon was finally connected to the National Grid, so we were able to go there to watch the FA Cup Final, West Bromwich Albion and Preston North End! Up until then the village had no electricity or running water to the houses.

Life continued, people came and went and the most marked loss was that of Rev. Lane who moved to a new ministry in Surrey. The church was never the same after that. The Rev. Lane was not a rural vicar, and did not understand that when the plum harvest began nothing much mattered to the villagers as for many of them that was their sole source of income. The harvest only lasted for 2 or 3 weeks and church was the last thing on their minds so the congregations were small, the poor vicar laid into them on their return and many were not seen in church again. A sensible man would have taken the church to the orchards. I often felt that this, plus the fact that he was a relatively young man looking for advancement, motivated his move from the village to suburbia.

Village life, on the surface, seemed idyllic but there often were undertones of discord. Village fetes ran smoothly on the day but when one got a stall or activity that another thought was theirs by right there was tension! Whist drives also were a great source of friction!

There were several people who I regard as making the village a community. Cedric Etherington, himself a newcomer to the village during the war, was master of ceremonies for many of the village events. Sir Lancelot Crawley Boevey of Flaxley Abbey was a great supporter of the churches and schools of the combined parishes. Mrs Eggleton, sadly killed in a road traffic accident, was a leading light and after her death, electric lighting was put in the church in her memory. This detracted from the atmosphere created by oil lamps although the heating was most welcome! The organ was converted to an electric air pump not the old traditional hand pumped bellows powered by a small boy who, in the early days, was Norman Penny, from

Heather Martin outside The Old Mill,
showing the dormer that housed the hoist that lifted sacks of grain
to the higher level for grinding in the mill.

Woodgreen, followed by yours truly after my voice broke and I could not sing in the choir.

There were other characters that made the village; Mrs Chuggy Lane who used to take in the runt of a litter of pigs and hand rear it to bacon! The pigs lived in the house

28

until they got too big. A pig in the back yard was quite common. On slaughtering there was more meat than one family could eat and it was given to friends in the village. Goats also were a popular animal to keep. Cedric and Chuggy each had one. Cedric used to take his on a lead to feed off the roadside verges especially down the Mill Pitch. Chuggy's goat had a nice little paddock to roam in.

Elderly Mrs Goddard ran the post office and often asked how Herbie was doing; Herbert was Granddad's brother who remained in Canada and she had a soft spot for him. Mrs Dowding, who lived on Nottwood Hill, was cleaner for the school and church. Mobile shops came to the villagers; Stevens the butcher, Mabel and George Beard fruit and vegetables, a fishmonger, whose name escapes me but he lived near Elton Corner. Mr Bailey delivered the post always on time and in all weathers! Mrs Etherington delivered the local Citizen newspaper. Mr Pugh delivered the milk every day.

In 1961 I found a job in a Toxicological Laboratory owned by Shell Research Ltd, based at Sittingbourne, Kent. It was an operating company of Shell Transport and Trading. While I was in lodgings at Woodstock Road in Sittingbourne, my landlady, an elderly Mrs Venner, remembered serving tea to the "Gloucesters" in what was a cherry orchard but is now the King George V recreation ground. It was 1916 and they were waiting to go to the Somme in France and she remembered Charlie, my Grandfather. She took me to a small village 2 miles away called Milstead were they had been camped and there was a small memorial to 'The Gloucesters' at this field. My Grandfather remembered Sittingbourne but he never ever talked about the war.

My family stayed in the village until they moved to Gloucester in 1967. I look back at my 14 years in Blaisdon with rose tinted spectacles. Indeed, Cedric Etherington said to me many years later, "They were the golden years." He was probably right but I still remember the hard times when harvests failed or there was a surplus of plums and money was always in short supply. It was a hand to mouth existence for many of the villagers. What I could not fathom out was when there was a glut of plums and the growers were dumping them by the ton at the sale ground at Grange Court the prices in the shops never seemed to fall to reflect this."

The Old Mill viewed from behind taken from the Mill Pitch. Syston Cottage is in the background, c1975.

LONGHOPE BROOK

Although known throughout the village as Blaisdon Brook, the stream running past Syston Cottage and Bridge (Brook) Cottage is Longhope Brook. It rises on the west side of Mayhill and then passes through Longhope before following the valley to Woodgreen. It runs along the edge of Mugglewort Wood and then curves around Syston Cottage, and crosses Blaisdon Lane. It continues till it merges with the Westbury Brook between Boseley and Westbury-on-Severn. The Westbury Brook originates in East Dean and has passed through Flaxley. It now continues through Adsett and Westbury-on-Severn, running alongside the famous water gardens before entering the River Severn at Severn Mill.

The Mill Race was taken from Longhope Brook at Woodgreen and ran above the stream arriving above the Old Mill. Surplus water would pass under the road and ran along the opposite side of Bridge Cottage to the Brook, re-entering the brook just downstream of the cottage.

The Tunnel passing under the railway line, Boseley end.

Wild garlic continues to grow in abundance along the banks of Longhope Brook.

30

2 views of the tunnel carrying Longhope Brook under the railway
line at Woodgreen.

Elizabeth Etherington remembers the great fun to be had as a child with a brook to play in:

"The section I remember so well starts at Woodgreen with the weir and travels under a tunnel and alongside the old railway track where snowdrops graced its bank in January. It went under the road bridge at the bottom of the Mill Pitch and within feet of Bridge Cottage. It then wound its way through the lower meadow until it reached the far tunnel and disappeared under the road leading to Northwood Green.

When we were children we often swam in this brook, had picnics by its side and picked the daffodils and wild garlic which grew in abundance. We also shared the brook with Mr Grindon's herd of cows and the flies which accompanied them. The tunnels were something else and we felt very brave to go through them, not knowing how deep the water was! We filled our boots on many occasion and dreaded the journey home to explain how this had happened but we had had great fun so it was worth a ticking off!"

Top Left: Bridge at Woodgreen.
Top Right:: Cows alongside the brook.
Centre: Weir at Woodgreen.
Bottom Left: Road bridge at bottom of Mill Pitch.
Bottom Right: Brook in full Flood.
(E. Etherington)

THE FORGE

The Old Smithy at the end of the 19th century.
A horse waits patiently at the gate.

Above the Old Mill, the road rises steeply for a short distance. At the top of the rise, on the right hand side, is The Forge. The new cottage and Smithy was built by Peter Stubs during 1894/5. Attached to the cottage is a large shoeing shed and behind is a timber built loose box. Water was from an iron pump in front of the house on the village supply. The scullery next to the old kitchen had a copper water heater and furnace underneath.

This was not the first Forge in Blaisdon, an earlier one being the source of a major fire in 1699. The Blacksmiths Shop which also burnt down is thought to have stood near to the entrance Lodge to Blaisdon Hall. The event is recorded on a painted board in the belfry of Blaisdon Church:

"*On Friday about four of the clock in the afternoon on the 7th day of July 1699 from a Smith's happened a fire, which in the space of two hours burnt down and consumed Dwellinghouses, Barns, Stables, Outhouses containing 135 Bays of Buildings, which loss sustained by estimate on oath amounted to the sum of £4210.18.9.*"

"*A wholesome tongue is a tree of life, but perverseness therein is a breach of the Spirit.*" (Proverbs 15. Verse 4)

A number of Blacksmiths lived at the Forge after its completion in 1894 including; Mr John Gabb and his wife, Caroline, Mr Prosser and his family, and George Knight and his family. ***Frances Knight***, granddaughter of George Knight, remembers taking the shod horses back across the fields to Grange Court, then walking back to the smithy. The Forge ceased to be a smithy at the time Blaisdon estate was sold in 1935. In the early forties the Mathams family took up the tenancy of the cottage which at that time was owned by Mr Newman Grindon, who also owned the surrounding land and buildings. In the Spring of 1944 The Forge became the home of the Etherington family and remains so to this day.

The original anvil at the Smithy.

Elizabeth Ethrington writes of her childhood memories,

"I arrived at The Forge in Blaisdon in the Spring of 1944 at the tender age of nine months. My mother and father Dinah and Cedric Etherington and brother Roger left London as the bombs were getting too close for comfort. This proved to be a very good move as we loved village life and are still part of it .

Back in those early days all the necessities for living were delivered to the door. The grocer, Mr Williams, delivered once a fortnight from his shop in Little London. The baker came three times a week. I remember particularly the lovely warm crust, which Mum always cut off the loaf for me on its arrival! The Butcher, Mr Ackerman from Huntley, delivered once a week. The milkman everyday and the Oil man together with pots and pans delivered every week.

There was no electricity at that time and the water came from a pump outside the front gate. Mr Martin and his son Ronnie together with Joey the horse brought the coal up to the village by cart. I also can remember an Indian man in a turban coming to the door and opening a large suitcase full of tea towels etc. At times we also had a Missionary who turned up in a large van and the children in the village gathered in the van to hear him preach and watch his slides.

We didn't want for anything, except it would have been nice to have an inside toilet and not to have to go outside to sit on the loo, especially in winter when it was very cold and dark. Can you imagine that happening in Blaisdon now!!!

Roger & Elizabeth with Aunt Jean.
Outside The Forge 1946.

The Forge 1946.
A view of the back of the house from the open field behind.

34

The Etherington Family on a trip to Rodley Sands. The River Severn is behind them.
Left to right:
Roger, Dinah, Elizabeth, Cedric and cousin Malcolm Etherington.

Roger & Elizabeth Etherington
1948.

I remember my first days at Blaisdon School. We had beds to sleep on during the afternoons. My worst moment was when Mrs Smith, the headmistress, unfortunately heard me utter the word "bum" the result of which was that I was brought before the whole class and rapped over the knuckles with a ruler. Something never to be forgotten!

As a family we attended Church at least twice on a Sunday. I remember walking home after the evening service clutching on to Mother's fox fur as it was quite frightening at that age to be out after dark, even though the stars were a magical sight.

Elizabeth Etherington
1951.

Roger, Elizabeth & Dinah
Etherington.

Roger Etherington on his motor bike.

Cedric Etherington
with
Nancy the goat.

Elizabeth Etherington
with
Judy.

In the springtime Mum gathered snowdrops from the fields and packed them into a box covered them with wet cotton wool and took them to Mrs Goddard the postmistress, whereupon she duly got out her red wax, heated it up and stamped the parcel accordingly and it was then sent off to cousins Mona & Joan in St Leonards by Sea!

One of my great treats was being allowed to go to the Red Hart and ask Mrs Price, the landlady, for a bag of crisps containing the blue wrapper with salt in. Mrs Price was a lovely old lady with grey hair swept into a bun and wearing daps on her feet. Now, why do I remember that?

We loved getting on the steam trains at Blaisdon Halt, even though they took us to work every day. Most of the village girls embarking on this 30 minute journey spent their time doing their make up and putting their hair in order. One of us even ate our breakfast on board!

Christmas time was a special treat for the school children when we were transported to Flaxley Abbey where Sir Lance and Lady Crawley Boevey provided a party for us all. I will never forget the enormous Christmas tree at the top of the staircase with loads of presents for us underneath and we had to sit patiently for our names to be called out and then we were presented with our present from her Ladyship, usually a book!

I loved Mum taking us on a picnic. We usually went on Rabbit Hill behind The Forge. Now and again we would venture up through the woods behind the church and onto Nottwood Hill and that is where I am now, many years later, in Cherry Tree Cottage."

Cedric Etherington
1950s.

CEDRIC ETHERINGTON

Elizabeth Etherington's tribute to her father, Cedric Etherington, who spent the last thirty years of his life devoted to the village he loved and to recording its history:

"He was born in Twickenham in 1909. He had three brothers and a sister and during his early childhood he lived with his family in Richmond Surrey. He always had many tales to tell about this early part of his life as his family were involved in the music business. Not only were they sellers of Etherington Pianos but they were also responsible for organising and staging concerts attended by the Royal Family of the time. He clearly remembered the day when King George V and The Queen Mary visited their premises.

His school days were mainly spent in Boarding Schools, then at the age of 9 he had his first encounter with Gloucestershire when he spent two years at Yew Tree Farm in Huntley with the Ackerman family. Whilst there he attended Huntley Village School. His final school days were spent at Seaford College in Sussex where his great love of cricket and rugby began.

On leaving Seaford College he went to work at Harrods in Knightsbridge and remained there for fourteen years working in the furnishing Department. He still maintained a link with this Company right up until his death in 1996

with phone calls to the Chairman's Secretary and securing an invitation to visit them!

In 1940 he joined the RAF and served in Palestine during the war years. One of my first memories was waiting under the railway bridge at Westbury in my pram and he appeared from behind a bus in his uniform and carrying a huge bag. I think it was the day he was demobbed!

He married my Mother Dinah in 1933 and in 1944 they came to live at The Forge in Blaisdon. His working days were mainly spent at Elmbridge Court where he was a clerk with the Ministry of Agriculture.

He had a great love for the Church and in those days he spent days working in the Churchyard, cleaning up the tombstones and cutting the grass etc. He sang in the Choir and also in 1962 he was admitted to the office of Reader visiting many of the surrounding Churches and officiating when needed.

From his days amongst the tombstones stemmed his great interest in the village history and its families. This virtually took over his years in retirement. No family in the village escaped his attention. Page after page was written, visit after visit to the Gloucestershire Record Office was made and if anyone came to the village looking for their ancestors they were always directed to The Forge, where Cedric would be sure to have the relevant information.

Having served in Palestine he had great affection for the Holy Land and on numerous occasions accompanied his good friend the Very Reverend Eric Evans (former Dean of St. Paul's Cathedral) on trips to the Country. Eric sadly

Cedric Etherington at 84, the Gloucester Newspaper's oldest delivery boy.

died within weeks of my Father. As a result of his travels he became quite an authority on Egyptology visiting local schools and inspiring the children with his knowledge.

During the forties and fifties our summer holidays were spent in Brighton with his sister and family. Whilst we sat on the beach all day Father would be sat at the Hove Cricket Ground watching his beloved Sussex! We had the same ritual for at least thirty years visiting the Badminton Horse Trials as we children were dragged around the Course with no time to sit down as there was too much to see. Even the Queen Mother got a "Good morning Ma'am." Father would never miss the opportunity of speaking to anyone.

The world of rugby took over every Saturday and Kingsholm was sacred ground. He became a member in 1947 and this continued throughout the rest of his life.

In his later years he enjoyed five trips on Concorde. He loved attention at all times, especially from the ladies! He also enjoyed any publicity he got. He wasn't backward in phoning the local radio station and taking part in broadcasts. He even got as far as speaking live on Television.

For many years after my Mother gave it up he delivered The Citizen around the Village well into his eighties.

He died on the 13th May 1996 and his ashes together with those of my Mother, who died in 1992, were scattered on the Malvern Hills.

He so loved Blaisdon and its people and it was his intention to write and publish its history. He didn't make it, but we have done it for him. He will have known all the people who have contributed and made his dream come true."

Cedric never missed an opportunity to entertain the villagers by dressing up at Fetes etc:
Above: A city gent waits on the platform for a non existent train.
Top Left: Entertaining his grandchildren, Adam. Jamie, Lorraine & Kevin.
Bottom Left: Charlie Chaplin at Blaisdon Fete.
Bottom Centre: Cedric on coronation day, 1953, at Flaxley Abbey.
Bottom Right: An Arab Sheik.

THE OTTAGE

The Cottage in the 1950s.

The Cottage had at one time, been the home to Belgian refugees and was known as Belgian Cottage. They remained in the cottage for some time after the 1st World War, eventually leaving in around 1925. When Mr Bate took up residence there in the thirties it became known as The Cottage, simply because when he lived at The Tan House, Mr Bate always referred to it as, "the cottage next door." Today, it is known as Hill Cottage, as it sits overlooking the Mill Pitch.

Mr John Bate was a native of Warrington and came to Blaisdon in 1905, at the age of 28, to take up the position of Agent to the Blaisdon Estate. He soon identified himself with the social life of his new home and organised cricket, football and social clubs, to which later bowls and tennis clubs were added. At one time he was captain of both the cricket and football team. Mr Bate's interests included local government. He was a member of the Westbury Board of Guardians and for many years represented Blaisdon on the East Dean Rural District Council, of whose Finance Committee he was chairman. He was the manager of both Blaisdon and Abenhall schools and served as a Church Warden at our village church.

When the Blaisdon Estate was sold in 1933, he moved into The Cottage after making several alterations to it. He extended the house and garden and brought the water supply into the house. He planted an orchard of 21 fruit trees at the rear of the house and built two sheds next to the existing coal and wood shed.

Mr Bate and his first wife, Mary Alice, had a son, Jack, and daughter, Ruth. Mary Alice died in 1916 and Ruth sadly died at the age of 8 years in 1919. Mr Bate's second wife, Annie, was Mary's sister. Nancy was their daughter. Annie Bate died in 1928, when Nancy was 6 and, shortly after, Miss Evelyn Burgin came from Derbyshire to act as housekeeper for Mr Bate and to help with Nancy's upbringing. She was a regular churchgoer and made several friends in the village, returning to her beloved Peak District in early 1950s and Miss Eva Gough from May Hill took her place.

Left:
J.S. Bate walking up his garden path, lined with daffodils. Nancy's car was parked opposite.

Below:
J.S. Bate with Miss Burgin and, holding the dog, his daughter, Nancy.

Mr Bate continued to live at The Cottage with his daughter, Nancy, after his son Jack left to become Art Master at a High School in Cardiff. Nancy became a Domestic Science teacher, eventually moving to Essex.

John Smith Bate died on the 3rd December 1956 and is buried in Blaisdon Churchyard with his two wives and daughter, Ruth.

After his death The Cottage was sold to Mr and Mrs E King from Monk Hill Farm, Flaxley.

Mr J S Bate
Of Blaisdon

The funeral of Mr John Smith Bate (79) of Blaisdon, took place at Blaisdon Church on Friday, conducted by the Rev. C. V. Colman (vicar).

The family mourners were: Mr Jack Bate (son), Mrs Nancy Watkins (daughter), Mrs Jack Bate (daughter-in-law), Mr David Bate (grandson), Mr and Mrs Dunton (nephew and niece), Mrs Gough (housekeeper).

Among friends at the church were: Mr A. M. White (Chairman of East Dean Rural Council, representing The Council), Mr Newman Grindon (also representing Mr M. F. Carter, Newnham), Mrs Skelton, Mrs Allen, Mrs McNamara, Mrs R.G. Nicholls, Mr Wallace Akerman, Mrs Etherington, Mrs Pickering (also representing Mr Pickering), Mrs Hogg, Mr A. Vernall, Mrs W. H. Buckett, Mr H. J. Buckett, Mrs A. R. Green, Mr H. Nash (representing the Nash Family), Mr E. Dowding, Mrs Vernon Eggleton, Mr Chiswell, Mrs C. J. Webb, Cinderford (also representing Mr and Mrs James, Orpington, Kent), Mr P. H. Woodman, Mr William Brewer, Mr and Mrs G. Beard, Miss Davis, Mr J. W. Griffiths, Mr Young, Mrs Grabham, Miss Marshall.

In accordance with Mr Bate's expressed wish there were no floral tributes.

Apologies were received from Mrs Whiteman, Mrs Shannon, Mr and Mrs Riley, Mrs Goddard and Mrs Newman Grindon.

The bearers were Messrs. B. Sargent, J. Trippier, G. Keyse and C. Etherington.

The funeral arrangements were carried out by Mr Maurice Watkins, Wintles Hill, Westbury-on-Severn.

Above:
J.S. Bate with Nancy's Godmother in his garden.
The Tan House Barn can be seen in the background.

Left:
The notice of Mr Bate's funeral, taken from an unknown local paper.

AN HOUSE

In earlier times, the Tan House was the home of John Dowding who has been credited with the discovery of the famous Blaisdon Plum. A chance finding in a village hedgerow led to the area rapidly becoming a centre for plums with orchards all around. The plum is especially good for jam making and was bought for many years by Robertson's for their plum jam. Modern

The Tan House in the late 1940s when Mr Joyce lived there.

John Dowding
Of Tan House Farm.
Born: 1805.
Died: 1896.

transport and lower prices elsewhere in the world led to this source of income being lost to the village and as the orchards reached the end of their natural life, most were not replaced. However, it is still possible to buy Blaisdon plums at the village roadside during late August.

Mr Joyce came to live at the Tan House at the beginning of 1934. He was a widower with a daughter who would visit occasionally. A mathematician, he had spent his working life teaching in prep and public schools. Because of this, he was known affectionately as 'The Professor'. He was rather shy but always pleasant and friendly with his immediate neighbours. He was a regular churchgoer and was also friendly with the Rector and his family.

2 early views of The Tan House from the days when it was part of Blaisdon Estate.

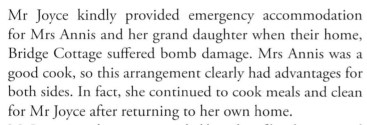

Mr Joyce kindly provided emergency accommodation for Mrs Annis and her grand daughter when their home, Bridge Cottage suffered bomb damage. Mrs Annis was a good cook, so this arrangement clearly had advantages for both sides. In fact, she continued to cook meals and clean for Mr Joyce after returning to her own home.

Mr Joyce was always surrounded by piles of books scattered over the floor. Kath Jones from The Cottage went shopping for him but never went into the house. Goods and money were exchanged on the doorstep. In later years, he found the upkeep of the house difficult and it showed increasing signs of deterioration. He died on 22nd April 1952, aged 81 years, and is buried in Blaisdon Churchyard.

Before Mr Joyce, Mr John Bate, the Blaisdon Estate Manager from 1905, had lived in the Tan House with his family. When the Estate was sold in 1933, he moved next door to The Cottage. His daughter, **Mrs Nancy Watkins** remembers the Tan House:

"Ivy covered the left side of the building which had the old office on the ground floor and a bedroom above. The front door entered into the office. The rest of the front of the building was covered then, as it is now, with a beautiful wisteria and a beautiful, dark blue clematis grew around the wisteria branches. On the right at the drive's entrance was a large lime tree."

After the death of Mr Joyce, the Tan House became the home of Vernon and Maud Eggleton. Mrs Eggleton was Mayoress of Gloucester. Tragically, on the 31st December 1959 she was killed in a road accident on the A40 at Birdwood. Her funeral took place at Flaxley Church on the 4th January 1960 and as she had been a great supporter of The Salesian School at Blaisdon Hall they held a full Requiem Mass for her. She was laid to rest in Blaisdon Churchyard. In her memory the oil lamps in Blaisdon Church were replaced by electric lights and there is a plaque on the church wall in recognition of this generous gift.

Mrs Maud Eggleton wearing her badge of office.

Christopher and Patricia Manners moved to Blaisdon in September 1961, shortly before their eldest child, Caroline was born. Their elder son, Charles was born at the Tan House in 1963, followed later by Tom. Still living in Blaisdon in 2010, they write of their early years in the village:

"We came to Gloucestershire in 1961 because Christopher got a job at Fielding & Platt, after completing his Graduate Apprenticeship. After hunting around for a number of months, we found the Tan House in Blaisdon, and immediately fell in love with it. The house had recently been done up by the previous owners and was considerably smaller than it is now. They also had re-vamped the garden and incidentally pulled out the old original Blaisdon plum tree that had been growing in front of the house, as they wanted a grass lawn there.

Village life in the early 60s was very different from that which it is now and was centred in the village, the Red Hart pub and the church. People did not travel out of the village much, to shop, eat out, visit friends and holiday, as they do nowadays, perhaps because it was difficult, and even if they did then Gloucester was about the limit of their expedition. For instance, there were only 2 houses in the village that had a car, Capt. Back at the Old Rectory and us. If folk needed to go to Gloucester to shop they walked to Hinders Corner and caught the bus, or caught the train at Blaisdon Halt, at the bottom of the village. Another big difference in village life was that in those days everything used to get delivered within the village, mostly weekly, so there was no need to go to Gloucester to shop, except for clothes etc. We had regular visits each week from various vans selling vegetables, fish, meat, milk, papers, pills and potions etc. Indeed the pharmacy van salesman more or less brought Caroline up in her early years, as he advised on what to do about the minor ailments she produced.

Christopher used to go to work at Fielding and Platt on the train. This deposited him at Gloucester Station at 8.00 am. A brisk walk down to Fielding's got him to a café near the entrance at 8.10, where his pre-booked breakfast of sausage egg and bacon was ready for him, leaving just enough time to eat it and clock in at Fielding's at 8.30!!

In those days, friends coming from London to stay the weekend would change trains at Gloucester, onto the Blaisdon train and, as instructed, get out at Blaisdon Halt. We used to go down to meet them, and hide out of sight.

You could see the look on their faces , 'Where on earth have we come to?'

The first person we met on arrival in the village was Bill Jones. He was the key holder for the Tan House. A retired signalman from the railway and a lovely man, he was, I remember, very skilled at propagating honeysuckle plants, which he then gave to villagers. Most of the older honeysuckle plants still in evidence around the village are his and a memorial to him.

Very good friends were Capt. and Mrs Back (Terence and Isobel), who came to the Old Rectory about 6 months before we arrived. They were a good deal older than us, and Capt. Back had suffered a stroke while on the bridge of his ship during the war, in the North Atlantic, which had left him paralysed on one side. They tried to get us to call them by their Christian names but somehow we never could. Capt. Back had

The Tan House in the 1950s.

a wonderful sense of humour. I remember going there for supper soon after we arrived, with Caroline, a wee baby, in a Moses basket. The Moses basket was put in the undecorated dining room on 2 chairs. When we went to collect her before going home, under the Moses basket was a huge puddle. Patricia, as a new mum, was covered in embarrassment but Capt. Back just roared with laughter, and then we noticed a watering can behind the door!! When the school in the village closed down, it was Capt.

Back who made it possible for the village to purchase it as a village hall. Every year he used to go off to Osborne House on the Isle of Wight, to give Mrs Back a chance of going on holiday, generally to Spain. On one occasion, also there was the lady who was responsible for government grants to villages. They played bridge together every night and while there he persuaded her that Blaisdon was a worthy cause for a grant!

A huge presence in the village was the Salesian School at Blaisdon Hall. They did a wonderful job teaching and looking after the boys who were lucky enough to be sent there by their Local Authorities. It is the only school I have ever heard of where, each year without fail, at least one boy ran away from home back to the school at Christmas time because his home environment was so awful, and he knew that the monks at school would look after him and be kind to him.

Our first encounter with the school was about a year after Caroline was born. Fr John Gilheney, headmaster of the school, came down across the field behind our house carrying a brown cardboard box. In it was a newly born lamb, which he had brought to show Caroline. This started a long and very happy relationship with him and the school. We got to know all the staff well and Patricia used to teach some of the boys the piano. Every year she provided piano accompaniment for the boys' annual pantomime, an event that was somewhat lengthy as every boy had to take part. I remember Fr Gilheney saying on one occasion after an hour, 'ten acts done and only 15 to go.'

In 1962 we extended the Tan House by building a kitchen at the back and above it 2 bedrooms and a bathroom. The work was done by Mr Hyett, a builder from Tibberton and a lovely man, plus the Potter brothers who worked for him. The contract price was agreed with him, over several glasses of whisky and then promptly painted over! There are not many builders I would trust on that basis. Every Christmas Mr Hyett would drive around all what he called, 'his ladies,' or his customers, and give each of them a large bunch of flowers.

Blaisdon was a very friendly village in those days and we remember well several of the people who lived there. Mrs Lane, who lived down the bottom of the village, used to come and baby-sit for us when Caroline was small. I remember her giving Patricia forceful lectures about allowing Caroline to cry outside in her pram. She had strong views which she expressed forceably and she was a bit eccentric on occasions, for instance she would only drink goats milk, but she was great fun.

Cedric Etherington and Mrs E. were one of our nearest neighbours, and very kind and welcoming to us and became good friends. Ivy Marshall (sister of Albert Pithouse) lived up on Nottwood Hill and used to help in the house. She would come to us and also to the Red Hart, walking all the way down through the woods and past the church at least 3 times a week come rain or shine. She laughed a lot and was great fun.

The vicar at this time was the Rev. Marchant. Most of his life he had been a policeman in Coventry. He suffered very badly from asthma and used to wheeze his way into church and through the service. Soon after arriving, Christopher was put in charge of the church heating, perhaps because he was an engineer by training. There was an oil-fired boiler down in the cellar of the church, which heated water that circulated through big cast-iron pipes beneath the floor in the church. Because the cellar was very damp, and flooded whenever it rained, the timer and electrics were a constant hassle and battle and quite often the boiler never came on, and we froze throughout the service."

Blaisdon Plums,
A watercolour by
R. Wagstaff.

AN HOUSE FARM BUILDINGS

The Tan House was originally the farmhouse of Tanhouse Farm. In the early part of the 20th century, it had been the Estate Office for Blaisdon Estate, while the land and the farm buildings opposite had been part of 'The Home Farm', Spout Farm being the remainder. The building nearest the road, on the right of the gateway, is the original tannery that gives the farm its name. When the Estate was sold, in 1933, Mr Newman Grindon of Poulton Court in nearby Northwood Green bought the buildings and adjacent land. Mr Grindon's farm worker Bob Sargent rode his bike from Northwood Green each day to attend the animals and the land.

Above & Below:
The original Tannery, part of Tanhouse Farm.

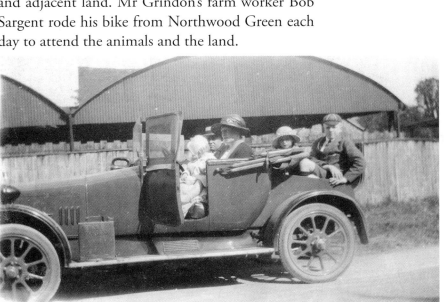

Left:
Jack Bate, son of John Bate (The Cottage) returning home when he lived at the Tan House. In the background are the cattle sheds, now demolished.

Ron Walton chatting to a friend next to some plum
boxes, labelled Walton, Longhope, Glos.

Above: Ron Walton watches David Lilley loading plum boxes.
Below: Ron & Mary's home from the late 1960s,
built adjacent to the barns & seen from the rear of the property.

The ownership of the Buildings changed to Mr Ron Walton during the fifties. Initially the Waltons lived at Hinder's Corner at the top of Blaisdon Lane but during the late 1960s, they were able to build a bungalow on land adjacent to the Tan House Farm buildings. Ron passed away on 13th December 2009 but his son, **Richard Walton** writes:

"Ron Walton was an "immigrant" from up north, Derbyshire to be precise. He moved to the more temperate climes of Gloucestershire after returning from serving as a Sergeant Major in Burma during the Second World War. He met and married a local secondary school teacher called Mary King, who taught for several years at Abenhall the then Secondary Modern school in Mitcheldean. Mary's parents, Ernest and Annie King, owned and ran Monk Hill Farm situated between Blaisdon and Flaxley.

Ron established himself as a landowner, livestock and fruit farmer, fruit trader and even an insurance broker! He grew some of his beloved Blaisdon Red plums and apples in his own orchards but also bought a great many more plums, apples and blackcurrants from farmers and fruit growers in Gloucestershire and Herefordshire. The plums were sent off in the well known Walton wooden boxes on the back of large articulated lorries to Robertson's factory to be turned into jam.

Young plum trees in full blossom.
(E. Etherington)

The apples and some pears, which were known as "bag fruit", were a smaller operation and were generally taken by Dave Lilley on the farm lorry to Bulmer's in Hereford or Showering's in Shepton Mallet to be made into cider or even Babycham! The blackcurrants were transported in shallower trays to avoid crushing the more delicate fruit and were made into conserve.

Inevitably, the fruit trade became more challenging after the UK joined the "Common Market" with Mediterranean countries such as Italy, Spain and Greece producing reliable, abundant and cheap crops of fruit. Unfortunately many British farmers, including Ron, grubbed out beautiful orchards in the face of such competition and returned to sheep and cattle as a more dependable source of income."

Ron & Mary Walton.

HOLMELEA

Situated between the Tan House Farm buildings and Blaisdon Nurseries are 2 modern bungalows. the first was built at the end of the 1960s and became the home of Ron and Mary Walton. The second is Holmelea, a brick bungalow. It was built in 1955 by George Keyse of Blaisdon Nursery on adjoining land.

It was initially occcupied by Mr and Mrs Mowbray and then by Mrs and Miss Smith. The present owner, Mr Brian Pearce, and his late wife, Rita moved into Blaisdon in 1967.

Above:
Holmelea with a dusting of snow.

Below:
Holmelea shortly after building work was completed.

BLAISDON NURSERIES

Since 1935, Blaisdon Nurseries has been the home of the Keyse family. The business has been run first by George and his brothers, then son Roger. Recently, Roger's daughter, Claire, has joined her father. The Nurseries were built as a kitchen garden for Blaisdon Hall and behind the house is a splendid walled garden. To one side of these is a series of barns and a large cobbled yard.

The story of the nurseries can be traced back to the early part of the last century. *Jenny Bomberg* has provided information about her family who lived at what was then known as 'Rose Bank.' Her grandfather, Arthur Statham moved to Blaisdon with his wife, Maggie, and was Head Gardener at Blaisdon Hall from 1905 to 1910. He then moved to become Head Gardener of Birmingham Hospital Saturday Fund Convalescent Home in Deganwy, North Wales. He later went on to open his own Alpine Nursery, The Rock Gardens in Llandudno. Jenny also has notebooks kept by her great grandfather who was clearly very proud of his son as he records his many achievements in flower and produce competitions.

In the 1920s. Mr Tipton was Head gardener and he lived at 'The Gardens' with his wife. When George Keyse and his brothers bought the nurseries, they renamed them 'Blaisdon Nurseries.'

Above:
Blaisdon Nurseries c1910
when it was known as Rose Bank.

Below:
Blaisdon Nurseries with the Tipton Family 1920s.

Arthur & Maggie Statham with their children, at Rose Bank, Blaisdon 1910.

Frederick and Roly, either side of their mother, were born in Penrith.

Alice & Edna were born in Blaisdon.

Pages from the notebook of Arthur Statham's Father.

This little paperback book is full of everyday information both domestic and gardening. He visited Blaisdon and proudly records Arthur's success at local shows.

The left page records Gloucester Rose Society 1909. The right page lists a series of 1st prizes at the Newnham Flower Show.
(J. Bomberg)

Greenhouses within the walled garden.

Ada Keyse (nee Price) married George in 1947 and lived at Blaisdon Nurseries for the rest of her life. In 1984, she wrote the following for a special fund-raising 'Blaisdon Chronicle.'

"I can vividly remember walking with my sisters through Blaisdon one spring evening in 1924, passing "The Kitchen Gardens" as it was then known, on our way to live at The Red Hart Inn, where our parents were to be the new Landlords. Little did I realise when sent on errands to The Gardens, it would eventually be my home.

Some eleven years later, The Gardens were sold to the Keyse family, who rechristened it "Blaisdon Nurseries'" and set to work building up a nursery business.

Over the next few years, one of the Keyse brothers, George, married, moved into the house and produced 3 sons.

Meanwhile, I too had married, moved to Frampton-on-Severn and had a daughter.

Then of course, the war years came and vegetables were the order of the day and George, being one of the lads left at home, joined the Home Guard. So, with hard work at the nurseries, helping the guard the home front and giving a helping hand at a farm during harvesting, the daily bread was earned.

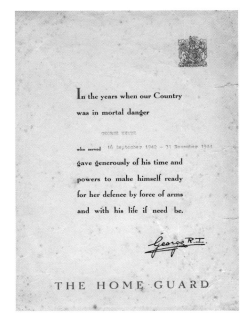

George Keyse's Home Guard certificate, issued after the war.

Shortly after the war, George and I met again, when I came to Blaisdon visiting my family at the Red Hart Inn. We had both lost our partners and, after a short courtship, we married on 7th June 1947. My daughter, Joey, and I moved into Blaisdon Nurseries and we settled down to running the business and bringing up four children.

Centre & Top Right:
George & Ada Keyse.

Top Left & Bottom Right:
George's prize-winning Vegetables.

Bottom Left:
Ada admiring George's prize-winning
blooms.

Life was really hectic then. Two or three mornings a week, George would deliver vegetables to local schools, often travelling by train to do this, though he did eventually buy a little van. While I sorted the family out, he usually started work before breakfast and working until dark. Watering greenhouses, planting seeds in due season and plenty of weeding in between. During the summer months we produced tomatoes and lettuce and the greenhouses in winter were full of chrysanthemums.

Late summer meant plum picking and preserving. Life was worked to the full. It was a great life if you didn't weaken.

Our Christmas preparations started long before most other folks, when we began to collect holly and all the other bits and pieces needed to create holly wreaths. We would spend many a long evening producing these Christmas decorations. George's large hands putting them together skilfully and quickly; a skill he has passed on to his son, Roger. This together with the killing and dressing of the Christmas poultry meant that by the time Christmas Eve arrived, we were all exhausted and in need of a break.

In the 1950s, we had the telephone installed. Eh! Oh! More work, to say nothing of running the length of the nurseries when it rang.

Still, the garden flourished and so did our family, particularly in 1958 when we increased the staff by producing son number four, Aubrey, but, alas, he showed little interest in growing vegetables and flowers, preferring to hammer away at the flower pots as he wandered around with a hammer in his hand.

It was in this year that George produced two new dahlias. The Blaisdon Red, a deep red, and The Aubrey Keyse, a delicate champagne colour and named after our last-born.

George Keyse's dahlias: Aubrey Keyse (Bottom left) and Blaisdon Red.

One of George's greatest loves was to enter local produce shows. In August each year, we would harvest the 'King-size' vegetables that had received such love and devotion and take them with pride to the various shows held at this time of year. Returning at the end of each day, jubilant with First Prize Cards and sometimes Silver Cups and Medals too.

But my husband was not content with local shows and we went national. Each autumn he competed in the Royal Horticultural Society Fruit and Vegetable Show. You can imagine what a proud moment it was for the family when George won the Riddel trophy for vegetables in 1967 and again in 1971. This cup was for attaining the highest marks in the whole show.

The years rolled on and I am a widow again but the seasons and life at Blaisdon Nurseries continue, as son number three, Roger, carries on the family business."

The Keyse family moved to Blaisdon in 1934 when George and his brothers, Jack and Dick, bought The Nursery. George married Pamla Gunter in 1938-9 and, in the following years, they had 3 sons, Michael, Terry and Roger. Sadly Pamla died in 1946, leaving George with 3 young children. Roger, the youngest was only 21 months old.

The Keyse Brothers: Dick, Charlie, George (back row) and Joe (front right) with Charlie's son, Ralph (front left) in the 1940s.

Roger Keyse says of his childhood:

"I was too young to remember my mother, though my father told me it was a difficult time. There was no state support for a single father but he had very supportive family and friends. The three of us spent a lot of time with various relatives so that my father could get on with running the Nursery. Happily, he met Ada Warlow (nee Price), a widow, and married her in 1947.

As a Nurseryman, my father had been deemed to be in a reserved occupation during the war and, as such was not allowed to enlist. Instead, he had to convert his nursery into food production. As he was a very keen vegetable grower, he did not mind this too much. After the war, he began the long, hard slog of rebuilding his nursery business, especially growing his beloved Dahlias.

I remember life during my childhood as quite hard. There was little money and always work to do around the Nursery. All three of us boys had our jobs around the place and we were never idle.

A Young Roger Keyse.

We kept pigs at Stanley on the Blaisdon Lane and they were our main source of meat. When ready to be slaughtered, a pig would be brought down to the Nursery. Jock Morris of Newnham was the slaughter man and he would kill the pig quickly and, for the time, humanely. The whole pig was used except, as the saying goes, for the squeal! We boys would grab the bladder as it made a great football.

There was also a plentiful supply of rabbits in the surrounding fields, if you could catch them, without getting caught yourself. We weren't supposed to go rabbiting on the Stud Farm then owned by the Salesians, as Brother Pat Flynn would tell us. However, he also told us that when the 2nd bell rang everybody would be in Mass and nobody would be around for 40 minutes. We took that as unwritten permission to venture forth with our ferrets. The big 50-acre field behind the Stud Farm had several ponds. These were a great source of Moorhen eggs. These made a great breakfast, though we made sure they were freshly laid and we always left some eggs in the nest.

In the hill above the Church is an old reservoir. In those days we used to swim in it thoughout the summer months. Eventually, we had to stop as there were health scares regarding the water quality. It then became a favourite spot for escaping to fish. We would also explore Ley Park woods. In those days the woods were filled with wild daffodils, so we always had a big bunch of flowers for our mothers on Mothering Sunday.

My school days were split between the village school and Abenhall School at Mitcheldean. Here, I was taught by John McGee, who was a teacher there before he moved to Double View School, Cinderford. Little did I realise that, a few years later, he would become a neighbour, living at Sharon. He was a good and kind teacher who was loved by all his pupils as much as he was by his flock in later years when he became a priest in the Church of England. Another connection we found out later was that his mother had been an evacuee to the village and had a room at the Nursery.

In the early 1960s the Rev. Bick decided to expand the carol singing that Flaxley youth club did round their village. Soon, carol singing encompassed Blaisdon, Nottwood Hill as well as Flaxley and Popes Hill. When he left, I took over the organisation and it continues to this day, spread over the week before Christmas. A collection is made and donated to the Children's Society. It's hard work but we hope it brings some enjoyment to local people. Indeed, if we miss people, they are often on the phone the next day, though we have also been paid not to sing!

George Keyse with his prize winning heifer.

My father, George, was a great Nurseryman. He won many awards for his vegetables, both locally and nationally. Going to the shows was a lovely time. They were real occasions and very competitive. I remember going to Shrewsbury, then the most important show outside London, and to the Royal Horticultural Show in London. Dad always seemed to come back with rosettes, certificates and cups. He also won awards for his livestock. His prize heifer was Reserve Champion at the Gloucester Christmas Fat Stock Show.

George Keyse at the Shrewsbury Flower Show 1958.
1st Prize
for 12 vegetables.

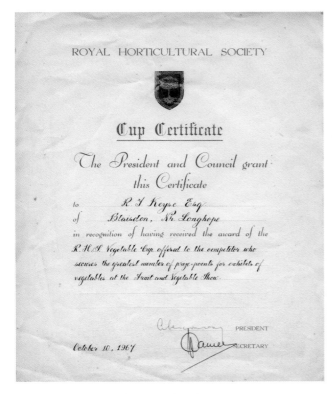

Royal Horticultural Society
Award of the RHS Vegetable Cup
To George Keyse in 1967.

I have inherited my father's love of plants and have continued to run the Nursery since his death in 1981. Plants, flowers, wreaths and produce are always available. As I have now reached retirement, the family business is now continuing with my daughter Claire in charge, while my wife, Ann and I have great fun with our grandchildren, Ella and George."

SUNNYSIDE

Sunnyside in the 1950s.
The orchard to the side is full of Blaisdon Plum Trees.

Opposite Blaisdon Nurseries is the first of three pairs of semi-detached houses. They were all built around the start of the 20th century. They replaced earlier buildings that were deemed to be of insufficient quality. Unlike their predecessors, the new houses were set back from the road and had the luxury of front and back gardens, though initially they all had outside toilets. In a further effort to improve the village, each pair of houses was constructed with different materials. Sunnyside and its neighbour, The Cottage, are faced with local Forest of Dean stone. The second pair is in a mock-Tudor style and the final pair is brick built. On the front of each pair is the date 1908 and the initials MH MI. These stand for Mary Helen MacIver who was, at that time, the owner of Blaisdon Estate. Initially, these were occupied by estate workers, though when the estate was sold in 1933, they were either sold to the sitting tenants or auctioned.

Sunnyside is the left side of the first pair of houses. In the years after the 2nd World War, the house was occupied by Mrs Berry and her son, Sydney. She taught the infants at Blaisdon Village School. They were followed by Mr and Mrs Eagles who lived in Sunnyside with their children, Katherine and Christopher. Katherine sang with us in the Church Choir. Mr and Mrs Chiswell then lived in Sunnyside before Robert and Margaret Pickering arrived in 1958.

Judy Badminton (nee Judith Pickering) remembers her childhood days at Sunnyside:

"I was born in 1951 and, with my parents, Bob and Margaret Pickering, moved to Blaisdon the following year, so I remember little of my very early years. My sister, Elizabeth, was born in 1952 and the dog we had throughout my childhood was called Blaize.

Bob and Margaret Pickering with Judith (standing), Elizabeth (on her bike), plus 2 cousins and Blaize.
1962.

I can remember most of the house being very cold in winter as the only heating was an open coal fire in the living room. My mother would hang our clothes on the fireguard to warm up prior to us running down stairs to get dressed in the morning.

Originally, the house had an outside toilet, coal shed and storeroom. When we moved into Sunnyside, these had been converted into a kitchen and bathroom, though the rooms were very cold and damp as they were only joined to the house by a glass roof and had thin walls. Dad would lock the original back door every night, so no heat from the living room fire would warm them up. I still have the solid stone step and a stone windowsill as a keepsake taken down from these outbuildings when they were pulled down for a new extension in the 1980s.

Judith Pickering with her dog, Blaize, in 1956.

We had one of the few telephones in the village as it was already there when we moved in. It was a shared line with "Blaisdon Nurseries." This meant that only one household could use the telephone at a time. As their phone was by the window we would look across the road to see if Mr or Mrs Keyse were using the phone, before using ours in order to avoid interruption or listening in to conversations. Neighbours who lived near us would frequently use it especially for emergencies, as it was quicker than walking to the phone box at the top of the village. Money would then be left by the phone to pay for the call. My bedroom window overlooked the glass roof and back door so being nosey, if I had heard someone call to use the phone after I had gone to bed, in the morning I would ask what the emergency had been.

We were fairly self sufficient as Dad reared chickens. We probably had around 100 at any one time. This provided meat and eggs and we grew all our own fruit and vegetables, some of which were preserved in various ways and any surplus would be sold. A very, very small box of groceries would be delivered from a shop in Littledean each week, but this was mainly baking ingredients. Fish, bread and pharmacy items were bought from the travelling vans.

A coach regularly called around the local villages picking up mothers and their young children to take them to the baby clinic held in Longhope village hall. I remember each chair had a potty and a bowl by the side of it. My sister and I would be changed ready to be weighed and the clothes would go in the bowl. After being measured we were given our quota of cod liver oil (ugh!) and orange juice (yummy!). This "outing" was also a chance for mums to get together and for the children to play.

My sister and I went to the village school. Despite being surrounded by open space Blaisdon school had no playing fields, but once a year we all marched down a footpath past the Old Rectory to a field that belonged to the Salesian School to hold our sports day. Occasionally we would be taken on a nature walk around the village. I remember each of the schoolrooms being heated by an open fire. Each child was allocated a free third of a pint bottle of milk as part of the Government's drive to improve the health of children. In winter, the frozen, expanded milk would lift off the milk tops and the teacher would put the bottles around the fire grate to thaw. When choosing a school for my children in the 70s I was adamant that they would go to a modern school with big windows as I always felt too enclosed in Blaisdon School as the windows were too high to see out of.

In the days before television, reading was an important pastime, though books were expensive. However, library boxes were delivered to the village school and we were able to go to the school to borrow books to read- this being yesterday's version of the mobile library.

The Red Hart pub had a corridor that divided the bar from the private areas and at the end of the corridor we children could purchase sweets from a stable door that was at the back of the bar. My favourite sweet was a Sherbet Fountain.

Another "outing" for Mums and their children was to the sewing parties that were held in the Tan House. Ladies gathered here to make goods in readiness for fete days. Patterns, ideas and materials were swapped, the children played and tea and biscuits were handed around. Children were also taken along to the Mothers' Union Meetings.

I loved collecting the free cards that came in the packets of tea. I remember going next door to see Mrs Bill Jones to swap duplicate cards with her. This was a treat as I also got to feed her tortoise. When talking to adults, we never used Christian names and to this day I only remember some neighbours as Mr... or Mrs..... Mrs Davis often had sick chickens or lambs keeping warm in her kitchen range. As we had no television I used to go down to my friend Jane's house to watch "Crackerjack" and also "The Secret Garden". It was there at Mill House that I helped pick plums in Mr and Mrs Martin's orchard and in "old" Mr and Mrs Martin's barn we would play in the hay bales. They were of a size that you could just about move in those days. I was aware that many of the villagers were related either to someone in the village or in a nearby village in contrast to we outsiders with our relatives being on the other side of the country."

THE OTTAGE

The Cottage c1950,
when Blaisdon Lane was quiet and often car free.
(R. Keyse)

Next door to Sunnyside is 'The Cottage.' Like its neighbour and the other houses in this row, it did not have vehicle access, only a pathway to the front door. This however would only be used on special occasions; everyday access was round the side of the house to the back door. When these houses were built, cars were virtually unheard of and it was not until the 1980-90s that these houses were given vehicular access from the road.

The Cottage was the home of Mr Samuel and Mrs Minnie Copner during the 1940s. They lived there with their two sons, Harold and John. Samuel Copner was a retired Shipyard worker. Their son Harold joined the Navy and spent a lot of time out in Singapore. John (known as Jack) became a Warrant Officer in the Royal Air Force.

Minnie Copner died on the 9th January 1947 at the age of 76 and Samuel passed away the following week on the 17th January 1947. He was 74 years old. They are buried together in Blaisdon Churchyard.

Following their deaths the house was to be the home of Mr and Mrs Oscar Jones and their two children Oscar

and Catherine until they left in 1956 after which Jack Copner returned to live in The Cottage until his death in 1968 at the age of 66. He is buried near his parents in the Churchyard.

Mr and Mrs Oscar Jones originally lived on Nottwood Hill before coming into the village. Whilst living on the Hill, Mr Jones and his family became involved with Blaisdon Church. Mr Jones took on the job of lighting the boiler in the church cellar every Sunday in order to have the church warm for the Sunday services. This was much appreciated by the congregation, as, like most old, English churches,

St. Michael and all Angels can be very cold, especially in the winter months. Like most of the men in the village he was also a bell ringer and hand bell ringer.

Above:
Mrs Oscar Jones with dog, Joe, outside the Post Office. Although the Post Office is closed, the red telephone box is still very much part of the village.
Left: Mr Oscar Jones snr.
Below:
Mrs O. Jones with Miss Nellie Marshall, walking up the church path. Stud Farm buildings can be seen in the distance.

Catherine Millin (nee Jones) recalls her childhood in Blaisdon:

"I remember cycling to Hinders corner and leaving my bike in Mr Nelmes' shed along with others who had to catch buses to work or school. It was fine during the daytime but very frightening when we came off the bus in the dark and only had a torch to enter Mr Nelmes' shed and find the correct bike.

During the fifties Blaisdon had plenty of activities to take part in, including a Club on Friday nights in the school, the ladies taking it in turn to do the refreshments. Mr

Above: Left to right
Ursula Howells, Mrs Oscar & Catherine Jones plus
Joe the dog.

Left: A closer view of The Cottage with Sunnyside on
the left, showing the stone construction.

Below: Catherine Jones is escorted to Blaisdon
Church by her father, Oscar Jones snr.
(1956)

Ricketts played the piano. We also had dancing classes with Miss Whittard at what was the old school room but is now Far View. Choir practise was once a week in church, Mr Buckett played the organ and Mr Etherington was choirmaster. I also remember going to Flaxley Rectory where, Mary Lane, the Rev. Lane's wife, supervised games. The village boys were invited to join the Hall boys at their Camps etc. The reservoir in the woods behind Blaisdon Hall provided a wonderful playground for all the local boys. And many learnt to swim there including my brother, Oscar."

Cath moved to Elton Corner in 1956 when she married Bernard Millin in Blaisdon Church and her parents moved to Little London. Oscar meanwhile married Joyce Bevan in 1960 at Huntley Church and returned to live on Nottwood Hill for the next 46 years at Alfred House.

Mr Oscar Jones senior died on the 25th April 1980 and Mrs Oscar died on the 22nd July 1994. They are buried together in Blaisdon Churchyard.

WESTERN VIEW

The middle pair of houses is built in the mock Tudor style. Western View is on the left. In the 1940s, it was the home of Mr and Mrs Young and their daughter, **Susan Young**, who writes of her memories of Blaisdon:

"I have lovely childhood memories of life in Blaisdon. I came to live there in the late forties having been staying with my Grandparents, Mr and Mrs Harry Young at Step-a-Side on Popes Hill. Once settled in, we would often cycle along the almost deserted lanes from Blaisdon to Flaxley via Monks Hill to see Granny Young at Step-a-Side.

Western View in the foreground with its neighbour, Halt Cottage. Belmont and Claremont are the next houses.
(R. Keyse)

Susan Young.

My parents were Jack and Bobbie Young and my dog was Rusty! He may have been the dachshund that killed Chuggy Lane's rats but I cannot remember that occasion!

I will always remember the steam trains to Gloucester with the banks of moon daisies by the station, as well as Aunt Ada and Uncle George Keyse's Nursery. It had so many greenhouses!

Visiting Aunt Mary Price at The Red Hart, I remember jumping elvers in the frying pan when I called on my way to school. Then there was Freddie Grace pulling my plaits whilst playing in the playground and my mother sending me back when I ran home from school!

These were carefree days and these cherished memories will always be with me. Oh, Happy Days."

Susan Young with her Father, Jack
& Grandparents,
Mr & Mrs Harry Young
from
Step-A-Side (Flaxley).

Jack & Susan Young.

Susan with her mother, Bobbie.

Susan with her father, Jack, and Rusty.

In 1957, the Young family moved from Western View and Bill and Evelyn Jones moved into the house. **Brian Jones** comments:

"Bill was the eighth child of Dan and Martha Jones and was brought up at Brookside Cottage in Woodgreen. He was married to Evelyn Young from Flaxley. She belonged to the Flaxley Youngs of "Garden Cottage" and left Blaisdon School to go into "service" in a London City house. Later she worked for the Payne family (well known Artists) at Amberley, Stroud. After their wedding in 1926 they lived at Streamways, a cottage at Woodgreen. Whilst living there two of their children Ena and Brian were born. Prior to the War they moved to Blaisdon where Barbara and then Nancy were born. In 1938 Bill helped in the distribution of gas masks. Due to work at Bullo Pill Goods Yard, he moved to Newnham and joined the Home Guard.

I do not remember much about "the War" in Blaisdon as I had just started school here. I recall walking out to see a small plane in a field along the Flaxley road and taking a gas mask to school. Later, at Newnham School, we had time off to pick up potatoes and gather rose hips to help the war effort.

In 1957 we moved back to Western View in the village where Bill was always very active. For many years he kept the churchyard tidy and in 1972 helped in getting the village ready for their entry into the Bledisloe Cup competition for the Best Kept Village.

It was whilst tying the roses on the fencing of the Village Hall that he fell from a ladder and died in Gloucester Hospital on the 29th of August 1974 (See report in Dean Forest Mercury). His memorial is the many honeysuckles he planted and which still flourish around Blaisdon. Evelyn continued to live in Western View and as there were 2 elderly Mrs Jones in the village, she became universally and affectionately known as Mrs Willie or Mrs Bill. She died on the 18th February 1995 and is buried together with Bill and their young son, William, in our churchyard."

Left:
Mr & Mrs Bill Jones outside Western View.

Below:
Evelyn Jones & her eldest daughter, Ena.

Following the death of Bill Jones, the following report was printed in the Dean Forest Mercury on Friday 6th September 1974:

A Shock when Blaisdon lost its beloved Mr. Jones

"The whole village of Blaisdon was stunned with shock and grief to learn of the sudden death of Mr William Jones. Mr Jones was tying up the roses and honeysuckle on the fence round the village hall when the ladder he was using broke in half and he fell to the ground. He died soon afterward last Thursday evening in the City General Hospital, Gloucester. An inquest was opened on Tuesday morning and adjourned to a date to be fixed.
Mr Jones lived at Western View, Blaisdon; he was 77. He is survived by his wife to whom he was married for 47 years, a son and two daughters.

Mr Jones was born at Woodgreen, Blaisdon and had lived most of his life in the village. He went to work on the railways as soon as he left school and, apart from serving in the Royal Artillery in the First World War, worked on the railways as a signalman until he retired in his 70th year. He completed a total of 54 years on the railways, latterly at Grange Court.

A real village character, Mr Jones was held in affectionate respect in Blaisdon. He was always ready to lend a helping hand to anyone that needed it and his help at gardening was often in demand.

Mr Jones loved his church and his village and expressed that love in years of devoted service and hard work. He was a churchwarden at the Church of St. Michael and All Angels, Blaisdon, a member of the P.C.C. and a bell-ringer.

He kept the churchyard in good order and helped with spring-cleaning the church interior. He spent hours, too, for the village, tidying up anything that needed tidying and helping to maintain the village Hall. He was one of those mainly responsible for Blaisdon's success in winning the Bledisloe Cup for the Best Kept Village in 1972.

He will be greatly missed in Blaisdon for many years to come and remembered with gratitude.

The funeral took place on Wednesday at Blaisdon Church. After cremation his ashes were brought back for burial to Blaisdon."

HALT COTTAGE

Halt Cottage and, to its left, Western View.

Next door to Western View is Halt Cottage. The Blake family lived here from 1949 to 1958, Frank and Edith and their children, Maureen and John. **Maureen Blake** recalls her life in Blaisdon:

"I spent a very happy childhood at Halt Cottage with my Mum and Dad (Edith and Frank) and my brother John.

Mum and Dad met at a cricket match in Madras India in 1938. Mum was a nanny to Colonel Atkins' family and Dad was in the army. They started their married life in Rangoon Burma (now Myanmar) but had to leave very quickly as the Japanese were invading the country. Mum and my sister Rosemary were put on a ship that was sailing to Calcutta in India and Dad had to fight the Japanese in Burma. (He didn't comment on it much but I was always well aware not to buy a Japanese car as he would not have got into it!). Mum arrived in Calcutta and was taken in by the nuns that were part of Mother Theresa's life and work.

Mum was then pregnant with my brother John and Dad arrived in Jalunder on the day John was born; Dad collapsed and Mum went into labour! Three years later my sister Judith was born and Mum, Dad, Rosemary, John and Judith led a contented life until, tragically, Rosemary and Judith died within six weeks of each other age 4 and 1 with dysentery. Fortunately for me I was already on the way and I was born in 1947 in Dalhousie in the Punjab and what an event that must have been because the whole of India became independent. Mum and Dad, John and I sailed to England in January 1948. We spent a year in Kent with my Mum's sister and then came to live in Blaisdon to be near my Dad's parents who lived at Popes Hill.

I met my best friend Margaret Ashcroft living in Blaisdon and we both started Blaisdon School aged 3. I remember Brother Joe at the farm taking us for rides on the tractor, being on the roundabout at Blaisdon Hall and the Hall boys pushing us round – what fun!

Sadly Margaret and family left Blaisdon to live in Brockworth but we still stayed friends. Mum would take me down to Blaisdon Halt and put me on a train, aged about 6 or 7, then Marg and her Mum would be there to meet me at Gloucester Station and Marg would do the same coming to Blaisdon and Mum and I would meet her off the train. Just imagine doing this now!!!

Maureen & John Blake. (1953)

Maureen, age 7 in Ley Park Woods, near Blaisdon.

Dad drove a Morris 8 car, registration GUA 875. (Isn't it funny the things you can remember). We had lovely family days out and picnics and, of course, we all went to the cricket matches when Dad was playing. Marg and I both remember being in the back of Dad's car with John in the front and we were going towards Westbury and on a sharp bend John fell out of the car and landed in the ditch! Marg and I laughed but Dad was not too pleased needless to say. Thankfully John was ok but after that he broke his arm falling out of a tree!

Dad refereed the football matches up at the Hall (he was very sporty in the Army) and I remember on baking day the Priests would always come to the house to chat to Mum and Dad, and demolish everything that Mum had baked. Marg's mum told me many years later that the Priests gave all the food they had to the 'boys' and people in the village fed the Priests!

I remember that we were the first house in the village to have a television and there was always lots of people around to come and watch - do you remember Quatermass and the Pit? I used to duck behind the chair when the frightening parts were shown.

There was no bathroom at Halt Cottage and Mum would fire up the boiler once a week for John and I to fill up the tin bath. The loo was brick built in the garden. We had four chickens called Hetty, Lotty, Fanny and Flo; names from a book that I loved called Chickweed. We also had a rabbit, a tortoise and a guinea pig called Oi Oi as that was the noise he made! John used to go and help pluck the chickens at Christmas time at the Keyse's Nurseries. I never eat poultry myself and I think that it stems from our pet chickens!

I will always have very fond memories of my childhood in Blaisdon: riding my fairy cycle and then a bigger bicycle, down the lanes to Flaxley, where, incidently, I was one of the ladies in waiting at the Coronation Pageant in 1953; making mud pies; and going to the whist drive with Dad where he brought home the prize that Mum had donated!

Sir Lance and Lady Crawley Boevey, who then lived at Flaxley Abbey used to give the school prizes and it was great fun being at the Abbey. There were nativity plays – John was a shepherd and I, of course, was a little angel. I won 1st prize as a Dutch girl in a fancy dress competition. Another time I was dressed as a flower girl.

Top:
Edith Blake with John & Maureen.

Right:
Maureen & photographer's dog.

Far Right:
Maureen winning 1st Prize as a Dutch girl.

I was also in the church choir. Mrs Trippier was my teacher when I passed my 11 plus to go to East Dean Grammar School. Mum and Dad decided that as Dad worked at R.A.lister in Cinderford and John and myself would both be at school in Cinderford that we should move there. I know that Mum enjoyed life far more in Blaisdon and kept in touch with people there. She joined the Women's Club in Littledean where Mrs Grace, who also used to live in Blaisdon went, and a good natter went on I am sure.

Sadly, John died aged 35 of a brain tumour in 1979. Dad died aged 82, 10 days before his and Mum's Golden Wedding Anniversary in 1989 and Mum died, aged 90, in 1997.

Marg Ashcroft (now Cookson) and her immediate and extended family camp in Blaisdon every year and I always visit them. I wouldn't miss it for the world. They were very Happy Days."

Edith and Frank Blake.
(12/9/1970)

BELMONT

The left-hand side of the third pair of semi-detached dwellings is Belmont, now called Nettlestones. It and its neighbour are brick built with a porch over the front door. A path led to the front door. Anne and David Warren, together with their son Leslie, lived in Belmont from 1936. *Leslie Warren* tells us of his memories:

"My Grandfather originated from Bury St Edmunds in Suffolk and travelled to the West Country seeking work, which he found as Gamekeeper at Blaisdon Hall working for the MacIver and Stubs families. He later becoming head Gamekeeper and lived at Stanley House up the fields. He married a girl from Adsett, Alice Butler. They had three children, May and, eight years later, twins William and Anne, my Mother. She worked 'in service' around the area; Malvern was mentioned a lot. She also did dressmaking and played piano. May married Harry Wilkins from Lymington who had a smallholding. William was educated at Ross Grammar School and went on to become a Fellow of the Royal Horticultural Society. He married Ruby a girl from Selly Oak in Birmingham and they had one daughter, Betty. He ran a Department at Birmingham University during the war and became Curator of the University and would visit us in his Morris Minor. My mother Anne married David Warren. He worked 8 acres of orchards growing fruit and cattle.

Belmont.

My first memory of Blaisdon was being taken to look over "Belmont" a semi-detached which my parents bought, it was empty and overgrown. The year was 1936 and I was aged 8 when we moved. Village life was very different in those days. We used to get our drinking water from a roadside tap in a metal bollard. We would lift the handle and a good flow resulted, fed from a spring somewhere at the top of the village. It never dried up and always was clean and tasted good.

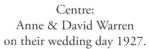

Centre:
Anne & David Warren
on their wedding day 1927.

Lower right:
David Warren building a hayrick, 1940.

Others:
David & Anne Warren
Haymaking, 1951.

A few residents had radios since these needed two accumulators (Storage batteries) as there was no mains electricity in our early days. Each week, one was taken for charging the other delivered charged. The man lived in Longhope and used a petrol or paraffin driven engine generator to charge them. You also needed a high tension dry battery of 120 volts. The 2 volts accumulator was needed to heat the 3 or 4 valves in the sets and take high tension to drive them.

There were no telephones. Cooking was on the black leaded range with a fire of coal or wood. We also had a paraffin cooker. Lighting was by paraffin lamps or candles.

Groceries were delivered weekly after orders were collected by a man calling each week from Longhope Stores. A fish and chip man came some weeks. Milk was delivered daily. We took our jug/container out to the man with a horse drawn cart. It was not unknown for a farmer to get taken to Court for watering the milk though I do not know of it happening to any of our local farmers.

Few people had cars. Gloucester could be reached by cycling or walking to Hinders Corner and catching a Cottrells' bus or catching the train from Blaisdon Halt, There was a corrugated shelter on one side of the track and a ticket office and animal pound on the other. Mr Sargent ran the office. It was very warm in winter as coal was plentiful. He came over to meet the train and unload parcels. Mr Martin was the local coal man with a coal yard near the ticket office. He always delivered your coal after good rainstorms, by horse drawn cart and 1cwt bags.

Rail travel had its problems. The platform was short and

Blaisdon Lane showing Belmont and the other houses on the right. The Van outside is owned by Francis Blakeway, Gloucester fruit & vegetable merchants.

many of the carriages had no corridors, so unless you boarded in the centre carriages the door opened onto a drop down to the track. As drivers were keen on timekeeping rarely would they move the train, so you stayed on to the next stop. This applied to many rural stations. There was a level crossing to a farm and cottages along Velthouse Lane near to the back entrance to Blaisdon Hall. There were several deaths there in my time including a local man with his motor cycle & sidecar.

I remember quite a few people who were our neighbours and lived in the village. Mrs Goddard ran the Post Office giving a good service. However, you only got your requirements after she had extracted all the village gossip you knew. Mr Lane lived by the Mill Cottage. He was a watch/clock maker/repairer – riding a bicycle with one leg, the other was paralysed. The Tan House at the lower part of the village was old. In the past the barn opposite had been used as a tannery. As far as I can remember an older man lived there, named Joyce, he was an academic or professor and something of a recluse. Mr and Mrs Harvey lived opposite us in a large house, with their two children, Sue and Mary. Mr Harvey was the first person in the village that I can remember owning a car. I recall that it was a Ford 8. I know little about the Red Hart Pub as I was not encouraged to drink and not taken there. My father did patronise it. Mr Bill Jones rode a push bike to Grange Court Station where he was a signalman. Mrs Jones went to the same school as my mother and was very clever. The Nursery was run by Mr George Keyse who was on the Council. Mr Copner was a retired Dockyard Engineer who lived opposite Mr Keyse and was great at fixing things.

Our neighbours were Mr and Mrs Davis and their four children. Mrs Davis being an Arts and Crafts person and her pictures were taken to many far away places. I have just counted 5 of them in our home, birds and squirrels. Mr Davis was a smallholder and he also had his own car. In later life we took them to London, as they had never been by train.

Opposite the Church in a nice detached house lived a Mr Brewer, Blaisdon Hall Maintenance Engineer, one of his machines I remember was in a building along a near by lane. It was a horizontal cylinder paraffin engine pumping water to Blaisdon Hall. It was always polished and gleaming. Stud Farm was The Hall's Farm and the Dairy, now made into a bungalow, is opposite the Pub.

My village life as a child was playing around the run down buildings opposite, riding around on my push bike, watching work being done, trees being cut down and pulled onto lorries by tractors and a steel rope. I would watch the farmers at work and enjoyed the chance to ride on horse drawn wagons during haymaking.

Sundays were always church days. Most people attended and talked about the sermon. After the outbreak of war in 1939 there was much talk of who would or would not be called up. Food rationing did not as far as I can recollect make much difference, eggs, rabbits and homegrown vegetables were always available, as was a communal pig that was slaughtered, the meat being shared around.

In early spring elvers were brought around door to door. Most of the local people were connected with the land and escaped the war, as they were required to continue in their occupations as food production was of major importance.

Left: Leslie Warren, 1939 age 11 outside Belmont.
Note the large Yew, now gone, outside Spout Farm.
Right: Anne Warren & Bingy outside Belmont.

There were no imported foods to supply the shops due to the German naval blockade, though I cannot remember a coal or paraffin shortage. Most householders burned wood on smoky fires. Best rooms were used at weekends or special occasions and heated by an open fire which, depending on wind direction, often smoked and heated one's front either too hot or not at all.

During the war a bomb aimed at the railway line blew a hole in the side of a cottage alongside the brook. The road was passable on foot only. I cannot remember if there were any casualties in the cottage. Another bomb caused a large earth mound in King's field near the railway line. Another incident I recall was a Hurricane pilot with engine trouble attempting to land in a field on the Flaxley road. It did not quite make it and crashed into a ditch. Mr King and others got the injured pilot out of the wreckage and looked after him until an RAF Ambulance arrived. After his recovery he called to see and thank them. My friends and I visited the wreckage after school. We took no notice of the strings of live bullets. I have a few bits of bent wreckage.

The Head Mistress, Mrs Smith, and the other teacher, Mrs Berry, ran the village school. In 1938/39 I remember Mrs Smith proudly showing us all her new Vauxhall car. The School Attendance Officer called weekly and I was very proud of being top of the attendance list on leaving the school at the age of 11.

At the age of 11 village children who did not pass a scholarship to the local Grammar Schools were taken by bus to Abenhall School near Mitcheldean. I remember doing well in algebra, wood and metal work. However, it was wartime and many teachers were called up. Those remaining in the schools were overworked and very stressed. I left school at 14 with no school certificates and cannot remember any exams. I served an apprenticeship in Electrical Engineering with L.C.Mitchells in Gloucester, travelling to work first by auto cycle then motorcycle. At the age of 17, in 1946, my father had a good year with his cattle and fruit and asked me to buy a car. I found a 10 H.P. Singer saloon for £200. It had 4 seats, 4 doors,

no heater, and a 3-speed gearbox and did 22 mpg. I had driven a tractor on the land since the age of 12 so I was able to get in the Singer and get used to driving it. We travelled at weekends to visit the various relations. On Saturdays the usual trip was to the Roxy Cinema at Ross on Wye, taking Mr and Mrs Davis (Tom and Ivy).

Someone approached Mr and Mrs Etherington at The Forge and we were allowed to garage the car there, as our house did not have a drive. They were a nice couple and they both talked to me but I can never remember taking them out in the car. The last time I met Mr Etherington (Cedric) was in Westgate Street Gloucester where he told me he was on "Borrowed Time" as he was over 70. At 81 and a half how much more can I borrow? Enough for 6 weeks in Tenerife Nov/Dec and four weeks in Mexico during mid Jan/Feb. Grandfather made 91 and Father 81 and smoked! He died in 1979, his gravestone reads 'A true and well liked countryman'."

Leslie Warren 1947.

A vehicle and passengers in Blaisdon Lane, just below the Red Hart Inn.
Left to right:
Ann Warren & her dog, Barry Davis, John Blake, Roger Keyse, ?, Brenda Davis, plus Leslie Warren attending the vehicle.
The vehicle is believed to be an old Morris 10 that Barry Davis had put together and made roadworthy.

CLAREMONT

Claremont is the final house in the row. For many years it was the home of the Davis family. **_Barry Davis_** recalls his memories:

"My parents, Ivor Thomas Davis (known as 'Tom') and Ivy Kibble were married at Flaxley Church in February 1930. Initially, they moved into a cottage and here their children Grace (1930), Barry (1933) and Brenda (1935) were born. Their third daughter Norma was born in 1938 at Claremont in Blaisdon where Tom Davis had bought five acres of orchard.

Above: Claremont.
Left: Brenda with Nipper and sheep at front door of Claremont.
Nipper sits on a milk churn. These were in common usage at this time.

We undertook our move to Blaisdon by horse and cart. Dad probably borrowed these from Ernie King's Farm (Monkhill) because he did some part time work there. The cart was loaded with all of our belongings and we set off with mum and Brenda riding on the front of the cart, dad leading the horse. Grace and I were hanging onto the back of the cart trying to keep up. We settled into our new home at Claremont very quickly.

There was an abundance of wildlife in the fields and woods around Blaisdon and we soon established where the nearest ponds and brooks were. There were moorhens, toads, frogs and snakes everywhere if you knew where to look.

I was lucky as my younger sister Brenda shared my passion for adventure and wildlife. Although young, she soon established pigs and lambs on the orchard at Blaisdon and was rearing them for markets. She had a passion for animals and continued her involvement in farming for the rest of her life.

Above:
Brenda with her dog, Nipper & pet sheep.

Right from the top:
Brenda with her animals at Claremont.
Cows do funny things!!
The family pig and litter.

The war started when we were living at Claremont and I remember that all the windows had to be blacked out and we had no lights. Mum had a passion for painting and she continued to paint throughout the war sometimes by candlelight during the blackout. This lack of light coupled with her very poor eyesight did not dampen her enthusiasm for her oil painting on silk. We all still have many of her paintings in our home today.

One very frightening experience during the war still stays with me. A German bomber flew over Blaisdon and dropped a bomb, which seemed to scream right past the windows of Claremont. We all panicked, Grace and Brenda hid under the bed and I got into the wardrobe. I don't think we slept at all for the rest of that night. Although the war was very scary for us kids, it also provided an opportunity for more adventure. Brenda and I were the first to discover and examine the wreckage of two British aircraft. One was, I think, a Spitfire, which crashed by Stud Farm and the other possibly a Hurricane we found along the Flaxley road by Ernie King's farm.

July, August and September were always a busy time for the Davis family. Every year the whole family picked fruit (blackcurrants and plums). The children picked alongside the adults to earn some pocket money and this family tradition continued until machinery took over blackcurrant picking in the late eighties. My own daughters were no strangers to the family fruit picking tradition and picked blackcurrants alongside us from a very early age. It was hard work out in the fields from first light until late afternoon, but Ann and Shirley have happy memories of those years when they had their own adventures building dens and exploring, as well as earning

some money to spend on their summer holiday. It kept us all fit too, carrying four buckets of currants (two on each arm) down the fields to the scales and lifting 56lb boxes of plums onto the trailer.

Tom carried on picking the plums at Claremont well into his seventies and fell off the ladder when he was in his mid-seventies and ended up in hospital for a while. This accident turned out to be a blessing in disguise as during his stay at Gloucester Royal the surgeons fixed up a stomach operation which dad had at 16 which hadn't healed up properly. This episode didn't put him off plum picking either and he was back up the trees as usual the following year. We didn't just pick the plums planted in the orchard at Claremont we also picked plums for other growers in the area, including Skeltons near Longhope and at Northwood Green and Flaxley. Dad, Brenda and I were skilled at moving around the 36-foot ladders, perfectly balanced and upright. We were all good pickers and Brenda once came second in a competition for picking a ton of plums a day.

Brenda
at the plum picking
competition where she
came 2nd.

Plum Picking Time for the Davis Family.

Above:
Grace, Ivy, Doreen, Ann & Shirley, Tom, Norma & Brenda.

In 1950 I joined the RAF, along with Oscar Jones a local boy I grew up with. During my time in the RAF I bought the Black Austin Tourer, which is in a photo taken at Blaisdon (page 91). I particularly liked this car and there is a photograph of the same model of car in an album by the American Band leader Glenn Miller who I really liked.

Barry Davis, left of 2nd row.
At RAF Cottesmore, 1953-54.

It was after I joined the RAF that I met my wife Doreen. We met at a dance in Newent. We married on 24th May 1958 and celebrated our Golden Wedding anniversary two years ago. When we were courting, Doreen and I used to spend a lot of time with my sister Grace, her husband Cecil Beard, my sister Norma and her boyfriend Terry Turner and a neighbour Stephen. We used to take Dad's white van and go to dances in Newent on a Saturday night. I don't know how we managed to squeeze so many people into one van, but we did. I often travelled in the back of the van, sitting with the doors open, playing my accordion all the way home with the rest of them singing

along. They were great times and we had a lot of fun. My accordion playing featured very heavily during that time of my life. I played it in the local pubs and in later years we would also go carol singing around the village with me accompanying everyone on my piano accordion. I am not sure how in-tune we were given that it was Christmas and everyone had been drinking, but this was another family tradition that continued for many years and long after the grandchildren arrived to join in.

Sadly Brenda died in 1992 after a long battle with cancer. Tom Davis passed away in 1993, on his and Ivy's 63rd Wedding Anniversary. Ivy followed him a year later and not long after, Claremont was sold. The people who bought Claremont made some alterations to the house and found the names Grace, Barry, Brenda and Norma written under the stairs. I don't know who did it as I don't remember putting our names there, but it is nice to know that we are all still part of the house as Claremont and Blaisdon were a big part of our lives for many years. The family still own the plum orchard and still pick plums to this day. We had many good times in the house and have fond memories of those days. Blaisdon village will always have a special place in our family and in all our hearts."

Barry's wife **Doreen Davis** also has fond memories of Claremont and Blaisdon. She recalls the time:

"I met Barry Davis on a Saturday night at a dance in Newent when I was 15. I remember he looked very smart in his RAF uniform. Very soon after we were courting and I spent a great deal of my time at Claremont with the Davis family. Grace was married to Cecil and they lived in a cottage in the village. In those days when I stayed over at

Claremont I shared a double bed with Brenda and Norma. Norma and I became good friends. Norma was courting Terry Turner and we used to all go out together. I easily fitted in with the family tradition of fruit picking as I had been brought up picking fruit myself. Most of the families in the area picked fruit to make extra money.

In the summer of 1957 Norma and I spent our holiday plum picking at Jeff Hart's. With the money we made we bought items for our 'bottom drawer,' the tradition of buying things in advance of marrying and setting up home. That year we each bought a tea set, mine was blue/white and I still have it to this day. We also bought tea, coffee, sugar and biscuit jars and tea towels. All of our items were bought in Woolworths because Norma had a job there and I think she may have got a discount! I don't think the tradition of buying things for a bottom drawer is so prevalent today, but Norma and I had a great time earning extra money and then buying things for our future 'home'. It made us feel very grown up, even though we were really still very young, in our teens. Girls today would probably rather spend their money on other things.

Barry and I married on 24th May 1958 and recently celebrated our Golden Wedding Anniversary, another family tradition as both my parents and Barry's parents celebrated 50 years of marriage. Indeed Tom and Ivy Davis achieved their diamond, celebrating 60 years of marriage in 1990. Norma and Terry married in 1960, Norma altered and wore my wedding dress and they celebrate their Golden Wedding in 2010."

Weddings:

Top:
Barry & Doreen's wedding,
Dymock Church.
(24th May 1958)

Centre:
Brenda's wedding to Roderick
Watkins at Flaxley Abbey.

Left:
Barry on his wedding day with
best man Cecil Beard.

More Weddings:

Top Left:
Grace with father, Tom, walking to church.

Top:
Mr & Mrs Cecil Beard.

Centre Left:
Blaisdon Church Choir at Grace's wedding.

Left:
Norma' wedding to Terry Turner (1960).

Right:
Local newspaper report of Grace's wedding.

Blaisdon Wedding

St. Michael and All Angels, Blaisdon, was beautifully decorated for the occasion of the marriage of Cecil Beard, only son of Mr and Mrs George Beard, of Nottwood Hill, Blaisdon, to Miss Grace Davis, eldest daughter of Mr and Mrs Tom Davis, of "Claremont," Blaisdon.

The ceremony was conducted by the Rev. Denis Lane, Rector of Blaisdon with Mr Roberts organist. The hymns, led by the choir were "Lead us Heavenly Father, lead us," "O Perfect Love" and Psalm 67.

The bride, who was given away by her father, wore a gown of heavy cream figured satin, with lace veil and orange blossom headdress to match, and carried a bouquet of orange carnations.

She was attended by the Misses Brenda and Norma Davis, sisters of the bride, Miss Margaret Beard, sister of the bridegroom, and Miss Hazel Godwin, niece of the bridegroom, dressed in gold mauve, green and blue taffeta respectively, with silver headdresses, and carrying bouquets of coloured carnations. The best man was Mr Gerald Bullock, the bridegroom's cousin.

As the couple left the church, the bell ringers formed an archway of hand-bells.

The reception was held at the School and attended by a large number of guests.

The honeymoon is being spent at Bournemouth, the bride travelling in a pale blue dress with navy accessories.

Top Left:
Barry & Doreen,
by the River Severn at Broadoak.

Above:
Norma & niece Gillian
on a tractor with Spout Farm
behind.

Left:
A Francis Blakeway lorry, driven
by Cecil Beard. On it are
Margaret Ashcroft
&
Maureen Blake.
Spout Farm is immediately
behind them & The Rectory can
be seen in the distance.

Above:
A painting on silk by Ivy Davis.

Above Left:
Barry's Car, a black Austin Tourer
with Noreen Tobin & Gillian Beard.

Left:
Tom's van with Brenda & Grace
plus sheep.

Above, left to right:
Norma, Brenda, Ivy & Grace Davis on Barry's BSA.
(This & some other photos shown here: L. Watkins, Brenda's daughter).

Opposite:
Aerial view of Claremont plus its five neighbours.
The orchards around the houses are those referred to in the text.
Most of the outbuildings have now been taken down.

SPOUT FARM

An early view of Spout Farm.
Sue Harvey is standing by the gate, 2 yew trees behind her.

Spout Farm lies in the centre of the Village and formed part of the Blaisdon Estate. When the Tan House became the Estate Office, the Tan House farmland was combined with Spout Farm and together, they were known as 'The Home Farm.' When the Estate was sold, the Tan House farmlands were sold separately and Spout Farm was bought by the Salesian Order, which also bought Blaisdon Hall and the Stud Farm.

Susan Harvey.

In the 1930s, Mr and Mrs Harvey and their daughters, Mary and Susan, lived in the Farm House. After Mr Harvey's death, the farmhouse was split with the Harveys living in the left side (looking from the road) and the remainder let to Mr and Mrs Ashcroft and their family. The Tobin family followed them during the 1950s. After Mrs Harvey left the village, her half of the House was let to Mr and Mrs Nicol and their two children who took up residence in the late fifties.

Memories of **Susan Harvey:**

"I went to live in Blaisdon in 1932 at Spout Farm which was renamed Home Farm. My parents, Harold and Kathleen, moved there from Ley Mill, Westbury-on-Severn.

94

The headteacher at the school was Mrs Smith, who lived in the adjacent schoolhouse. Mrs Berry was the infant teacher and lived at " Sunnyside" in the village. Some of the children came to school from Popes Hill and others from Nottwood Hill, and because of the distance they had to walk, beds were provided for them to rest during the afternoon. One of the things that we had to do every morning was to go to the village well, on the corner by Mr Wilce's house (Spring Cottage) and fetch the daily supply of water. There was also a village pump outside Home Farm where we had to draw water from.

The Gloucestershire Dairy Students used the Dairy, next door to Spout Farm and now called Dairy Cottage. Butter and cheeses were made at the Dairy.

Mr Grindon delivered milk to the villagers. I used to enjoy helping at weekends and holidays. Milk was in a large churn and served with a pint measure into jugs waiting on the doorsteps. Mr Green from Huntley was the Baker. He had a horse-drawn covered wagon. He always wore a black bowler hat. George Knight owned the Forge at the bottom end of the village. It was always a place we loved to go as children to see horseshoes made.

Above:
Miss Kathleen West driving the Lovegrove Dairy vehicle when employed as a dairy maid for the suffragette Pankhurst family. Kathleen undertook the milk deliveries when the Pankhursts were in jail. She married Mr Harold Harvey and lived at Ley Mill, later moving to Blaisdon.

Below, left to right:
Susan & Kathleen Harvey.
Kathleen.
Susan, Kathleen, Jack West(Uncle), Harold Harvey.

Blaisdon Halt had a sparse train service. The only other means of transport was to catch a bus from Hinders corner or the Weighbridge in Westbury. It was quite a walk either way!

I married Alec Baber from Awre at Blaisdon Church in 1949. We had a Guard of Honour of traditional farming tools as we walked from the church through the garden of Church Cottage."

The wedding of Susan Harvey and Alec Baber
on
17th September 1949.

Andrew Ashcroft writes:

"My parents, Frank and Joan Ashcroft moved into Home Farm with their three children Richard aged 9, myself aged 8 and Elizabeth aged 7. Margaret was born at Spout Farm in January 1948. At the age of 11, Richard and I went to East Dean Grammar School and Elizabeth went to St Rose's in Stroud. Frank Ashcroft was a designer at Gloster Aircraft Company in Brockworth, driving to work every day. The family moved from Spout Farm in 1953.

I remember the mysterious Mr Buckeridge! One day a strange man moved into one of the buildings in the yard. He was scruffy and unkempt, with a straggly ginger beard almost down to his waist and he was dirty. I don't remember him ever saying anything, but I got the impression he was very irritable and we were a bit scared of him. His name was Mr Buckeridge and apparently he was an artist, but I can't remember seeing any of his art. I can't remember how long he stayed but he left as suddenly as he arrived.

I got the impression that Dad didn't have much time for him and used to call him "Abu Ben Buckeridge" but Mum was always sympathetic and used to give him meals and do his washing. My abiding memory was the sight of his threadbare long johns on the washing line. As I say, we never saw anything of his art, but Mum's washing line looked like an installation by Tracy Emin.

Old Pad was the best dog that ever lived; a beautiful straw-coloured English mastiff, as patient as Job, and at least as intelligent as Einstein. She was getting on a bit when we lived at Blaisdon and although we loved her, she wasn't active enough to be of much interest to us youngsters.

One day she was in the paddock sleeping in the sun, while we played darts. This was outdoor darts without a dartboard, the object of the game being to see how high we could throw the dart. One throw went off target, veering towards the sleeping dog. It seemed an age falling to the ground and we were sure Pad was about to be punctured and she was. The dart pinned her big floppy ear to the ground. We weren't that relieved at first because she was sure to leap up and tear a lump out of her ear. In the event she didn't even stir. She survived, and eventually died of natural causes without any help from us, being laid to rest, coincidentally, in the exact spot where she had had her ear painlessly pierced.

The big event in 1953 was the Coronation of Queen Elizabeth II. Our local celebration was to be a garden party at Flaxley Abbey. The highlight for me was the fancy dress competition. This was the dawning of the space age, and every boy's hero was Dan Dare in the "Eagle" comic. Anthony Jones and I decided to go as spacemen. With our war surplus gas masks and overalls and our best wellies, we really looked the part. When the winners were announced, first prize went not to the spacemen but the divers. It took a while for us to realize that we were the winners and, frankly, we would have preferred to lose rather than be

taken for divers. What would Dan Dare have thought? The prize, a Coronation Crown, was some consolation, as I was able to flog it for 5 shillings (25p) when I was out of funds.

Whenever I begin to tell my grandchildren how things were better in "the good old days", for some reason they feel it necessary to look up at the ceiling. 'I used to leave my bike at Hinders corner, where I caught the school bus, without a lock, and it never got pinched,' I'd say. To tell the truth, it did get "borrowed" once. When we reported it to the police at Westbury they said 'Come and get it, it's been handed in.' When I got there the desk sergeant gave me an address on a bit of paper, and said 'This is the man who found it, you must write and thank him for his honesty.' As I cycled home I figured that he had probably borrowed it, and as he had made me walk all that way I wasn't going to thank him at all. I stopped under the railway bridge and tore the paper into tiny pieces, so small that the police would not be able to put it together and identify it, and dropped it down the drain. I was convinced I was committing a serious crime by not doing what the police had told me to."

Elizabeth Ashcroft also remembers Blaisdon:

Having struggled for several years with the ancient paraffin cooker, Mum decided that a Calor Gas cooker would have a modernising effect on her kitchen. The contents of a house in Newnham were up for auction including a gas cooker, so off she went, taking with her the grand sum, for those days, of £10. In the evening Dad asked whether she had been lucky in her bid for said cooker whereby Mum rather sheepishly had to admit that she had bought a

Left: Andrew Ashcroft in his 'spaceman' outfit.
Right: A close-up of the 'spaceman's helmet!'
(Also known as a war surplus gas mask)

previous lot – 2 antique carver chairs for £8. So the cooker would have to wait for a while.

Dad as they say 'was not best pleased' and, not that he needed an excuse, went for a pint in the Red Hart where he related the story to the landlord, Gideon Price. "I'll take them off your hands Frank" old Gid said, here's a tenner. Dad thought about it for all of 10 seconds before saying "No, I think we'll keep them," and keep them they did. The chairs are still with the family now, sixty years later, and I'm looking at one now. The gas cooker did arrive later but hasn't lasted as long!"

Margaret Cookson (nee Ashcroft) writes about her son, Flight Lieutenant Christopher Cookson:

"Chris was born on 18th May 1969 the second child and only son of Margaret (nee Ashcroft) and Kevin Cookson. Chris joined the RAF in 1987 as an Aircraftsman. In 2000 as a Sergeant he applied for a Commission. He attended his officer-training course at RAF Cranwell and graduated as a Pilot Officer. He soon gained promotion to Flight Lieutenant.

Chris was diagnosed with leukaemia in the spring of 2003. Sadly he died on 31st October 2003. Chris spent many happy summers camping at Blaisdon Hall and because of his love for Blaisdon his dying wish was that he should be buried in Blaisdon Churchyard. His grave is marked with a stone bearing the RAF insignia."

Flight Lieutenant
CHRISTOPHER W
COOKSON
Royal Air Force
31st October 2003 Age
34

Beloved Husband Father
Son and Brother.

The Tobin family moved into Spout Farm in 1953. ***Tony Brady,*** an Old Boy of Blaisdon Hall, knew Pat Tobin for many years and has written the following tribute:

"Pat Tobin came to Stud Farm as Head Cowman from the Tibberton/Taynton part of Gloucestershire in 1953 taking over from John McCrossan who had left for Ireland. Pat served in the Royal Navy as a turret gunner As a result of terrible conditions he experienced on the seas off Russia, he suffered poor health and his once fine teeth often plagued him. After the Navy, he worked for the Bradley farming family, whom he idolised. Pat had met Joan Pittman during the war; they married and had 3 children, Denny, Patsy and Noreen. When they came to Blaisdon they lived in the house at Harvey's Farm.

Pat had a weather beaten face and a striking thick jet black head of hair. Joan was stockily built and had a down to earth nature. She was a loving mother and very tolerant

Left:
40 head Friesian Milking cattle
with Stud Farm behind.
Nottwood Hill in the distance.

Right:
Pat Tobin(left)
with Lawrence Stanton.

of Pat's weakness for the cider. She would go to the pub and get his drink for him, though she never drank alcohol herself. Their home was very rough and basic with no refinements whatsoever. I remember for a number of years being expected to attend there every Friday night to watch TV. Pat loved 'Take your Pick' with Michael Miles, followed by 'The Army Game'. Bootsey and Snudge were particularly appreciated. As guests in their home we often felt awkward and embarrassed because Pat tended to be coarse with Joan calling her 'the old scrubbing brush,' supposedly as a term of endearment

Joan and Pat's children were lovely and we were very fond of them. Fr Dan saw to their religious education and they attended Mass in the farm chapel most Sundays at 9.30 in the morning. Joan was not a Catholic then, though she became one later. For a time Pat and Joan were often short of money and Fr Dan helped them out. He engaged Joan as Dairy Supervisor and this was a great boost to the family finances, and to Joan's self esteem.

Pat was a person whose standard of work was excellent.

He had a natural affinity for animals and a patient temperament which brought out the best in them. When he arrived at Stud Farm the dairy herd was mainly mixed crossed Shorthorn and Friesian stock; there were some Ayrshires and Herefords too. Pat gradually introduced, by artificial insemination methods, a full bred pedigree Friesian herd which produced the highest butterfat milk content yield in the whole of Gloucestershire. The three original standing bulls were sold off and an Aberdeen Angus bull bought in from Perth, Scotland. This breed produces a small hornless calf, perfect for a first calving. These calves were sold for beef. Second calvings were then by AI. The pedigree calves were hand reared by Lawrence Stanton and, later, by Joan. They were retained as breeding heifers.

By 1961 the Stud Farm Friesians were known far and wide as best quality maintained stock. Each cow had its own name plate above its head in the 40 standings milking byre. Its milk yield was shown and level of feed concentrate required. Pat was particularly skilled with first lactating heifers; these can be awful vicious kickers but he was brilliant in his management of them. The herd was a great achievement and source of pride to everyone on the farm, mostly due to Pat's assiduous care.

Pat Tobin with Bill Harte. In the milking parlour. c1957

Pat set himself the highest standards and always sought to maintain them through practice and example. Pat's hedge laying was legendary. Each spring he and Johnny Dunbar, cut the hedges from Stud Farm, along Blaisdon and Hinders Lanes. His rick building in hay and straw was of the highest standard, not to mention his neat use of the winter silage knife on the pits where he had spread the spring grass out so thoroughly and smoothly. Pat was an "all rounder" in every farming skill. He had trained with horses and rarely drove a tractor. One particular feature of his horticultural outlook, which would go down well today, was his prophetic views about organic vegetables. Fr Dan let Pat have land next to George Keyse's high brick wall on the Harvey's field side. Here he tended a most productive vegetable garden. This was a sight to behold and we often ate the rewards of Pat's good husbandry which he brought to our farmhouse table.

Following the sale of the Stud Farm to Mr Bert Knight in the early 1960s Pat continued to work there until 1964 before moving back to Tibberton to work on Mr Lifely's farm. Pat's wife, Joan, died of a heart attack when she was 41 years old. Pat's alcohol dependence increased after Joan's death. Pat died when, at the age of 64, he fell into the path of a passing vehicle whilst leaving the Travellers Rest public house at Malswick.

He was very much a "character" in the Blaisdon village in the 1950s. Pat's children made their way and did well in the world having aquired skills to ensure productive and purposeful lives. That's the measure of Pat as a successful father despite the drawbacks of his early life that provided only the most minimal early opportunities."

Tony Brady, age 16 with Aberdeen Angus Bull. "So tame you could sit on its back" Stud farm piggeries behind.

Dennis Tobin, who works in Cinderford with his brother, was 5 years old when he came to live in Blaisdon, during the summer of 1953. His brother, Patsy, was 4 and sister, Noreen, 20 months. He recalls:

"Stefan Orysiuk, who lived at the Dairy with his parents, drove a lorry to Tibberton to collect our belongings. On our first day in the village, father acquainted himself with the Red Hart Inn and spent the rest of the day there in company with Albert Pithouse.

My brother, sister and I regularly attended Mass on a Sunday morning at the Stud Farm and following my first communion I became a server at Mass. Fr Dan Lucey, who was the Rector, conducted the services entirely in Latin. Following the service, they would all stay for a cooked breakfast with the farm staff and afterwards we would often go up to the Hall in time for the next service.

Left:
Father Dan Lucey with Dennis & Patsy Tobin on the day of their 1st Communion at the stud farm Chapel.
Right:
Jim Meenaghan, Bro. Joe Carter, Lionel Williams & Noreen Tobin at the front, c1959.

On Saturday mornings, at the age of 10 or 11, I would go to Gloucester on the train, alone, to do the shopping for mother. When I had to work on the farm for a while, this shopping trip was taken over by Patsy.

Mrs Lane from Syston Cottage was friendly with my mother and the family and she would often waylay us on

our way home from the train station for a friendly chat. She tried teaching us the tongue twister: 'Shut up the shutters and sit in the shop,' and laughing when we got it wrong.

We used to go fishing in the reservoir in Blaisdon woods, catching tench, roach and daice, which weren't edible and were thrown back in. My brother and I also went elver fishing at the Old Mill at Westbury. We caught a load of elvers and these were sold at the pub. In those days elvers were caught around Easter, sold and enjoyed by most country people along our stretch of the Severn. Once, my father, Pat and some of the customers from the Red Hart, decided they would go elvering along by Garden Cliff at Westbury. As elvering was mostly done at night, it goes without saying that those going on the elver expedition had probably had a few to drink beforehand. Pat and company were walking along Garden Cliff when Pat slipped and fell over the edge. The men with him hurried down the cliff to see if he was all right. Meanwhile, Pat had picked himself up and scrambled back up to the top of the cliff. Albert Pithouse happened to look up and see Pat looking down on them, to which Albert, with his usual dry humour, exclaimed: 'Christ, he's gone to heaven already!' Needless to say, not many elvers were caught that night.

At the age of 11, I developed a rash all over my body, which didn't respond to any treatment. As a result, a biopsy was taken and sent to America for analysis. The diagnosis was Granuloma Annulare, a complaint, which it was discovered affects only 1 in 5 million and stays with you but is controlled with the right medication. My brother and I stayed with the Brown family at the Vectis when mother was hospitalised following a miscarriage.

Pat Tobin on left with his catch of elvers.
Also other Red Hart regulars including Sam Bullock,
Jim Marshall, John Vick & Albert Pithouse.

Following the sale of Blaisdon Hall and the Stud Farm, we moved back to Tibberton to live. I eventually left school and took up a 3 year apprenticeship as a slaughter man with an abattoir in Hempsted. As I was not paid much as an apprentice, travelling to work on the bus proved too expensive and I eventually got a bicycle and cycled to Gloucester each day. At the age of 16, I bought a BSA Bantam motorbike, which made my journey to and from work a whole lot easier. My father liked to come back to the Red Hart for a drink in the evening so I would give him a lift on my motor bike, dropping him off on my way to Flaxley to meet up with my pals, and picking him up on his way home, around closing time. Pat would usually be well oiled by the time I picked him up and I would stop right outside the door of the Hart so that my father only had to take 2 steps from the front door of the pub and then cock his leg over the back of the motorbike. This was done on a regular basis. Elsie, the landlady would bring

out Pat's take home cider and hand it to Dennis and then hold the door open for Pat to take his 2 steps to the bike. On one night however a car was parked outside the door and I had to park further along the pavement. Pat came out of the pub took his usual 2 steps and cocked his leg as he thought over the passenger seat of the motor bike but instead wrapped himself around the car, much to the amusement of the onlookers. I got an ear bashing from Pat for not parking where I should have been!"

Will and Linda Nicol in a school photo.
(the poodle was the photographer's dog).

Will Nichol moved into the left-hand side of Spout farm in 1957, living there for about 2 years.

"I came to Blaisdon with my parents, Tom and Chris, and my sister, Linda, by train from Liverpool arriving at Blaisdon Halt. My father was to be Head Chef at Blaisdon Hall. With the job came 2 Home Farm Cottage, one of two semi-detached cottages that is now Spout Farmhouse. Our neighbours at No.1 were the Tobin family, with three children, Dennis, Patrick and Noreen.

My sister and I went to the village school. I excelled at PE, holding the high jump record of 3 feet and 3 inches landing on a harsh coconut mat placed in the playground. It produced very sore knees; Health and Safety would have a fit! During the summer, at lunchtime, the head teacher would let us watch her TV in the schoolhouse attached to the school. I remember watching Garfield Sobers playing cricket. I think her TV was one of only two in the village, the other being owned by the Blake family. They had a daughter, Maureen, who I had quite a crush on although she was a little older than me! They once moved their TV somehow to the garden and a number of chairs were put out so that villagers could watch a big event. At school, maypole dancing was popular, I had never seen it before and always got in a tangle. Country dancing was another popular item.

Summer holidays from school seemed eternal, collecting frogspawn, tadpoles and newts from a stream across fields near the last cottage by the halt. Cricket seemed to be the sport played most. One day I broke the handle of my cricket bat, so decided to make my own bat in a workshop at the back of our cottage, using dad's tools. A wood chisel slipped and badly cut into the thumb of my left hand. Blood sprayed everywhere. With no car in those days, hospital was not an option. Mum took me to a farmer just over the road, who dipped my thumb in a white powder, which was used for cattle with cut feet. It set in a pink (bloody) plaster of paris cast. I finished the bat and played cricket later but I still bear the scars on my

Above:
Will & Linda plus pet cat, outside their home.

thumb to this day!

We used to hike out to Nottwood Hill, taking pop and sandwiches to play on the summit, it was one of our favourite places. In spring we collected bluebells for our mums somewhere out that way. One day feeling bored, Dennis Tobin and I were up by the large house next to the School, The Rectory. It was empty and derelict, and very spooky. We proceeded to throw stones at the windows, breaking nearly every one facing the track between it and the school. Someone must have seen us as we both got a severe roasting that evening.

Blaisdon was at that time famous for its plums. The pub had extensive orchards and everybody helped pick the fruit. We got 2/6 (12½p) for every crate we picked, but that took some considerable time. Out on the road towards Huntley, an elderly lady sold sweets from her house. It wasn't a shop, she just had sweet jars, but it was heaven to us kids.

We never used the front room of our cottage except for Christmas and visitors. It was all wood, panels and floor, with a huge fireplace. We tended to live in the back part of the house with its red tiled floor and huge black range, where mum used to make home made bread. It was always warm in that kitchen even in summer.

Next door were a Polish family. We soon learnt the expression 'Dzien dobry panie,' which means 'Good day, Sir.' As Catholics, we attended Sunday service at Blaisdon

Hall's Chapel. I remember one time when the clocks went forward, coming out after the service, we met the Polish folk arriving. Nobody had told them about the British eccentric idea of summertime.

These were the halcyon days of my childhood, out after breakfast, playing all day and coming home for tea, parents did not worry about us, doors were left unlocked, and my how things have changed! But after visiting Blaisdon in 2010, I found that there was still a peaceful air to the village, even though it had changed…"

Fire in the hay barns at Spout Farm.
The fire brigade quickly on the scene. Water had to be pumped from the village brook.
Nancy Bate was on hand to record this photograph.

Spout Farm in the 1950s.

Blaisdon had a 2nd 'Great Fire' as well as the fire of 1669:

'In the year of one thousand nine hundred and fifty or thereabouts the second great fire of Blaisdon took place at Home Farm in the centre of the village.'

It is thought that some young village boys decided it was a good idea to cook breakfast in a hay barn. Needless to say, the fire spread rapidly and so did the boys! Many of the then village boys admit to being around when the match was struck but it remains a secret to this day as to who actually did it.

THE AIRY

The Dairy was situated in the orchard between the Spout Farm and the Rectory. In the days of the Blaisdon Estate it took milk from the estate farms in the village. Butter and cheese were made from the milk and sold around the village and the whey from the cheese making was sold for cooking purposes.

Until Abenhall School was built at Mitcheldean, pupils stayed at Blaisdon School until the age of 14, when they left and started work. The Dairy was used by the school, which sent 14 year old girls there for a period of three to four weeks during the summer term to learn to cook. A peripatetic teacher would teach the girls and in the process use oil cookers which were brought in for the purpose.

At the age of 14 **Peggy Gregson** was sent to the dairy in Blaisdon on 2 days a week to be trained in the process of butter making. Miss Colnett was in charge and she was assisted by Miss Lilla Smith and Miss Nicholas. Lilla Smith came to live at Little Garth in Blaisdon many years later. Also at the dairy at this time were Joyce Grindon, Dorothy Sparrow, Dorothy Young, Mary Harvey and Mary Lewis.

Peggy says: "I was highly regarded as a good butter maker being able to get a 'fine grain' in the butter making process. However, on one occasion I had an accident when I tipped the curds I was processing onto the dairy floor. Fortunately,

The dairy, after it was converted to living accommodation and became known as Dairy Cottage.

neither Miss Colnett nor her assistants were present, so I quickly scraped what I could up off the floor and the other girls gave me some of theirs to make up, and no-one was any the wiser. As well as learning to make butter, the dairy maids also had to learn how to milk a cow by hand, and how to prepare poultry for the table. I represented the dairy in competitions at the Three Counties Show and at Earls Court in London. Meetings prior to these shows would take place either at Gaulett Farm or Poulton Court for us to receive our instructions from Miss Colnett, as the Dairy was not big enough to hold such meetings. I would ride my bicycle from Elton to Waldron Farm in Flaxley to meet Marjorie Bullet and then walk up through the Park by the Abbey and onto the track through the wood leading to Gaulett Farm.

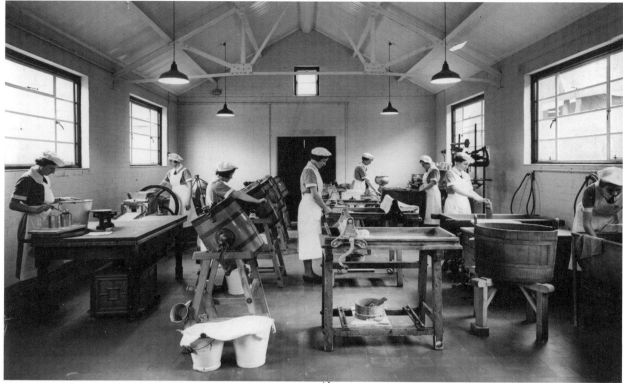

Above:
Inside the new Dairy School that was opened by the Duchess of Beaufort. Peggy Gregson is 2nd left & Miss Colnett 3rd right.
Below Left:
The staff & students at the new Dairy School. Front Row, 6th from the left is Lilla Smith & 2nd row 4th from left is Mary Harvey.
Below Right: Taken in the Shire Hall c1937-8.
Front Row: Mrs Sparrow, Mary Harvey, ?, Lilla Smith, Miss Colnett, Mary Lewis, Daisy Davis, ?, Dorothy Young.
Middle Row: 3rd from left is Peggy Gregson.

Judging at these events included the dairymaid's uniform and if we were not properly turned out then we would be disqualified from entering the competition. No talking was allowed. I recall when entering one competition that one of the cows provided was barren and it just so happened that I got it. After washing the cows udders, which had to be done before milking, I quickly realised that my cow had no milk so, instead of labouring on trying to get milk out of a barren cow, I quietly got up from my milking stool and returned to my seat in the waiting area. I was later highly commended by the judges for my quick deduction and the quiet way I retreated. Miss Colnett also praised me, saying that she was proud the way I had conducted myself. I received many awards for butter making, junket making as well as in the poultry classes." Peggy is now in her 91st year and lives at Walmore Hill.

The Blaisdon Dairy closed in the 1930s transferring to the basement of the Shire Hall in Gloucester where the butter and cheese making processes continued. Eventually, a new purpose built dairy school was erected between the prison and the Shire Hall.

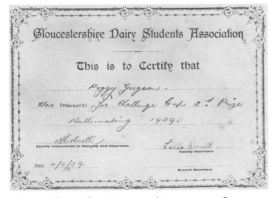

A certificate for Buttermaking: one of many awarded to Peggy Gregson and signed by Lilla Smith.

Tony Brady remembers a family who lived at the Dairy:

"During the 1950s the farmyard and buildings between Blaisdon Nursery and Spout Farm were used to winter-shelter steers and sheep and store crops. Until demolished in 1956, a row of brick-built piggeries formed an outside wall between the two main gates. In the winter months, the grain spread in the two overhead granaries was turned regularly, bagged and lowered by winch onto tractor-drawn trailers and conveyed for crushing at Stud Farm. The potato crop, harvested by the schoolboys each Autumn, was stored under knee-deep straw in the former cow byres, riddled, sorted, weighed and bagged up for sale in Gloucester. Cecil Beard, who lived in the village, drove the 10-ton flat bed lorry loads to the wholesaler.

As Father Dan, Kevin Keating, Lawrence Stanton and various other farm workers paused from their work on the potatoes, they would have observed the activity of Muscovy ducks, geese, chickens, sheep with fostered lambs, various cats as well as a vegetable garden being tended by an aged couple. They were dressed like peasants straight out of a 19th century Russian novel. They lived in the former Dairy, now a small two roomed cottage, set in an orchard below the towering height of Blaisdon Rectory: they were the parents of Brother Jan Orysiuk, who was in charge of electrics at Blaisdon Hall, and his brother Stefan.

Presently, the old couple would approach the sheds bearing a tray fashioned from a shallow fruit box. From this they dispensed tea and bread they had baked themselves. The bread was black and sesame seeded. Neither could speak English but the elderly woman smiled often, revealing broken blackened teeth, while her husband looked on unspeaking. When we expressed our thanks, Mrs Orysiuk cackled and her husband bowed. Father Dan communicated with the couple somehow and, sometimes, the wizen-faced old man stayed and helped sew the sack tops with a bodkin and twine.

Stefan, leanly built, in his thirties, flat capped and

Stefan Orysiuk with an intact tractor on stud Farm.

invariably grinning, worked as a driver of the two lorries at the Salesian School, Blaisdon Hall. His manner of driving varied from erratic to nightmarish. Once, when driving the flat-bed lorry, he took a corner at speed near Over, on the road close to Gloucester, and the dozen or so large boxes of fresh eggs destined for market ended up all over the road and in nearby hedges. From then on it was known as Omelette Corner. Another time, when supposed to be collecting sawdust at Forest Products, Huntley, he could not lower the hydraulics of the tipper so drove it, raised, all the way back to Stud Farm and some telephone lines were snagged near Hinders Corner. Continuing narrow escapes got Stefan transferred as a tractor driver to Stud Farm. There, he managed to overturn tractors, drive into ditches and wreck various implements to the increasing concern and frustration of Brother Joe Carter.

Brother Jan was the complete opposite to his brother. Squat,

bespectacled, serious-minded speaking broken English, he possessed brilliantly applied skills in mechanics, engineering and electronics. He was particularly remembered far and wide for the way he lit up Blaisdon Hall as part of the community celebrations for the Coronation of the present Queen in 1953. The great crown he installed on the tower was his homage to a realm that had provided him and his family refuge from certain slavery under the communist regime: a political system that was to dominate Poland behind the Iron Curtain during the years of the Cold War. For weeks, people visited Blaisdon from all over Gloucestershire to see the 'Blaisdon Illuminations.'

Brother Jan spent the rest of his life in Blaisdon as a Salesian

The Coronation Lighting of Blaisdon Hall by Jan Orysiuk in 1953.

Lay brother. His parents died in the 1960s and he followed them in 1993. 'The Dairy' became the Parish House of the Salesian priests serving the local community. Stefan found his life companion among the Polish community in Gloucester, married, had children and died in 2009.

A group of Stud Farm workers once accepted the hospitality of The Polish Club in Gloucester on the invitation of Stefan and his brother, and enjoyed a traditional Dinner and Dance. Stefan performed a lively crouching dance with the arms akimbo, held chest high, to wild gypsy music. We joined in with great gusto aided by Old Krupnik or polish vodka."

RED HART INN

Gideon & Mary Price, with their daughters, Elsie, Ada & Daisy, outside The Red Hart Inn.

In 1924, Gideon Price, together with his wife Mary and 3 young daughters Elsie, Ada and Daisy, moved from Popes Hill to take up the tenancy and become licensee of The Red Hart Inn, Blaisdon. The tenancy of the Red Hart Inn remained in the family for 67 years over 3 generations until sold by Whitbread Brewery into private ownership in 1991. ***Margaret Hogg***, Gideon's granddaughter, tells the story of the earlier years.

"The Red Hart Inn, with its flagstone floors, in those days had no electricity or indoor sanitation. There were spittoons placed under the wooden seats which had to be cleaned out every day and sawdust was spread on the floor. The only lighting was by means of oil lamps and candles and much later calor gas lights were installed in the bar and downstairs living quarters. At bedtime hurricane lamps or candles were used to light the way and Mary Price almost always had a Price's nightlight (a small candle) in the bedroom window which would stand in a saucer surrounded by water and usually burn itself out by morning. On one occasion I remember we were woken up to lights flashing across the bedroom ceilings and a commotion outside. It was a fire engine. Mrs Back from the Rectory opposite, who happened to be up early and looking out of her window, saw the night-light flaring up and thinking the house had caught fire, called the Fire Brigade. Following an explanation which was taken in good spirit they departed and we all went back to bed.

Mary always kept a jar of goose grease in the corner of her bedroom in case of colds when it would be liberally applied to the chest of the infected person and the chest then covered with a piece of red flannel. Bluetts ointment was also kept in the medicine chest as a cure-all remedy for all manner of ailments. Jars of Bluetts ointment were always available for sale over the bar both for human use and also one for animal use. Bluetts was made to an old

The Price Family.

Above: Mary.

Below: Gideon.

Left:
Elsie, Daisy & Ada.

and secret family recipe handed down through the Bluett family of Cinderford and sold in and around the Forest. Unfortunately, the Bluetts era came to an end when the family member who held and made the secret recipe died without fully passing it on. Attempts to recreate the famous ointment following the death were sadly never successful.

As well as the Bluetts ointment which was kept in the display case behind the bar there were a couple of mouth organs and a Jews harp which Gideon Price enjoyed playing. I believe he could also get a tune out of a violin.

In the bar sitting room, which was the first door on the right along the passageway as you went through the front door and was not licensed, was a piano on which my mother and her sisters had learnt to play. This piano was tuned once a year by Mr Wasp, a piano tuner from Gloucester, who would post a card in advance of his visit to say what day and time he would be coming. I remember Iris, Josephine and myself would way lay Bertie Buckett and plead with him to play us a tune on the piano. He would always protest that he had to get

Gideon Price outside the Red Hart.

back to do something or other but we usually managed to persuade him and once settled at the piano he would play and sing heartily the songs from the music we provided from our sheet music box. I think his favourite was Peggy O'Neill which he played and sang with gusto, thumping the keys at certain points and almost jumping up off the piano stool, we thought this was hugely funny but we knew once he'd performed that one that we wouldn't get anymore from him that day.

Gideon Price was a great believer in Old Moore and a copy of the almanac was always available over the bar to check the month-by-month predictions and weather forecast made by Old Moore. A poster hung on the bar wall advertising the forthcoming film to be shown at the Hippodrome picture house in Gloucester. There was a shove halfpenny slate on the corner of the bar counter. There was a quoits board on one of the tables and cards and dominoes were always available for those who wanted to play and although gambling was not strictly permissible in pubs a blind eye was often turned if money was involved on a game.

Beer was drawn straight from the wooden casks which were kept aloft on wooden 'trams' in the cellar adjacent to the bar. Each new barrel had to have a hole drilled in the top and a wooden plug tapped in; this was to gradually introduce air into the barrel. Once the beer had been allowed to settle, the barrel had to then have a brass beer tap inserted. This required an element of experience because if you didn't get the tap in with your first hit of the wooden mallet you likely as not got liberally sprayed with beer and much of the profit was lost. We were in fact serving what today is known as real ale and customers came to the Red Hart because the beer was always good, coming from a cool cellar and straight from the wood. Similarly we served draft or rough cider as it was known and this was also much liked by the regulars. In the winter months this rough cider would be warmed by customers on the bar fire in a saucepan especially kept for that purpose. If anyone had a cold then root ginger would be added to this warmed cider as it helped to sweat out the germs. Still a good remedy today!

In those early days the Red Hart Inn, the Church and the Post Office were the only establishments in the village not owned by the Squire who lived at Blaisdon Hall. The fact that the Squire did not own the Red Hart and therefore had no control over Gideon Price was a constant source of annoyance to him. He would ride his horse through the village to check that his workmen were not spending too much time drinking at the Inn and is reported to have rebuked Gideon one day for encouraging his workmen to drink too much ale so that they wouldn't be fit for work the next day upon which Gideon retorted to the Squire, 'you don't pay your workmen enough money for them to drink too much of my ale' and bid him good day.

Top:
Gideon, Mary & Elsie Price
in the Citroen.

Centre:
Elsie with her father Gideon.

Right:
Mary & Gideon Price.
The Rectory is behind them.

The Red Hart had a large productive vegetable garden, which kept the family in fresh food and any surplus would be sold to boost the income. The orchard was stocked mainly with Blaisdon plums along with several varieties of apple, pear and plum trees, including Cox's Orange Pippin, Brown Bury pear, a Prolific Plum, and Victorias. Also in the orchard was a big old hollow walnut tree which as well as giving us walnuts was good for our games of hide and seek. Gideon Price grafted several apple trees and produced a variety of cooking apples which he called Price's Seedlings, these apples were much prized by the family for their wonderful flavour and the fact they stayed very white when cooked. Sadly I think the trees have all now gone. In the bottom corner of the orchard opposite the Rectory was a small pond in which grew watercress, which again was gathered and eaten by the family. The pond was also much appreciated by the ducks and other animals kept in the orchard. An old willow tree grew on the edge of the pond, on the road side; the water from the pond then flowed into a brook which ran down along the boundary hedge fronting the pub garden before disappearing into an underground culvert situated on the corner of the garden boundary near the house. During heavy storms the grill in this culvert would often become blocked with debris and the water would overflow into the road and unless the grill was cleared the water would often flow into the house via the front door.

When war broke out, an air raid shelter was dug out into the bank opposite the kitchen door by Gideon and anybody else who was available. Fortunately, it wasn't needed during the war but in the ensuing years it came into its own for storing surplus apples to see us through the winter, it being both dark and having a more or less

Above:
Gideon Price at Grange Court Christmas Market.

Above Left: Gideon with yolk & pails.

Left: Mary Price digging the garden in 1939.

constant temperature was ideal for this purpose. Mincing the horseradish roots, which grew in the garden, was a performance. This was done in relays by the family. Due to the pungent odour given off by the root, which would almost take your breath away and made your eyes water as it was minced, it was almost impossible to do more than a couple of minutes at a time before having to run outside to recover. Then Uncle Les hit upon the idea of wearing a gas mask (left over from the war years) whilst operating the mincer. This act caused a great deal of fun and laughter but the problem was solved!

The orchard also had a stable, 2 pigsties, fowl house with a scratching shed attached [so called because fowls like to scratch and wallow in the dry dusty earth and this shed enabled them to do this all the year round]. Free-range eggs were always available and the surplus was sold, again to add to the income. In the fowls' run were a flat stone and a hammer, which was used for smashing broken or cracked crockery for the hens to peck up to aid their digestion and strengthen the eggshells. Pigs were reared in the sties both by Gideon and later by Elsie.

During the fruit season the pigs would eat the fallen fruit and as it fermented in their stomach they would become quite tipsy. Gideon also kept rabbits and ferrets in hutches down the side path, and I remember always giving the ferrets a wide berth when passing because they smelt and always seemed rather fierce. He would take the ferrets with him when he went 'rabbitting' together with his Jack Russell, 'Snorter' who was also a very good rat catcher. By day, Gideon worked as a traveller for Lydney Farmers Association whilst Mary served in the bar. He drove a

Above:
Elsie Hogg tending her pigs.

Left:
Snorter, age 13 (1958),
the renowned Jack Russell.

Citroen car in order to get around to meet his customers with much of his business being conducted in the local hostelries. Knowing this, Mary would send Elsie with him on his round to discourage him from having too much liquid refreshment. Unfortunately, the law eventually caught up with him in Westbury and he was charged and brought to Court for being drunk in charge of a motor vehicle. As a result, he lost his licence and declared he would never drive again, which he never did.

On 13th May 1940 Elsie and Ada had a double wedding at Flaxley Church. Gideon apparently was too emotional to be able to give his 2 daughters away so this privilege was passed to his brother-in-law, Jack Harris, who lived in the Dower House at Flaxley. Elsie and Ada, 11 months later, both gave birth to daughters within a week of each other Elsie first, giving birth to Iris, and Ada, a week later, giving birth to Josephine. Sadly Ada's husband, Victor Warlow, died at Standish Hospital from TB after only 3 years of marriage and Ada and Josephine returned to the Red Hart to live. Ada later married George Keyse from Blaisdon Nurseries. Daisy had married Leslie Clifford who was from Yorkshire in 1939 also at Flaxley Church.

Gideon died in 1952 and the licence passed to his wife Mary Price who held it for 3 years until she retired and the licence passed to my father, her son-in-law, Francis Henry Hogg, and his wife Elsie, who up until then had lived at Frampton-on-Severn. During her short tenancy as Licensee, Mary's granddaughter, Josephine Warlow, who at the time was living at Blaisdon Nurseries with her mother Ada and step father George Keyse and his sons Michael, Terry and Roger, moved into the Red Hart and both she and Mary remained as part of the household.

The Double Wedding Of Ada & Elsie Price 13th May 1940.
Victor & Ada Warlow are the couple on the left, Frank & Elsie Hogg on the right.
Mrs Mary Price is on the far right.

Frank, as he was known, and Elsie together with their daughters, Iris and myself, Margaret, moved into the Red Hart in 1955. I went to Blaisdon School and Iris transferring to Abenhall.

Life in the Red Hart was a step back in time for we 2 children. Coming from a house with electricity and a somewhat new indoor flush toilet and bathroom we now had to get used to gas lights which hissed and were not terribly bright and an outside Elsan toilet. On washdays a fire had to be lit under the boiler, which was in the corner of the kitchen. I think the electricity must have arrived shortly after we moved in and eventually this labour intensive boiler was removed from the kitchen and replaced with an electric Burco boiler. Friday night was bath night and water for a bath had to be heated up in the boiler in the kitchen and carried upstairs in buckets. We always washed our hair in rainwater and this was collected in a water butt situated outside the back door. At night we went to bed with either a hurricane lamp or a candle to light our way as the gas lights were only fitted on the ground floor. When electricity was eventually laid on we thought we were in heaven, for one thing we could now see to read in bed at night. No more hissing gas or gas mantles to be changed. At the flick of a switch our darkness was lightened, but the Elsan toilets would remain until the licence changed hands the next time. Suffice to say, the pub garden grew very good vegetables!

Growing up in the fifties and sixties we didn't have the benefit of 24-hour television, nor computers or ipods that are taken for granted by today's generation. What television we did have was black and white and started in the afternoon and finished at about 10 o'clock each night. Most households owned a wireless and would tune in to listen to their favourite programme. Mary Price was an avid fan of the Archers, as we probably all were. Whatever she was doing stopped just before a quarter to seven so that she could listen to the next edition on her Roberts radio. I think we all went into shock when Grace Archer was killed off when trying to rescue her horses when the stable caught fire. It was almost like losing a member of the family!!

But for the most part, we had to make our own amusement. I remember on hot summer days Elizabeth Etherington and myself going down to the Blaisdon brook to try and learn to swim, and playing tennis in the road outside

the Forge with Elizabeth. Not too many cars passed through the village back then. Elizabeth's father, Cedric Etherington, was a bit of an eccentric and enjoyed dressing up in different outfits and taking on the character of that particular outfit. I remember on one occasion we were playing in the back garden at the Forge and we had been given instructions that when he came outside we were to run up and ask him for his autograph. When he eventually came outside he was dressed in a silk dressing gown with a towel round his neck fists held up like a boxer and he was pretending to spar in the fashion of a prize fighter. We dutifully ran up and asked him for his autograph much to the amusement of Mrs Etherington.

On sunny days we would wander across the fields and on one occasion I remember we were scrumping apples in an orchard belonging to Newman Grindon, who was a local Magistrate, until we spotted him watching us. We were terrified but fortunately we got away with it. In the early spring we would go 'snowdropping' along the brook, which ran through the fields behind the Mill House and later pick bunches of wild daffodils in Ley Park. I can also remember the gypsies would go along to Ley Park and pick them by the cart load and bunch them up to sell on the roadside. Few of these activities would be allowed today, either because of conservation or health and safety.

The local policeman during the fifties was PC Root. He was based in Longhope and would ride his bicycle down to Blaisdon, stopping off at the Red Hart, to check that all was in order. He was not strictly allowed to drink alcohol when he was in uniform and on duty but he never refused the pint offered and would sit in the cellar out of sight and remove his helmet so that he was not then in full uniform.

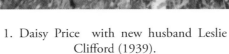

1. Daisy Price with new husband Leslie Clifford (1939).

2. Margaret & Iris Hogg, 1950s.

3. Iris Hogg.

4. Elsie Hogg & Ada Warlow with daughters, Iris & Josephine.

5. Josephine Warlow.

6. Elsie, Daisy & Ada.

7. Margaret with nephew, Neil.

Nos 4, 6, 7 were taken on the wall outside the Red Hart where the stream was diverted under the road as it passed the pub.

CASK BEERS	Trade price	Public Bar Price
Best Bitter	337/- per barrel	1/7 per pint
Cheltenham P.A.	288/- per barrel	1/4 per pint
Stroud XX	288/- per barrel	1/4 per pint
Mild Ale	288/- per barrel	1/4 per pint

KEG BEERS

Whitbread Tankard	(10 gallon casks)	
	12/8 per gallon	2/- per pint
Flowers Keg	(9 gallon casks)	
	12/8 per gallon	2/- per pint

DRAUGHT CIDER (GLOUCESTERSHIRE CIDER Co. Ltd.)

Country Dry	216/- per barrel	
Medium Sweet	(6/- per gallon)	

KINGSTON BLACK

Dry	246/- per barrel	
Medium	(6/10 per gallon)	

H. P. BULMER and Co. Ltd.

Dry	216/- per barrel	
Medium	(6/- per gallon)	
Sweet		

COUNTRY CIDER

2 Gallon Jar		16/- per jar

BOTTLED BEERS	Trade price per dozen Bots.	½ Bots.	Public Bar price Bots.	½ Bots.
West Country Ale	—	11/6	—	1/4
Cotswold Ale	—	9/-	—	1/0½
Cheltenham Ale	14/2	7/7	1/9	11d.
All Bright	14/2	7/7	1/9	11d.
Brown Chelt	14/2	7/7	1/9	11d.
Nourishing Stout	14/2	7/7	1/9	11d.

WHITBREAD

	Per Dozen Bots.	½ Bots.	
Pale Ale	19/6	10/10	1/2½
Forest Brown	18/-	10/-	1/2
Mackeson	24/-	12/6	Nips 1/5½
Final Selection	—	14/5	

			Nips
Guinness	—	12/7	
Bass and Worthington	—	13/6	10/6
Heineken Lager	—	14/-	
Skol Lager	—	14/-	
Carlsberg Lager	—	14/6	
Tennant's Gold Label	—	—	16/11
Bass No. 1	—	—	18/1

Deposit Charges:—
All bottles 3/- per dozen.
1 dozen cases 3/- each, 2 dozen cases 6/- each.

To meet the requirements of the Acts of Parliament

BOTTLED CIDER	Trade Price Per Dozen Flags. ½ Flags. ¼ Bots.	Public Bar Price Flags. ½ Flags. ¼ Bot.
GLOUCESTERSHIRE CIDER Co. Ltd.		
Dry	25/11 10/2	2/9 — 1/1
Medium Sweet	23/6 9/8	2/6 — 1/-
H. P. BULMER and Co. Ltd.		
Extra Quality	— 9/8	— 1/-
Woodpecker	23/10 13/10	2/6 1/6 —
Dry	25/11 —	2/9 — —
Perry	23/6 —	2/6 — —
Strongbow	29/3 11/8	3/3 — —
No. 7 Still Cider	— 11/5	— — —

FLASKS

Golden Flask and Strongbow	5/3 per flask	
Vintage Cellar	6/7 per flask	
	3/8	¼

BOTTLES *Deposit Charges*

Flagons 8/- per dozen, ½ Flagons, ¼ Flagons, ¼ per dozen, ¼ Bottles and Nips 3/- per dozen, Flasks, 2/6 each, ½ Flasks 1/- each.
Cases 3/- each. 4-Flagon crates 1/- each.

			Bots.	Nips
Pontange	56/9 doz.	11/2 doz.	7/-	1/5

Wines, Spirits, Minerals and Cordials
ARNOLD PERRETT and CO. LIMITED
Lower Tuffley, Gloucester *Telephone* 24054
Branches:
BEWELL STREET, HEREFORD *Telephone* 2426
51, WESTGATE STREET, GLOUCESTER *Telephone* 22901
137, HIGH STREET, CHELTENHAM *Telephone* 23103
7, FOREGATE STREET, WORCESTER *Telephone* 23373

Clockwise From Top Left:
Frank Hogg at the Harvest Home.
Frank at the bar of the Red Hart.
Margaret, Frank, Elsie & Iris Hogg.
Price list from West Country Breweries, 1964.
Painting: The Hunt at the Red Hart (Roger Etherington).

Harvest auctions began in the Red Hart during Frank and Elsie's tenancy. Customers would bring their produce to the pub on the allotted Saturday and Hazel from Littledean would arrange the produce and flowers into a wonderful display for sale by auction that evening. The evening would commence with the vicar attending to say a prayer and bless the produce and those present and then Jake Harris, Hazel's father, would start the auction. He had a gentle way of coaxing that extra bit of money from the punters for a lovely bunch of flowers. The harvest loaf would be bought and sold many times raising lots of money and the eventual purchaser often donated it to be eaten by the assembled crowd. After Jake retired from this role, Jack Waite took over. He had a louder more robust way of coaxing those extra few shillings out of you. These auction sales were a lot of fun and together with the raffle raised hundreds of pounds for the Royal National Institute for the Blind and other charities.

The Red Hart was more like a home from home to some customers. A word of sympathy and an aspro would occasionally be handed over with the first pint of the day. The button tin would often be brought out and a near enough match for a missing button be found and stitched on by my mother. A sympathetic ear was given in times of stress. All these things and more were part of everyday life growing up at the Red Hart Inn and if we had to do it all again, we probably wouldn't change a thing. The Red Hart Inn has always attracted colourful characters. Gideon himself was a character and was remembered fondly or otherwise long after his death. ***Jim Allum***, who lived at the Rectory, wrote a poem after hearing that Gideon had taken his gun and shot his Gleany out of the plum tree mistaking it for a pigeon. Jim's poem is alongside:

Gids Pigeon Shoot or The shooting of the Glea-ny

Down in the Village behind the Pub,
The pigeons were giving old Gid quite a rub,
He swore that he would get his own back,
So he loaded the gun that he took from the rack.

He slunk from the Pub, when the sun was quite high,
In search of the pigeons he thought were nigh,
He walked the garden round and round,
But not a pigeon was to be found,
Until at last up in a tree
He spied a Pigeon He laughed with glee.

As he crept close as in rugger,
He was heard to say, just stay two minutes more you
BUGGER.

He took his aim with the greatest care,
Then bang his shot went into the air,

The bird was hit well and true,
In fact he'd drilled the darn thing through.

It fell through the branches of the tree,
And crashed to earth for all to see.

But it was also alas, alack and a day,
Twas not a PIGEON but a GLEA-NY they say.

Old Gid looked down with great remorse,
Chit Tah, the old man does shoot accurate of course.
But out of bad can come some good,
That Gleany has stopped cackling for good.

The moral of this story misters,
Is don't get your sights mixed up in your whiskers.

Hunting days were an excuse not only to exercise the horses but also for the huntsmen and followers as well as Gideon to consume large amounts of alcohol. One notable record of a hunting day was when Harold House, an eccentric farmer from Taynton, led his hunter into the bar and banged his riding crop hard on the bar leaving a dent before ordering drinks for himself and his companion.

Jimmy Jenkins from Popes Hill with his horse & cart. Sam Bullock in the foreground & Oscar Jones Snr. behind.

Residents of Westbury Hall, which was home to many unfortunates and had once been the local Workhouse, became regular customers of the Hart. One who we called 'Old Shakey' because he was old, slow and very shaky had difficulty eating a bag of crisps because Snorter the pub dog would sit on the seat beside him and before the crisp had got from bag to his mouth Snorter had snatched the crisp and eaten it. Old Shakey was lucky if he managed to eat a couple. Another was Old Parry who had a liking for old clocks and watches. He would always be after a watch or clock when he came in and if he was handed one, broken or not, he went away happy.

Growing up in the 'pub' meant that family life was somewhat restricted compared to a 'normal' household.

However this was offset by the experiences, the amusement and the insight we gained from the antics of the many and varied characters who were our regular customers. I recall on one occasion during a hot summer evening, and being unable to sleep, we 3 children (Iris, Josephine and I) watching from a bedroom window the awesome sight of grown men pretending to be red Indians and doing a war dance and singing and whooping noisily around a lighted cigarette packet in the middle of the road.

At closing time such sights were not uncommon especially on a Saturday night. Having spent the evening drinking men liked to finish up with a singsong. I recall Len Cox from Flaxley would perform a credible version of the laughing policeman becoming very red in the face in the process much to our amusement.

Men never seemed in any great hurry to get home. Once turned out at closing time they would spend another half hour at least outside the pub putting the world to rights and on occasions tossing up to see who would drop Sid Cripps off at his home knowing that whoever did would get the sharp end of Mrs Cripps' tongue for taking Sid home in the drunken state he would almost certainly have got himself into. Sid was known to some by the nickname 'Sir Stafford' after an eminent politician of the day, I suspect he had been given the nickname by Albert Pithouse who seemed to attach a nickname to quite a few folk. He always referred to my father, Frank, as 'Sinatra,' not that my father could sing!

Sunday lunchtimes again were times when men liked to have a singsong. Most had a party piece, which they would be encouraged to perform. I remember Hubert Lord who came from Huntley would sing about Colin and his Cow much to the delight of everyone present. Ernie Sterry from Longhope would sing The Crystal Chandelier, but the worst singer was 'Spanker' who rode his bicycle up from Broadoak. My father had to ban him from singing in our pub. His voice was so loud and so awful he could clear the place in less time than it took to draw a pint of beer. He also banned Lil Hart from Shapridge from singing her particularly vulgar version of 'I'm Popeye the Sailor Man', especially if ladies were present, but she could be persuaded to defy him and would perform it for the price of a pint of beer much to my Father's aggravation.

Right:
Gideon Price and Snorter
with
Mr Oscar Jones snr.
outside the Red Hart.

Far Right:
Pat Tobin, Albert Pithouse, John
Vick & Keith Walker,
Around Albert's Van.

Sunday lunchtime was also the day when the Nottwood Hill dwellers would come to the Hart for a drink. Albert Pithouse and Ted Pithouse, Jim Marshall, Sam Bullock to name but a few would walk down through the wood in all winds and weathers. I remember in particular one Christmas they wheeled Sam Bullock into the pub in a child's pushchair dressed as a baby complete with cider bottle with a teat on the end for him to drink out of. I think they had all had a few to drink beforehand and were all in high spirits. As we used to say where there are no fools there's no fun.

Mrs Etherington from the Forge was for many years the paper lady delivering the Citizen newspapers around the village. She had never been known to have a drink in the pub until one day Albert Pithouse spotted her and asked her in. Her protestations that she had to get home to get her husband's tea went unheeded, so in she came and Albert duly bought her a drink and chatted to her no doubt pulling her leg about something or other as he was notorious at doing. She seemed to enjoy herself laughing at his nonsense and when she said she had to go he insisted on buying her another in spite of her saying repeatedly that Cedric would be wondering where she had got to. Needless to say Albert worked his charm and she had another drink.

Albert Pithouse was known to like nothing more than to say something jokingly which he knew would be controversial and cause the assembled company to start arguing amongst themselves, often heatedly, whilst he sat back silently and watched developments with a wicked grin on his face. However, one day the joke was on him when a rubber hose he had bought to fit to his van went missing from where he had left it in the passageway. Albert accused one after the other of taking this pipe and it got

Aerial View of the Red Hart, showing the grounds before the car park was installed.
The Rectory & Dairy Cottage are in the foreground.

The Red Hart Inn.
Note the old fashioned school road sign.

quite heated but of course no one in the bar had taken it. The culprit was Timmy, our black poodle, who had a habit of taking things and hiding them away. Seeing the rubber pipe in the passage he had picked it up and taken it into the cellar and buried it under the trams where it was discovered the following week when the new delivery of beer was made.

Left to Right:
David Read
Margaret Hogg
Albert Pithouse
Jim Marshall
Ivy Marshall.
Front:
Gillian Read
David Marshall
Carol Read.

I think Timmy the dog warrants a mention here because he too was a character. Mrs Chuggy Lane had a habit of walking her bitch up through the village and at certain times of the year this played havoc with Timmy's natural instincts. On one occasion, he took himself down to Mrs Lane's house went into her kitchen and cocked his leg against her kitchen table leg. Fortunately for him he made off before she could punish him. Unfortunately for Mrs Lane a few days later she mistook Mrs Day's black poodle for Timmy and put her stick across him. Mrs Day saw this and remonstrated with her whereupon Mrs Lane apologised saying, 'I thought it was that sexy poodle from the pub.' Mrs Pickering said she always knew when her bitch was coming into season because Timmy would be sat on her lawn in anticipation for the week beforehand. My mother tried tying him up one day outside the pub door

only to go out half an hour later to find he had chewed through his lead and made his escape. He was incorrigible.

Mrs Pitt from the Church House trimmed and shampooed Timmy on a regular basis. Mother would deliver him to Mrs Pitt and Mrs Pitt would walk him back home on his lead when she had finished. On one particular occasion Mrs Pitt said she wouldn't be able to bring him back and my mother didn't have time to collect him so when she delivered him she paid Mrs Pitt and said turn him out when you've finished and he can find his own way home. Sure enough, in due course he came trotting down the road proudly sporting his new haircut (he was quite vain) and thereafter this arrangement stood.

There were so many colourful characters who frequented the pub during this era that a whole book could probably be written about their many and varied antics and anecdotes. Sadly many pubs seem to be bland in comparison and pubs are no longer simply the drinking establishments that they once were. Instead of the simple bread and cheese that we once served they offer a full a la carte menu in order to survive in modern day Britain. The Red Hart does this very well and, for different reasons, is as popular as ever."

Timmy 1965.

THE LD RECTORY

Apart from Blaisdon Hall, this is largest house in Blaisdon, The Rectory sits across the road and overlooks The Red Hart and is now known as Blaisdon House. **Nancy Bate** recalls:

"The last Rector to live at the Blaisdon Rectory was Rev. Ensor in 1911, who lived there from 1911 till his retirement in 1923. At that point, Colin MacIver asked Rev. McNamara from Flaxley to take on a second parish, thus combining the two. He continued to live in Flaxley."

The Old Rectory during the Smith family residence.
(1940s)

The Rev. & Mrs Ensor.
Rector Of Blaisdon 1911-23.

The late **Ruth Magee** in her reflections on life in Blaisdon has written:

"Besides seeing the Rector, the Rev. Gilbert Ensor in his usual surroundings, I well remember seeing him in quite an unexpected spot, writing his sermons, on summer days, beneath a shady apple tree in Parry's Orchard. He used to say Matins and Evensong every weekday at 10.00 a.m. and 6.00 p.m. ringing the bell to invite parishioners to come, before he began The Office. Every Sunday, men, women and girls and all the hymns filled the four choir stalls and varying chants were sung in four-part harmony. The choir practised regularly every Friday evening and the bell ringers had their practice on Tuesdays. The bells were rung for Matins and Evensong, with a full peal for at least half an hour before each Service."

Following the departure of the Ensor family, Colin MacIver who lived at Blaisdon Hall and owned The Rectory, let it to a Mr. A. C. Harmer at £65 per annum. At this time in the late 1920's Elsie Price, daughter of Gideon and Mary Price at the Red Hart, went to work 'in service' for Mr Harmer. The property was sold in 1933 along with the rest of Blaisdon Estate and it is thought that it was bought by the Salesians, who bought Blaisdon Hall as well.

Elsie Price 'in Service' c1930.

A Mrs Pennington and her husband Dr Pennington (apparently an ordained Church of England Minister and Doctor of Medicine) were the new tenants. Mrs Pennington was a very strong willed lady with several Pekinese dogs. Betty Hickie was their daughter and her husband, Mr John 'Jack' Patrick Hickie, and their three-year-old son John completed the family. By 1938 Jack Hickie who was a hotel valuer was ill and in hospital in Gloucester where he subsequently died in 1939.

During the 1990s Jack Hickie's First World War Victory medal was dug up in the garden of The Rectory, by the present owner Mrs Sheila Evans and eventually his son, John was found and the medal returned to him. John's only memory of the house was his grandmother's Pekinese dog getting its head stuck in the banister on the landing!

During the Second World War the Rectory was requisitioned by the Government of the day and divided into three flats. This provided homes for the Thomas family who lived on the top floor, the Allum family on the first floor and the Smith family on the ground floor.

In 1956 the Salesians put the Rectory up for sale and it was purchased by a Mr Evans who came to live there with his family, his wife, three children, Richard, Margaret and Joyce and Granny came along too!

In the early sixties the property was sold again, this time to Captain and Mrs Back and their family. Captain Back along with others, including Mr R Pickering, Mr G Keyes and Mrs Keating worked tirelessly to secure the redundant school for use as a village hall. It was purchased with the yard for £500. No funds were available so an appeal was made. Every household in the parish donated at least two

Capt. Terence Back & his wife Isabel.

pounds and a special fete was organised in 1965 at which £55 was raised, making a grand total of £315. In the meantime Capt. Back negotiated with the Ministry of Education and Science for a grant towards the purchasing and furnishing of the school and in January 1966 they confirmed their willingness to grant the sum of £265. With Capt. Back, Messrs Pickering and Keyes acting as trustees the conveyance was signed in March 1966. The Village Hall remains in regular use and is a great memorial to the Late Captain Back.

Sale Particulars from The auction Catalogue of Blaisdon Hall Estate (1933)

LOT 4

(Coloured Pink on Plan No. 2).

The Gentleman's Residence

known as

The Old Rectory

built in the Elizabethan style with mullioned windows with nicely-proportioned rooms, situated in Blaisdon Village just back from the road, on high ground facing South, overlooking a large garden with kitchen garden adjoining. The House is substantially built of stone and rough cast and has a stone slate roof and contains the following accommodation: Porch, Entrance Hall, heated by radiator and having adjoining a lavatory with lavatory basin and W.C. Drawing Room, 22-ft. 6-in. by 16-ft. 8-in., exclusive of bay window with a marble mantelpiece and radiator. Dining Room, 19-ft. 5-in. by 15-ft. 8-in. with a Serving Hatch from the kitchen passage. The Dining and Drawing Rooms have a South-west aspect and overlook the Lawn and Garden. Study or Morning Room, 14-ft. 6-in. by 14-ft. 6-in., fitted with radiator.

ON THE FIRST FLOOR are the following: Bed Room, 15-ft. 11-in. by 14-ft. 7-in., facing South, fitted with large cupboard. Dressing Room. Bed Room, 16-ft. 4-in. by 15-ft. 4-in., facing South and Dressing Room adjoining. Bed Room 15-ft. 2-in. by 14-ft. 2-in. with cupboards in recess. Bath Room with Bath and W.C.

ON THE SECOND FLOOR are Three Attic Bed Rooms, Box Room and Tank Room.

The Domestic Offices comprise large and well-lighted Kitchen with tiled floor and fitted with "Herald" Range—the "Ideal" boiler for the domestic hot water supply is the property of the tenant. Larder with shelves, Scullery with shelves, sink and draining board, furnace and force pump which is not now required as water is laid on by gravitation. Housemaid's Pantry and sink (h. and c.) and China Pantry. Underground Cellar with boiler and Wine Cellar.

At the back of the House is a timber and slated building containing Battery Room and Engine House with 2¼ h.p. Lister petrol engine and dynamo. Servants' W.C. and Tool House. The House is supplied with water by gravitation.

The Electric Lighting installation is the property of the lessee with the exception of the wiring and the Purchaser will be required to take from the lessee at valuation the whole of the plant and fittings with the exception of the wiring in the house.

There is Central Heating with radiators in the Hall, Drawing and Morning Rooms, but the radiator in the Morning Room is the property of the lessee and shall be taken by a Purchaser at valuation, as also shall the whole of the fixtures which are the property of the lessee.

The Stable Yard

has direct access from the road and the buildings comprise stone and tiled Two-Stall Stables, Garage, Coal Shed and Fowl House.

The Gardens

are very simple, attractive and inexpensive to maintain and comprise a Tennis Lawn, Rose and Flower Garden and an excellent Kitchen Garden sloping to the South with fruit trees.

The whole extends to about

1a. 0r. 4p.

This lot comprises Ord. No. 156 and Pt. Ord. No. 178a in Blaisdon Parish and is let to Mr. A. C. Harmer on lease expiring the 1st July, 1934, at £65 per annum.

The Tenant, however, has agreed to give Vacant Possession on the 1st January, 1934, subject to his being paid for his Tenant's fixtures and the electric light plant, by valuation, and to receiving reasonable notice.

Apportioned Tithe: 8s. 3d.
Land Tax (if any) as assessed.

The Village Water Supply (violet system), is laid on and the pipe line is continued to a trough in Field Ord. No. 173a on Lot 11.

The Hydrant Supply (red system) is laid on from Lot 11.

The Drainage from this lot flows to a ditch by the roadside adjoining Lot 11j, continuing down the ditch between Lots 11 and 40a.

Rights-of-Way for Lots 1, 11, 40a and 11j are reserved over the roadway, Part Ord. No. 173a.

This lot probably also drains into the Village Sewer.

If Lot 4 is not sold this lot will be withdrawn.

LOT 5

(Coloured Blue on Plan No. 2).

A Semi-detached

Modern Cottage

Situated in Blaisdon Village, well built of brick with a slated roof, extending with large Garden to about

26 poles

It contains Sitting Room with cupboards, Living Room with cupboards and Three Bed Rooms.

Left:

The Old Rectory with Croquet hoop on lawn.

Below:

The Old rectory from the road, the wall was covered in roses.
c1940s

The Smith family have memories of Blaisdon in the 1940s. First, *Jackie Smith*:

"We came to The Old Rectory in 1943, my mother and Father, my older brother John and me. My sister Jenny was born there in 1944. There were three families living there at this time. We were on the ground floor, the Allum family were on the first floor and the Thomas family at the top. No electric, no gas and only cold water pumped from a well in the garden, but what a wonderful place to spend your childhood with absolute freedom, not only within the Rectory grounds, but over the whole of the village. We lived there for ten years and left in 1953 but Blaisdon stays in your heart for ever."

Janet Morris (nee Mockford) :

"During the mid 1940s I lived at The Rectory Blaisdon with my grandparents and 'The Smith' family. I attended Blaisdon School where I remember Mrs Smith, the Head Teacher and especially 'the cane,' which she kept for the boys mainly. My memories are of learning to knit in a lesson outside in the summer and of eating condensed milk sandwiches at playtime! The Rectory held a few mysteries for us as some of the rooms were locked and shutters closed down. Looking through a keyhole confirmed they were full of furniture! The garden was a great place with outbuildings to hide in. What happy days – time seemed endless!"

John Smith writes as follows:

"I went to the village school. On my first day at school, Mother promised to wait outside for me. When I saw she wasn't there, I ran home. One day, Mr Turner, the School Inspector who always had very shiny brown shoes, stopped

Anthony Jones and myself in the village whilst we were playing on a pram wheel trolley. He asked why we weren't at school and, after much telling off, we were taken home

From Left:

Mrs Smith with Jackie, Jenny & Janet.

Janet Mockford.

John Smith.

to our respective parents, where he was informed we were suffering from chicken pox.

My Mother once lost her bicycle for a fortnight, before she remembered that she had ridden her bike down to the station, caught the train to Gloucester and then came home on the bus.

The village seemed to be full of larger than life characters. There was Mr House, from Tibberton, who rode his horse into the bar of the Red Hart. I believe he also set fire to Gideon Price's beard! Mr Roberts lived in the woods and made the charcoal. I remember his tent with the camp bed, and what sticks in my mind is his alarm clock. It was very important that the wood was fired for the right amount of time if the best charcoal was to be produced. There were Gipsies who arrived each summer to do the plum picking. Ronnie Martin sold his plants door to door from the back of his bike and Mr Stevens, the butcher, came around in a van with the chopping block and the spring balance scales hanging in the back of the van.

Cedric Etherington had us all in fear for our lives as he explored the school looking for a gas leak with a flame and very nearly committing arson! Mr Joyce's house being broken into by persons who will remain unnamed.

There was always something happening in the village. I remember the Christmas parties at the Latchen Rooms, Longhope, and being given sugar mice with string tails. Another time, I won a fancy dress at Flaxley Abbey fete dressed as a spaceman. We had great fun when the "Brothers" took us village boys camping to Uphill near Weston-Super-Mare. One of our pigs died for no reason, and we had to wait for the Policeman to come to see if it was infected before we could bury it. I used to deliver the "Citizen" in all weathers for a pittance. I think Roger Etherington took it on after me.

On the day the Spout Farm barn was set on fire, a Policeman came to the door and told Mother it was me that 'did the dirty deed.' IMPOSSIBLE it was bath time and I was in the bath.

The winter of 1947 was one of the hardest on record. My father and I had to dig the car out of a snowdrift along the Flaxley Lane. A Private Essex of the 'Glosters' lodged with us, maybe during or just after the Korean War. Finally, I have a hazy memory, of the old Queen Mary driving through the village. Blaisdon was the place for one of the best childhoods one could wish for."

During the years of the Second World War families moved out of the cities and into the countryside for their safety. Blaisdon was a village that welcomed the city dwellers and they in turn embraced the country life and few ever returned to their roots. Mr Robert and Mrs Annie Allum moved into the first floor of the Rectory when their son, also Robert came to work in Mitcheldean. In 1940 his company, J.R.Rank, sent him to take over The British Acoustic Company based at the Old Brewery in Mitcheldean. When J.R.Rank acquired BAC, the new company became known as Rank Precision Industries and, later, Rank Xerox.

Robert (junior), his wife Kathleen and daughter Jean, who was born in 1941, stayed some of the time with his parents, but also spent six months at a time back in London. Jean actually stayed in Blaisdon with her grandparents, as they all loved the countryside so much and when the time came she couldn't wait to go to school. Mrs Smith arranged for her to go early.

Robert junior's brother, Jim, arrived at The Rectory after the war having served in Burma. For a short time he drove the school bus for Cottrells and took outings to the seaside when required. Then he also went to work for Ranks where he stayed for 25 years until his retirement.

Mrs Annie Allum worked in the kitchens at Blaisdon Hall and also worked as a home help in the village when needed. Mr Allum senior spent a couple of years with Ranks before retiring to village life.

Annie Allum, Mrs Grace & members of Blaisdon Hall kitchen staff.

Mr and Mrs Allum junior's second daughter Pam was born in Shepherds Bush in London during the winter of 1947, after which sister Jean, at the age of 7 returned to London to be with her parents and new baby sister. This left Mr and Mrs Allum senior and their son Jim to continue life in Blaisdon. Mr Allum died in1949, at home in the Rectory.

The family would often visit and Pam Allum recalls being told the times they would go to Gloucester Market. This entailed pushing her in the pram up to Hinders Corner, leaving it with Mr Nelmes and then going by bus to Gloucester. On return the bags of shopping together with Pam were placed in the pram and plenty of rest on the long trek back down the lane was taken with stops at various houses for a chat!

Pam Allum remembers the story of her Nan going to the Red Hart:

Pam Allum.

"She asked Landlord Gideon for a bottle of Milk Stout to drink, to which Gideon replied 'I do not serve women in this pub.' Annie told him that her money was as good as anyone's in there at which he asked her to leave. Annie stayed put and Gideon relented and opened up his sitting room and asked her to sit in there, which she did. Other women followed suit later on and the snug bar was formed!

Jean and I remember being told that when you go into the Pub, you are standing on the old head stones from the Churchyard following the Great Fire. The broken head stones were laid there as the heat of the fire had cracked and broken them, so when the pub was rebuilt they laid them on the floor instead of having an earth floor and as far as I know they are still there to this day. The last time the family were there together with Mr Robert Allum junior was in the 1990s for the Plum Festival, the floor was still the same so he told the then owner of the Red Hart the story. The person behind the bar did not know this, but it was true as my uncle and father always told people the story when they spoke of Blaisdon.

I also remember going to the pub when I was young and my sister Jean and I would call in at a stable door at the front of the pub and ask for lemonade and crisps. They would always ask if dad knew. We would say 'yes', he would pay when he comes tonight for his pint. Poor dad would go for his pint. When told the price, would say, 'god you put your price up Gid,' only to be told that his daughters had put their drink on tic at lunchtime! Gid was told not to serve us any more if we did not have the money. We had a stern talking to that night but we still enjoyed the drink and crisps!

Nan kept chickens and one day I was bored. Jean had gone out without me, Nan said 'go and dig up some worms for the chickens,' which I did. Looking at the worms I thought they were too fat for them to eat, so I put them through Nan's mangle to flatten them for the chickens. Mum and Nan were very cross. It made my Mum sick and Nan had to wash it all off. All my hard work for nothing. Mind you the chickens were not impressed with the skins!"

1. Rank Precision Industries C1940.
Taken at The Old Brewery, Mitcheldean.
2. Jean & Pam Allum, Mrs Allum, Jackie & Jennie Smith.
3. Robert jnr, Kathleen & daughter, Jean.
4. Jim Allum outside The Old Rectory.
5. Robert snr & Annie Allum & granddaughter, Jean.

Jean Stone (nee Allum) writes:

"I was born in 1941 and came to Blaisdon when my father, Mr Robert Allum, came to the area to start the factory for Ranks. My grandfather had retired from the Post Office so came to work with my Dad at Ranks. My grandfather loved it here so my Nan, Annie Allum, came to live at the Rectory. They rented the upstairs and Mr and Mrs Smith with their three children rented down stairs. Their children were John, the eldest, Jackie, who was the same age as myself, and Jenny, the youngest. My Uncle Jim arrived after the war having served in Burma.

I stayed with my Nan at the Rectory until the war finished. I went to school there. I used to stand at the gate, so they let me start school early. One time I wouldn't eat my school dinner. I can remember it so well it was Macaroni Cheese. They made me stay at the table until the bell went for home time, but I still wouldn't eat it. My Nan was called to collect me and I am afraid she gave them a row. I didn't have school dinner again.

We would play in the stream, which was a big attraction to us kids and we had many a clip round the ear for getting wet. There was a small stream of

Jean Allum: off to school, age 4.

water running in front of the school and also alongside the drive to the Rectory. I left Blaisdon when I was 6yrs 10 months old as that was when my sister was born.

When we came down for our summer break when I was older, say 12-13 yrs, I would help down on the farm that the brothers of the Hall used to run. I remember they had lots of pigs that I helped with and the entire village helped one another with the haymaking.

I remember in the pub it was always popular to play shove halfpenny and Quoits. Uncle Jim used to play cricket for the local team. He also drove the school bus and coach for day trips and loved his motorbike.

I remember having to walk all the way up to the main road to catch the bus into Gloucester for market day. We would stop at different houses, though I can't remember any names. We would visit on the way home to rest from carrying the heavy bags of shopping."

When Annie and Jim left Blaisdon they went to live in Mitcheldean. In 1957 Annie died in her sleep at the age of 74. Jim died in 1987 at the age of 67, the same age that his father had died. Following the deaths of Mr and Mrs Robert Allum (junior) in 1996 and 1995 respectively, it was their wish that they should come back to Blaisdon to be laid to rest with his parents and brother Jim. In 2010 Elizabeth Etherington met Pam in the churchyard and sat and talked about the past and how they came to live in Blaisdon, and now in death they are all together again in the same grave, in the village they loved.

1. Kathleen, Jean, Pam & Jim Allum,
Herding Bertie Buckett's Friesian cattle past The Lodge.
2. Jean Allum, Jackie & Jennie Smith.
3. Jean Allum walking past The Old Mill.
4. Jean & Pam Allum crossing the railway line at Blaisdon
Halt.

THE SCHOOL

& SCHOOL HOUSE

The village School building was built in 1896 at a cost of £1,156. It comprised of 2 school rooms with an entrance in the centre and a School House on the left of the building. This was the home of the Head Teacher until the school's closure. It was built to replace an earlier school near the church and accommodated 143 children, but in 1964, sixty-eight years later, with only eleven children attending, it ceased to be a school and

Blaisdon School with The School House on the left (1904).
Miss Emily Wright, Head Teacher 1896-1910, with her mother.

Above:
Mrs Alice Martin
Headmistress 1910-1914.
Left:
Mr Percy Garner
Headmaster, 1919-1929,
with his wife & daughter, Poppy.

the remaining children were transferred to Westbury-on-Severn Church of England School. 1964 was a sad time for our village, not only losing its school, but it was the year that Blaisdon lost its railway. Since 1964, the School House has been a private residence and the school is now the village hall, though the exterior appearance and the interior layout remains largely unaltered.

School life was very different from today. Until 1930 when the senior school was built at Mitcheldean, those not passing their exams to go to the Grammar school spent their entire school life at Blaisdon School, leaving at 14 to start work. Additional life skills were taught at places like the Dairy as described earlier. Once Abenhall was opened, the older children went there, leaving Blaisdon at 11.

Mrs Ethel Smith
Headmistress 1929-1954.
Her Husband Albert died in 1936 & they are
both buried in Blaisdon Churchyard.
The inscription on her gravestone reads:
'Her children shall rise up and call her blessed.'

Over the 68 years the school had seven Head Teachers. Miss Emily Wright was the first teacher at the new school followed in 1910 by Alice Higgins-Martin, the wife of Charles Martin. They lived at Bridge House. She was Head Teacher from 1910 to 1914 and was followed by a Mr John Page. In 1919 Mr Percy Garner took over and stayed until 1929.

Mrs Ethel Smith (affectionately known as 'Polly Smith' by her pupils) arrived in 1929 and stayed until 1954, a full 25 years! Mrs K.L. Trippier took her place for four years and

the last teacher at Blaisdon School was Miss Agnes Rees who stayed until the closure in 1964.

In the post war years there were three infant teachers: Mrs Berry who lived at Sunnyside with her son Sidney; Miss Priest, (who later became Mrs Nelmes) and travelled from Grange Court each day; and Mrs Small, who lived with her husband in a caravan behind the school and was there during the last years before its closure.

When Flaxley School closed in 1901 most of the children transferred to Blaisdon School. Children from Flaxley and Pope's Hill walked to and from Blaisdon each day, two and a half miles each way for five days every week from the age of five years! Children also walked to Blaisdon School from Northwood Green another couple of miles each journey.

When **Ada Price** came to live at the Red Hart Inn in 1924, she and her sisters went to Blaisdon School:

"Elsie, was 12 years old, I was 10 and Daisy was 8. We all attended the village school, a stone's throw from our home, The Red Hart, but we often climbed out of bed at a ¼ to 9 and dressed hurriedly, eating breakfast with my father saying 'Come on you girls, you'll be late,' but we always managed to scramble into the lines and walk in with the rest of the pupils. The schoolmaster, Mr Garner, had his classes named 'A' and 'B' and a Miss Wilcox taught in the same room. Her class had children aged 6 to 11, so when I started, I went straight into Mr Garner's 'B' class. It was very different from the Littledean School where I started when we lived on Popes Hill, but we all settled down and learned Reading, Writing and Arithmetic. We were taught script and longhand. Mr Garner used to say, 'I always like to see good writing, although I don't write very well myself,' but we could always understand his writing on the blackboard and he was very keen that we should all learn to spell so for any word that was wrongly spelt in our compositions we were made to write our correction 3 times.

Miss Workman taught the infants and she also taught Elsie and me to play the piano. I'm afraid my practice, which was supposed to be one hour a day, was neglected in favour of games of spinning top and skipping. I can recall playing a duet with Elsie at a school concert. The 'Yorkshire Bells' was the name of the duet, I played bass and Elsie played treble. We were very proud and highly honoured to play before the village mums and dads and some of our fellow schoolmates. I'm sorry to say that I can no longer play. My daughter, Josephine, can play "by ear" and amused herself whenever she saw a piano. Her father, I may add, being a Welshman, was musical and he learned to play the piano in 9 months.

We learnt to sing and dance at school and Miss Wilcox taught us in sections in our age groups. She was also expected to take us in needlework and knitting. My favourite lesson was needlework and Miss Wilcox, who was a good all round teacher, taught the girls to hem, run and fell seams, French seams and also some embroidery stitches. We were studying for the 11 plus and after a while several of the children at the age of 11 or 12 left and went to the Grammar School in Cinderford. I'm afraid we did not pass so we stayed at Blaisdon until we were 14 years of age and then we were expected to work. My younger sister, Daisy, was one of the first pupils to attend the newly built Secondary Modern School at Abenhall, Mitcheldean.

Mr Garner was a very good teacher, strict, but that is perhaps what is needed to educate children and looking back I think he did his best to teach us. He would set us a lesson then sometimes walk outside and look through the classroom windows to see if we were misbehaving and woe betide anyone who did but no-one except Billy Brewer was ever caned in front of the other pupils. The culprits were asked to step into the lobby and hold out their hand and many a lad returned to his desk with tears in his eyes. Master W Brewer was caned in front of all the rest of the children for playing truant from school during the time his father was away from home, after a spell of ill health. Our Billy was a "Just William" devil may care boy, and I can see it all now. Miss Wilcox was taking the girls in needlework in the afternoon and all of a sudden the classroom door opened and Mr Garner bringing back his class of boys and Billy Brewer with his father saying to Mr Garner, 'I give you permission to cane this boy for not attending school although his mother had sent him.' So it was 'Hold your hand out you naughty boy,' and I'm sorry to say the devil may care look changed and 'Ouch!' escaped our lad's mouth and I did hear the comment later from someone that Mr Garner had said 'I don't know who the episode hurt the worse, me or Billy.' You see, young Billy could be a likeable lad but he had spent three days down at Mr Nash's farm behind his own home. What excuse he gave them each day I don't know as Mr Nash was a genuine man and had asked Billy why he wasn't at school.

I, myself, was known to spend time standing in the corner by the piano. Oh yes, we were punished this way if we transgressed. After a time I was told to go and sit down and unfortunately I had to pass my cousin Nancy's desk and I just smiled at her. A voice roared 'come back here Ada

14 Blaisdon School Pupils c1926.
All are cousins related to the Young family from Flaxley.
Front Row, L-R: Ada Price, Nancy Young, Percy Young, Phyllis Young, Joan Young, Dorothy Young, Daisy Price.
Back Row, L-R: Reg Young, Leonard Young, Gibbs Young, Lilly Young, Jack Young, Cyril Young, Irene Young.

Left: Elsie & Daisy Price.
Centre Left: Prize certificate awarded to Elsie Price for needlework, signed by Mrs MacIver of Blaisdon Hall (1926).
Far Left: Ada Price.

Price. What do you think you are doing? I saw that grin' and with that he pushed me back in the corner whereby I let out a good yell and sobbed my heart out for quite 5 minutes as I thought, the injustice of it. One can't even smile at one's cousin without getting into trouble.

I remember the drill we had to do in the playground after Assembly. We were spaced out in rows and it was - arms stretch, arms bend, hands on your shoulders, hips firm, raise your heels, knees bend and lower your body onto your heels. After a few more orders we had to run around the playground twice. Then we had about 8 minutes for a quick game before a whistle would be blown and into school we went. We thought we were hard done by but I guess it all helped make true and strong men and women of us. The girls made up a little ditty about Mr Garner and sang it while they skipped:

4 Friends at Blaisdon School, 16th July 1926.
L-R: Ruth Brewer, Gladys Vernall, Elsie Price, Elsie Lane.
Ruth & Elsie Price lived their adult lives in Blaisdon.

'Mr Garner is a very good man
Tries to teach us all he can
Reading, Writing and Arithmetic
But didn't forget to use the stick
But disobey, disobey, naughty girls to disobey.'

Looking back to those school days, all in all, we were given a good start to prepare us for life's ups and downs."

Nancy Watkins (nee Bate) was the daughter of Mr J.S. Bate the Estate Manager to the MacIvers at Blaisdon Hall. She is an amazing lady with the most detailed of memories. She lives in Essex but still visits Blaisdon on occasions. She writes of her years at Blaisdon School:

"I attended Blaisdon School from 1927 to 1932. In addition to those who lived in the village others came from surrounding farms and cottages, which could mean a very long walk, especially for the young children from Northwood Green, even if they took the shortest route across fields. There were no buses at all and I can remember only one bicycle, ridden by an older boy who lived in Flaxley.

Mr Garner was the Headmaster and with one junior or student teacher taught all those aged 6-14 years in what was called the 'big room.' An infants' teacher in the 'little room' prepared the 5 year-olds for what was to come; to count, using an abacus, do simple arithmetic, to learn to read, to write and draw. Here, pencils were used and sometimes a kind of waxy crayon for colouring. Large clear charts of letters and numbers, as appropriate, for every child to copy were placed on the blackboard.

After a year or so we moved from the rather dark infants' room, with its one window facing north into the bigger room. This was light, often sunny, and full of desks and many large boys and girls, most wearing dubbined boots. We started off at the road end of the room, sitting opposite the main entrance from the girls' 'lobby' but fairly near the solitary coal fire. In the winter, wet clothes would be hung from the fireguard to dry. There were 3 other doors, at or near the far end, one leading directly on to an open yard. By the time we were old enough to leave the school we had travelled the length of the room, away from the one source of winter warmth, via a series of double desks. These, with windows behind, faced the inner wall, the teacher's desk, a piano, a blackboard and easel, the fireplace and 3 of the 4 doors. Here too we progressed from infant room pencil script to joined up writing with loops, dipping pens in inkwells filled by 2 senior boys on Monday mornings. All the village children could go home for their midday meal, others brought sandwiches, some made with bread and lard or bread and black treacle.

Washing facilities in the 'lobby' were basic. Each morning 2 older girls drew water from the supply opposite the War Memorial. Some of this was transferred into enamel bowls in a washstand and shared, as was the soap and towel, by whoever needed to use it. Presumably the boys collected their own supply for the day, but at a different time. Girls' lavatories, earth closet type, were outdoors across a small uncovered but enclosed rough yard at the back of the school and reached by a door from the big room.

Left: Nancy bate being pulled along by a cousin.
Right: Evelyn Burgin.
Both taken outside the Tan House.

The whole playground area was of hard, uneven, compacted earth and stones with numerous puddles after rain. The girls' playground was at the front of the school and playtime was very lively. Two flattish areas made hopscotch and skipping possible. A few girls were adept at spinning a top, using a stick and piece of string, though, try as I might, I could never keep the top spinning. Various ball games were played, using old tennis or Sorbo rubber balls. Occasionally, we were taken outside for P.E. This was limited, mainly to arm and leg exercises, bending and stretching, things that could be done 'on the spot'. Most children got enough exercise in walking to school and in the playtime periods. I can only remember one sports day. Races were held in Perry Orchard from the stile into Nottwood, downhill to a certain pear tree. There were sprints, egg and spoon races, 3 legged and sack races. I wonder why didn't we go to the much flatter cricket ground?

A railing and flower border divided the girls' yard from the School House garden. I can remember large red poppies, wild sweet peas, red-hot pokers, some roses and large border daisies. This garden was well tended by the boys. They also had a vegetable garden in Velthouse Lane, alongside a path, which led through the park to the Hall. I am guessing that they were taught and supervised by Mr Garner and that this was when all the girls did needlework or had nature study walks with the Assistant Mistress followed by drawing and colouring flowers and leaves.

Pupils' paintings and drawings, and written work were fixed to the walls just below the window ledges which held jars of flowers, bulbs, sprouting seeds and twigs according to the time of year. Harvest time and Christmas were particularly colourful.

Every year the Dairy in the village was used for cookery lessons. A peripatetic teacher stayed for a few weeks. The 13-14 year old girls had a concentrated course of basic cookery, going to the Dairy every day instead of attending school. Whenever possible the results could be taken home and shared with the family.

I do not know if there was a similar scheme for the boys in things like carpentry or metalwork but they were encouraged to take up apprenticeships on leaving school.

When District Secondary Schools were built, Mr Garner left to be Head of a larger school on the Cotswolds. Mrs Smith was appointed Head and Mrs Berry Assistant Teacher for infants. The rolls of all village schools were greatly reduced. On the plus side, Abenhall was purpose built, in a beautiful location, with plenty of space for playing fields, unlike many city schools where the children would be in old buildings, adapted slightly to cater for practical subjects and a Science Lab, but with no Assembly Hall, Gymnasium, or playing fields anywhere near. Any extra buildings would use up existing playground space.

In Mr Garner's last years, and my first term in the 'big room', one late November afternoon it became very dark with strong gusts of wind and heavy rain lashing the school windows. Suddenly a loud and long cracking sound was followed by a tremendous crash. The junior teacher leapt on to a desk by the window and shouted, 'My God! The poplar tree has come down.' There may have been pandemonium but I don't remember any. We were allowed, under supervision, to climb on the desks to see for ourselves. Mr Garner left to check any damage to his house and soon returned. The tree had uprooted, fallen across the road, across the schoolhouse garden landing inches short of the house.

The loud noise and its guessed location brought others living or working nearby. Soon Estate workers using axes and handsaws started to clear the many lower branches. Those of us living down the road were shepherded out of the school gate, allowed a good look at the tree and then sent home. I have no idea how children from the Lodge side managed to get home. The men worked in teams throughout the night. Others held lanterns in the still driving wind and rain or brought out food and hot drinks. With daylight, horses came to haul away the huge pieces down to the sawmill and to clear away the many smaller branches. There was a lot of damage to the schoolhouse garden with gate, railings, bushes and trees all crushed.

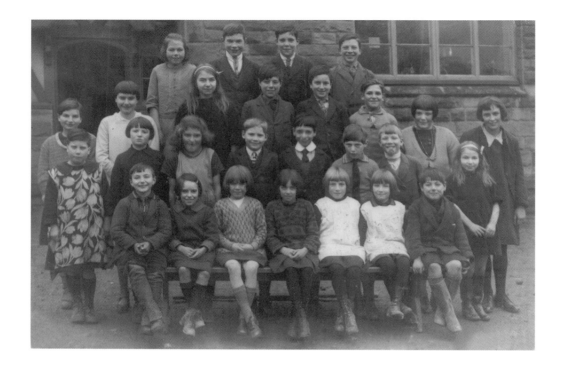

Blaisdon School 1928.

Top: Juniors

Front Row: William Brewer (1st on left).
2nd Row: Joan Young (1st on right)
Cyril Young (2nd on right)
Ivy Marshall (3rd on left).
3rd Row: Ruth Brewer (1st on left)
Lily Young (3rd on left)
Daisy Price (2nd on right).

Left: Infants

Nancy Bate (Back row, 2nd on left).

(D. Marshall)

When Blaisdon School became a Junior School, the 'big room' suddenly seemed spacious with obviously far fewer desks. Wooden boxes of textbooks and pictures would arrive each term from a small town in the Lake District - Ambleside I believe. We were taught by the PNEU method (Parents National Education Union). Similar boxes came from the County Library with suitable books for children and their parents to borrow. There were pictures in the box for Picture Study, black and white prints of pictures well known at the time. I can only remember 'The Laughing Cavalier' and 'When did you last see your father?' The lesson for your age group started with discussion with Mrs Smith about the picture. She then left you to write your own observations on the picture while she taught other subjects to other age groups. We read a lot, learned to use a dictionary and atlas. We read poetry and some Shakespeare (Midsummer Nights Dream, Julius Caesar, Macbeth, Merchant of Venice - possibly abridged.) Arithmetic, History, Geography, Scripture, Nature Study, Art, Needlework, P.E and there was now room for Country Dancing. We sang daily, hymns, psalms, folksongs and shanties.

We occasionally would have concerts, though all fair-haired girls were destined to be the fairies unless they could prove an exceptional talent and be chosen for the speaking parts. My destiny was tinsel, wings and a wand. At a different concert, with headscarves and aprons of sackcloth as our costumes, I was one of a pretty tuneless trio who invited the audience to 'Buy my caller herring,' thrusting a cardboard cut out herring at front row guests at regular intervals. There was what seemed like endless practising for church services like Ascension Day with responses, psalms and hymns all to be sung. Then we would walk in a crocodile to the church to play our very large part in the service.

When 10 or 11 you could sit the scholarship exam. Depending on the results, we would go to Abenhall or East Dean Grammar School in Cinderford, though the latter was difficult to reach for village children, as the nearest buses were 2 miles away in either direction. From my year, the Gloucester Director of Education was persuaded

BLAISDON SCHOOL CONCERT.

Help For Summer Outing Fund.

A successful concert, the proceeds of which will be devoted to their summer outing fund, was given by the scholars of Blaisdon C. of E. School. The large number of parents and friends present were agreeably surprised at the talent and humour shown by the youthful performers.

The first part of the programme consisted of various marketing songs, which were all applauded, notable favourites being "A Pedlar Song," by Master Arthur Smith, "Caller Herrin'," by six small fisher-lassies, and "The Violet Song," by Misses Hilda Pye and Violet Lewis.

Part two was a medley of songs, recitations and dances, the two most popular items being "The Babes in the Wood," by the Infants, and "The School Jazz Band," conducted by Master Jim Richardson. This latter item, which the children thoroughly enjoyed, caused roars of laughter.

The third part of the entertainment consisted mainly of a play entitled "Presented at Court." This was well acted by the children, and began by being amusing, and became funnier as the play proceeded. Master Jack Young as the Magistrate and Master Sidney Berry as The Naughty Boy were very good. The concert concluded with "good-night songs" by the Infants, and a "bed-time song," in which all the scholars appeared in fancy costumes.

The Rector (the Rev. A. E. T. McNamara) proposed a vote of thanks to the children, to Mrs. Smith (head mistress) and the staff, and also to Mrs. A. C. Harmer, who fulfilled the duties of Chairman.

Newspaper report of concert at Blaisdon School.
c1930

to allow pupils from Blaisdon School to go to a High or Grammar School in Gloucester, travelling by train from Blaisdon Halt.

Friends were made at School, but often left when their parents moved to other jobs away from the village and contact was lost. They included Peggy Sparrow, Poppy Garner, and Jean Richardson (also fair haired) from the house now called Vectis. Phyllis Young stayed for a longer time, she with sister Vera and brothers lived at Grove Farm, Flaxley."

Arthur Davies can be seen on the 1935 school photograph (1st on the right of the front row). He describes his childhood journeys from home in Northwood Green to Blaisdon School:

"I lived with my parents, Tom and Nellie Davies, and nine brothers and sisters in a two up two down cottage near Ampney Lane in Northwood Green. The cottage was one of four situated alongside Ley Woods, though the cottages no longer exist and I'm the only one of my siblings still alive.

Along with three or four of my siblings and other children in all weathers, I would set off each morning around 7.30.a.m. We would cross the fields at Northwood Green and head off towards Blaisdon. This brought us down across the Warag field, through the kissing gates over the stream and more fields and eventually coming

Arthur Davies, age 16, having just shot a rabbit.

out alongside The Forge Cottage. I remember watching the horses being shod in the Smithy. We then went up through the village, arriving at the School in time for the nine o'clock bell! At the end of the school day we would do the return journey arriving home around 4.30 just in time for tea!

On leaving Blaisdon School I attended Abenhall School, which meant each morning again embarking on a long walk from home to Boseley Corner where I would get on the school bus. If by chance I missed it I would then continue the walk to Abenhall. After leaving school I went to work at the Poultry Farm at Grange Court."

David Kibble walked to school from Flaxley and Popes Hill:

"The nearest primary school to Popes Hill, where we lived, was at Littledean, a walk of about a mile. As a clean-living Christian family (snobs to some of the locals), mum decided Littledean was too rough for us. Instead, we were sent to Blaisdon, some 2½ miles away, through the country lanes. At 5 years of age, in all winds and weathers, this was pretty demanding. Joining

David Kibble.

other children from the Flaxley area, there were quite a number of us by the time we left the village.

The journeys were not without incident. On many occasions we had to pass gypsy camps and undergo threats

Blaisdon School 1935.
Back Row:
C Warren, Mary Preece, Marian Nelmes, Dorothy Wilks, Pat Frost, Kath Davis, Kitty Wilks, Frank Gardiner.
2nd Row:
Mary Lewis, Dorothy Nelmes, John Haile, Jim Young, Sid Berry, Vic Warren, Margaret Woodyat, Mary King, ?.
3rd Row:
Lucy Phelps, Kath Daniell, Jose Haile, Grace Davis, Barbara Green, Sue Harvey, Dot Gardiner, ?, Jean Arnold.
Front Row:
John Reece, Len Gardiner, Gilbert Daniell, Harold Gardiner, Lee Warren, Humphrey Phelps, Bert Nelmes, Arthur Davies.

from children, sometimes from parents, and almost always from the half-wild dogs they kept. We certainly learnt how to run!

Often we were offered lifts by dubious looking characters, difficult to resist when you were hardly able to put one foot in front of the other. Luckily, the older children had the sense to refuse unless we knew the driver.

We had no idea of the time of course, only by experience, as none of us possessed a wristwatch. If we had to do a detour to avoid the gypsies, or the field shortcuts were too muddy, we could be late for school. We always reckoned to be at Blaisdon Halt to see the train, which gave us 10 minutes to do the last ¼ mile. If we were late, we had to stand in a line, often dripping wet, while the eldest was admonished for letting us be late. This was unfair of course, as it was the young ones who couldn't keep up. I don't think we realised that trains could also be late!

It had its compensations at harvest time. There were blackberries and hazel nuts to be taken, and a lone pear tree at the roadside, which was still there, I noticed, a few years back. Also, there were apple trees within reach. We also played a distraction game with a lovely old gentleman, Mr Joyce, who had apples, pears and peaches in his garden. The girls would engage him in friendly chat whilst the boys crept round the back and scrumped his fruit. He probably knew what we were up to all the time.

When we first started school, the youngest ones had to lie down for an hour in the afternoon on stretcher beds on the classroom floor, to get our strength back ready for the walk home. Of course, we couldn't sleep with the infants'

classes taking place in the same room, but spent most of the time picking the grey paint off the adjacent wall. Within a few months our efforts revealed large patches of bright burgundy paint underneath.

Some respite came after I had been at school a couple of years. Italian prisoners of war, who had been put to work on local market gardens, stayed on after the end of the war. Their old grey bus travelled through Flaxley and Blaisdon, so they gave us all a lift. I remember that they all used to sit one in each seat, so we had to sit by them. They always chatted and were very interested in our school library books. We never felt threatened in any way, despite the fact that the only Englishman on board was the driver. Salvation came a little later when the bus carrying pupils to Abenhall Secondary School also took us to and from school, leaving us only ¾ mile each way to walk each day. We didn't mind standing or the intimidation of some of the older boys. It was a small price to pay for saving our legs and the soles of our shoes.

David Kibble was at Blaisdon School from 1945 to 1952:

"We had no running water in the early years, so 2 seniors were despatched to the tap just up the road from the school entrance and two to the tap by the Red Hart pub. Occasionally, an extra duty was to get the landlord to refill the headmistress's soda siphon. Often we lost a bit on the way!

There was a huge roaring coal fire, suitably guarded of course, which heated the school milk but was also reachable to ignite our drinking straws. Smoking milk soaked straws was an art, at least trying not to cough and give the game away was! We also used to smoke honesty twigs.

Blaisdon School 1950.

Back Row L-R:
Josephine Warlow, Gillian Phelps, Betty Howells, Doris Bowkett, Norma Davis, Marjorie Jones, Susan, Josie & Janet Kibble, Katherine Eagles, Jackie Smith, Mary Dunn.

Middle Row:
Roger Etherington, Michael Keyse, John Smith, Norman Penny.

Front Row:
Terry Keyse, David Kibble, John Martin, Anthony Jones.

Blaisdon School 1938-39.

Back Row:
Henry, Derek, & John Haile, Don Hawkins, Peter Haile, Derek Hart, Bert Nelmes, Les & Chris Warren, Dennis King, May Harper, Dorothy Kibble.

Middle Row;
Jean Arnold, Sue Harvey, Mabel Brooks, ?, Barb Reece, Grace Davis, Marg Dowding, Jean Hart, Ethel Watkins, Jose Haile, Lucy Phelps, Kath Daniell, Ena Jones.

Front Row:
Mary Keyse, Jean Kibble, Muriel Dowding, Ted Davis, N Frost, Barry Davis, Brian Jones, Monica Hart, June Young, Iris & Sheila Daniell, Joan Kibble.

We had two teachers, Mrs Smith, the Headmistress, who taught the juniors, and Miss Berry (affectionately known as 'Misspery'), who taught the infants. Both were nearing the ends of their careers and were strict but very well respected.

For morning assembly, the infants marched in two's into the 'Big Room,' to the accompaniment of a march played by the Headmistress on the piano. Once assembled, prayers were said, followed by a short resume of the day's schedule. Before we were dismissed, hankies had to be shown and, on Mondays, clean towels, as these weren't provided. I was often asked to lift mine up for the class to see how a clean towel should look, as Mum's Persil really did wash whiter - and it showed!

On the first two days, we learnt the alphabet and before long our chalk and slates were abandoned for pencils and paper. Most of the lessons were common to all of each group, of course. Arithmetic was worked from textbooks, so we could go at our own speed, but history, nature and writing were taught to all from the blackboard. Every year there were prizes for the best pupils in each year, and a present for everyone at Christmas, all due to the generosity of the Headmistress, I believe.

The boys' toilets comprised two boards with holes above buckets. The stench was terrible. The ceiling was about 5 feet high - no prizes for guessing how you joined the 5 feet high club!

The girls' playground was nicely asphalted and served for outdoor gym, etc, in the fine weather but the boys' playground was bare earth. This resulted in many gashed knees from the protruding stones. Much more interesting for playing marbles though, and fooling the batsman with an unexpected googly! Unfortunately, the railings didn't retain small balls. The field on one side was not a problem as the fence was easily climbed and you were unlikely to be caught. The other side bordered old Mrs Goddard's orchard. She was also unlikely to spot us, as she ran the Post Office, but as soon as you'd reached the furthest point a deafening chorus of 'Pig's in the garden' went up. Some kids would panic and run back without the ball. This was a real error of judgment, as they had to go back, by which time it was far more likely that the old lady had made it into the orchard. If she complained to Mrs Smith, you were really in trouble.

One day, David Compton (Curly Top) mis-judged the width of his shoes when trying to jump off the railings to recover the ball. His feet lodged between the rails, leaving him hanging upside down. Fearful of a scolding from Mrs Smith for climbing the fence, we tried to release him without success. Heeding his screams of, 'Help, I'm dying,' we decided to get Mrs Smith. She came running out and immediately summing up the situation shouted, 'Norman Penny, don't just stand there, do something!' She hadn't chosen Norman for his skills or brainpower. Norman at 11 years old had the body of a 15 year old. To our amazement he casually walked over and, grabbing the shoes, lifted Curly Top clear of the railings. That stopped our game of cricket for the day.

There was a huge shed at one end of the playground, where various pieces of furniture were stored. We were allowed in when it was raining, which was quite exciting, climbing over it all and hiding. It was, of course, very damp as it

Blaisdon School 1954.
L-R, Back Row:
Mrs Nelmes (nee Preest), John Blake, Roger Keyse, John Watts, Tony Young, Paul Phelps.
2nd Row:
Doreen Jones, Valerie Keyse, Margaret Green, Susan Young, Elizabeth Etherington, Janet Smith, Sylvia Price, Barbara Watts, Mrs Smith(Headmistress).
3rd Row:
Patricia Young, Jacqueline Hewitt, Maureen Blake, Susan Evans, Margaret Hogg, Anne Daysh, Vera Jones, Anita Martin, Diane Smith, Heather Martin, Shirley Green, Ann Cooper, Irene Green.
Front Row:
Wilfred Keyse, Graham Keyse, Billy Davis, Peter Smith, Patrick Tobin, Brian Young, Dennis Tobin, Ian Hewitt.

was open at the back and wasn't well maintained. An old piano was stored there. The damp had melted the glue. It wasn't long before all the key facings were pulled off, the hammers were dismantled and little by little the piano was almost completely dismantled. Needless to say, when Mrs Smith at last decided to inspect the shed contents she went absolutely berserk. As one of the senior boys, and up to this point thought to be a fine upstanding lad, I took the brunt of her anger and I felt very ashamed of myself.

As you can imagine, with 8-11 year olds sharing a single teacher, it was difficult to get much individual attention. For bright kids this was fine, as you just got on with it, the incentive for doing well being a prize at the end of term. For the less bright ones, however, it wasn't too good. I remember many occasions when kids and the teacher were mutually reduced to tears of despair. There were no 'Teaching Assistants' in those days.
So many of us were poor that there was no shame in wearing 'hand-me-downs.' I remember when I was given a pair of second-hand hobnailed boots, quite popular in those days. Mum would never buy me boots, but free was a different matter, and it was a dream come true for me.

Christmas was a very special time. For children from poor families who had very few luxuries, we had such fun, such a magical time, and it cost us so little. Firstly, the decorations were put up, all rather tattered after many years of use. Putting up the Christmas tree was fun too. The best was yet to come; Christmas dinner, prizes for the best pupils of the autumn term and, for everyone, a present. Mrs Smith asked us all what we wanted and usually, within reason, we got it, paid for by herself.

Norman was mad on trains; his dad worked on the railways. He wanted only one thing, a stationery set. Mrs Smith explained it was nothing to do with trains but writing paper and envelopes. 'No, that's what I want,' he insisted. So that was what he got. He was so disappointed. Despite the fact that we all treated him with disdain, I felt so sorry for him.

The other great thing was the 'Jolly Miller.' We did a lot of country dancing at school, but this one was saved for Christmas. For the uninitiated, the dance was accompanied by a song, which went:

'There was a jolly miller and he lived by himself,
As the wheel went round he made his wealth.
One hand on the tiller and the other in the bag,
As the wheel went round he made his grab.'

The Kibble Family:
Back row; Tony, Shirley & Jean.
Front Row: David, Josie, Janet & Susan.

At this point, the music stopped and, as partners were changed, the 'miller' had to grab a partner, leaving a new 'miller' and so it continued. With the euphoria of Christmas coming up, it was danced with great gusto and got faster and faster in a bid to outwit the 'miller.' On one occasion it got too fast and, as we swung round the circle, someone's leg dislodged the plum box, which was supporting the corner of Mrs Smith's desk as the leg had fallen off. In an instant, the desk toppled over and the most incredible mixture of miscellaneous junk scattered in all directions. Dance over. For a moment we stood there, taking in this incredible sight then, down on our knees clearing it all up. To this day I cannot believe that old desk could contain so much junk.

We all remember the day that King George VI died. Terry Keyse's dad had a market garden, which supplied the school with vegetables. Terry had heard the news during his lunch at home. Returning with vegetables for the next day he knocked on the canteen door. As Mrs Cox opened up he greeted her with a blunt 'the King's dead.' She promptly collapsed. Luckily, Miss Berry was on hand to offer assistance.

Canteen meals were pretty plain in those days - we weren't used to fancy food. One day we were served Macaroni Cheese, ugh, poison, or so you'd think. Nobody would eat it, until we were told no second helpings for the rest of the week unless we did. Colin Keyse and myself couldn't accept that, so we soldiered on until it was gone. Lots of little faces looked enviously on!

Roger Etherington, a really nice lad, just couldn't eat his meat. He used to cut it up into such small slices before starting the painfully slow process of eating it. Miss Berry would get so annoyed as he held everyone up. One day she lost it and he got a pudding spoon rapped on his knuckles, something normally reserved for naughty boys. Most of us boys scoffed our dinners down very quickly, as we always seemed to be hungry.

One day, having just learnt that if you dug a tunnel through the centre of the earth you'd come out in Australia, we promptly decided to do just that! Using a pick and shovel we found in the shed, we were down about 2 feet before our plan was discovered and we were ordered to fill it up again! On reflection, we were somewhat relieved, as it had been hard going thus far!

The year I left Blaisdon to move up to East Dean, six of us took the 11+, three passed. The total number of pupils at Blaisdon infants and juniors was less than 40. Imagine how we felt, arriving at East Dean to find almost that number from Bilson School alone!"

The Old School Bell, still hanging in the old school, above a plaque commemorating the building of the school in 1896 with a donation by Mr P. Stubs and its closure in 1964.

Blaisdon Church of England School,
Showing where water used to run in front of the railings.
(Allum)

Mrs Smith, during her 25 years as Headmistress, made sure that her pupils never forgot anything they were taught. Times tables and spellings were reinforced until known perfectly and poems were learnt and recited by heart, from the lighthearted, 'Underneath the Spreading Chestnut Tree,' to the epic, 'Hiawatha' by Longfellow. How many of her old pupils can still recite some of the poems she taught, such as the extract from Hiawatha reproduced here?

Hiawatha's Departure.
By the shore of Gitchie Gumee.
By the shining Big-Sea-Water
At the doorway of his wigwam,
In the pleasant summer morning,
Hiawatha stood and waited.
All the air was full of freshness,
All the earth was bright and joyous,
And before him through the sunshine,
Westward toward the neighbouring forest
Passed in golden swarms the Ahmo,
Passed the bees, the honey-makers,
Burning, singing in the sunshine.

Bright above him shown the heavens,
Level spread the lake before him;
From its bosom leaped the sturgeon,
Sparkling, flashing in the sunshine;
On its margin the great forest
Stood reflected in the water
Every tree-top had its shadow,
Motionless beneath the water.

From the brow of Hiawatha
Gone was every trace of sorrow,
As the fog from off the water,
And the mist from off the meadow.
With a smile of joy and triumph,
With a look of exultation,
As of one who in a vision.
Sees what is to be, but is not,
Stood and waited Hiawatha.
                    H.W. Longfellow.

Blaisdon Church of England School Nativity Play,
Christmas 1952.

Angel Gabriel: Mary Dunn.
Joseph: John Watts.
Mary: Valerie Keyse.
3 Kings: Jean Dunn, Jenny Smith, Margaret Green.
Shepherds: Roger Keyse, Michael Adams, John Blake.
Angels: Maureen Blake, Diane Smith, Heather Martin, Irene Green, Margaret Ashcroft.
Adoring Throng: Doreen Jones, Susan Young, Margaret Hogg, Elizabeth Etherington, Vera Jones, Mary Adams, Wilfred Keyse, Peter Smith, Paul Phelps, Graham Keyse, Anita Martin, Barbara Watts, Sylvia Price, Janet Smith, Iris Hogg, Anne Daysh, Susan Cox, Jackie Smith, Colin Keyse.

Blaisdon Church of England School, 1957.

L-R, Back Row:

Brian Young, Tim Magee, Edgar Green, Dennis Tobin, Jacqueline Hewitt, Ann Cooper, Sheila Boughton, Patricia Young, Shirley Brown, Wilfred Keyse, Eric Brown, William Day.

Middle Row:

Anita Boughton, ?, ?, ?, Janice Hyett, Janet Kibble, Sally Brown, Margaret Townley, Margaret Green, Noreen Tobin, Judith Pickering, Jane Martin, Hilda Davis, Shirley Green.

Front Row:

Patrick Tobin, ?, David Phillips, Stephen Young, Ashley Green, ?, Alan Smith, Phillip Cooper, Edward Keyse.

Blaisdon School c 1959.
Left Desks from Back:
Lynette Price, David Phillips (Blakemore Farm), Edward Keyse (New Road), Pat Tobin.
Centre Desks from Back:
Peter Smith, Tim Magee, ?, David & Eric Brown (Twins).
Right desks from Back:
Peter Brown, Russell Watts, Alan Smith (Hay Farm, Elton Lane), Anthony Jenkins, Janice Hyett (Velthouse Lane), Judith Pickering, Noreen Tobin.

SPRING COTTAGE

Spring Cottage in the early 1960s.
(B. Jones)

Spring Cottage is situated at the cross roads where Blaisdon Lane meets Velthouse Lane and is opposite the War Memorial. It is a 17th century timber framed cottage, the original cottage being largely unaltered though there is a large modern extension built in the later years of the 20th century and dormer windows have been placed to increase light upstairs. Inside, it is a classic 2 up 2 down with a large inglenook fireplace with bread oven. Although the roof has been tiled for many years, there is evidence in the roof space that the cottage was thatched in the past and the pitch of the roof would also support this suggestion. It is presumed that it was named because of its proximity to the village spring.

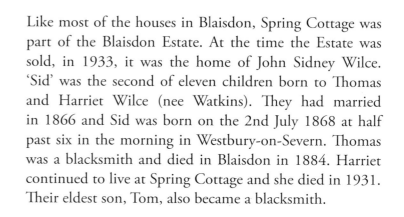

Mrs Harriet Wilce.

Like most of the houses in Blaisdon, Spring Cottage was part of the Blaisdon Estate. At the time the Estate was sold, in 1933, it was the home of John Sidney Wilce. 'Sid' was the second of eleven children born to Thomas and Harriet Wilce (nee Watkins). They had married in 1866 and Sid was born on the 2nd July 1868 at half past six in the morning in Westbury-on-Severn. Thomas was a blacksmith and died in Blaisdon in 1884. Harriet continued to live at Spring Cottage and she died in 1931. Their eldest son, Tom, also became a blacksmith.

Mr Neville Pailing the grandson of Florence Alice Wilce, Sid's sister, sent the following information given by Cedric Etherington during the eighties when they spent time in Blaisdon researching their family history. Cedric wrote:

"Sidney was a woodcarver who displayed his wares in the end window of the cottage, overlooking the road. At each General Election, he would carve a bust of the new Prime Minister and display it. When the Whigs were in power, the Lord of the Manor, a staunch Tory supporter, would send a message to him to tell him to remove it! Spring Cottage was only rented. The rent for the cottage and the smithy across the road was 1s.6d. a year and, I suppose, this is why the Lord of the Manor, who probably was the Landlord, could insist he removed the bust!"

Bust of Gladstone.
Carved by Sid Wilce.

Sid, who was a gardener by trade, continued to live at Spring Cottage and, in 1934, bought it with his brother, Walter, who was a florist's assistant in Hereford. Sydney never married but employed a housekeeper who was rather old-fashioned and was in the habit of wearing large hats. She was known locally as 'Madame Butterfly,' though her real name is not known.

Michael Jones who lived at Vectis remembers Mr Wilce with fond memories and writes as follows:

"Sid was an extraordinary gardener and skilled wood and metal carver. He liked to make furniture and walking sticks. Whether his carpentry and skills was a trade or hobby, he never said.

The tale I liked about Sid came from the Reverend McNamara, the village vicar. He stood outside Sid's gate one day viewing the beautiful flowers and said to Sid, 'You and the Good Lord have done a wonderful job in your garden this year.' To which Sid retorted, 'Yes, but the Good Lord didn't do very well last year when I was ill!'"

Sidney died on 16th September 1947. In December of that year, Walter Wilce sold Spring Cottage to Miss Violet Lethcourt Lorimer, who moved from Weston-under-Penyard, Herefordshire. Miss Lorimer died on 3rd November 1952 and she stipulated in her will that her companion, Susan Anna Dagger, should be allowed to continue to live in Spring Cottage. This she continued to do until deciding to move to London in 1953. The cottage was then sold to Mrs Emily Lydia Townsend, a widow from Gloucester, who lived there until the mid 1960s.

Centre:
An early picture of Spring Cottage.
For many years, it was known locally as 'Sid Wilce's Cottage,' as he lived there for
so long.
Clockwise from top left:
Minnie (niece of Sid) with Alice (wife of Walter Wilce) and children, Olive & Tony.
Minnie Pailing, Sid Wilce, Walter & Alice Wilce & their children Jack, Olive, Ken
& Tony (centre).
Minnie & cousin Jack.
Florence Alice Fossey (nee Wilce) c 1920.
(photo: Mrs M. Pailing)

POST OFFICE

The Post Office lies just behind Spring Cottage. It underwent alterations in the 1970s with the roof height being raised and the exterior rendered, so that it is much changed to the time when it housed the Post Office. Although the post box was removed from the wall when the Post Office closed, the old red telephone box remains working and in its original position. It is now protected by being within the Blaisdon Conservation Area.

The Post Office.
The sign above the door reads 'D. Parslow.'

Like the village pub the village Post Office remained in the same family for about 70 years. Mrs Goddard or Annie as she was affectionately known, was the village postmistress for 46 of those years. She was the longest serving sub postmistress in Gloucestershire and received the British Empire Medal for her service to the Post Office in 1967 when she was 85 years old.

Annie Goddard was born in 1882 in her words 'in the shadow of the village church.' One of a family of eight, Annie had 2 sisters living in America and 1 in Canada. One of her brothers, Frederick Parslow, was killed in the First World War and his name is commemorated on the village war memorial. Her father, Mr David Parslow, was the first village postmaster, a post he held for 24 years. Her mother was the schoolmistress and church organist.

Annie married Sgt-Instructor James Goddard of the old Newnham Volunteers. They lived at the old School House in Flaxley until his death in 1927. She never remarried and Annie returned to Blaisdon to live and eventually took over the role of sub postmistress. Mrs Sherratt, Annie's widowed elder sister, came to live with her and helped out with running the Post Office until prevented by old age and failing health.

Annie will be remembered for different reasons by different people but most will remember her for the way she wore

Mary Elizabeth Annie Parslow
before she became Mrs Goddard.
(R. Etherington)

Regimental Sergeant Major James Goddard (seated left)
in the uniform of the 2nd Gloucestershire Rifle Volunteer Corps.
His rank is denoted by 4 chevrons surmounted by a crown on his
right sleeve. The crossed rifles on his left arm indicate he was a
marksman. He was also entitled to carry an officer's pattern sword.
The other seated figure is a Colour Sergeant.
c1900.

her spectacles - always on the end of her nose and over which she peered when she spoke to you. She had a canny way of keeping you there talking and in so doing managed to extract every last bit of village gossip which you might know before you left. And therefore, if you wanted to know something, she was the one to ask.

Blaisdon postmistress kept her secret

FOR three days, Blaisdon's 85-year-old postmistress, Mrs. Mary Elizabeth Annie Goddard, had to keep a big secret from her customers. She had to wait until the Queen's Birthday Honours were officially announced to tell them that she had been awarded the British Empire Medal for "meritorious service."

Three days before the announcement Mrs. Goddard had a letter from the Prime Minister telling her of the award. "It was difficult keeping it a secret with customers coming in and out all the time. I felt I wanted to tell somebody," she said.

The whole village of Blaisdon was delighted for their postmistress has served them for as long as most people can remember.

She has spent most of her 85 years there . . . "I was born in 1882 in the shadow of the village church. My mother was the schoolmistress and organist."

Apart from a period of seven years, Mrs. Goddard, a widow, has been at Blaisdon Sub-Post Office since 1914 and it was in the family for 24 years before that.

Newspaper report of Annie Goddard's British Empire Medal.

When Annie became too old to care for herself she went to live at Townsend House in Mitcheldean. She died at the Dilke Memorial Hospital, Cinderford, in 1975 aged 92 years and was buried in Blaisdon churchyard.

Post destined for Blaisdon was sorted at Longhope Post Office and delivered to the village each morning and afternoon by the postman of the day. The village post box was set into the boundary wall of the Post Office and emptied twice a day by the postman. Mr Joe Bailey, the postman during the 50s, would cycle twice daily down the Velthouse Lane in all weathers. In those days, [before automation] you could count on the postal service to deliver next day, and, if it were a local address, something posted in the morning would often be delivered in the afternoon.

As well as delivering the post Joe Bailey would also collect prescription medicines for Blaisdon people which would have been dispensed and left by the Mitcheldean Doctors with Bonnie who ran the café in Longhope and from whom the Mitcheldean doctors' practice rented 2 very small rooms which they used as a surgery and a waiting room for those unable to get to Mitcheldean. The building was of wooden construction and conversations between Doctor and patient could often be overheard, so privacy was not high on the agenda but nobody seemed too concerned in those days.

Sally Wynn, Granddaughter of Joe Bailey, writes:

"Joe came to work in Longhope, from Hereford, in the 1920s as a very young man, working initially as a messenger boy. He met Lily Jackson, the local blacksmith's daughter and they married.

Joe became a postman, a very respectable and important position in those days. He was employed by the Longhope Post Office and took on the Blaisdon 'round'. He was called up to serve in the Second World War, leaving his beloved Longhope and Blaisdon behind for several years. Joe was part of the Medical Corps and took a front line role in Italy and the Middle East.

At the end of the War, Joe returned to his job with the Royal Mail at Longhope. In those days mail was a vital form of communication and he would make two deliveries a day to Blaisdon, cycling from Longhope, up Hopes Hill to Nottwood Hill and on to Blaisdon. He would recall times of abandoning his bicycle and trudging through very deep snow to get the post through to the residents of Blaisdon. Joe had a very strong relationship with the residents of Blaisdon and very fond memories of his round there. Lifelong friends were made and countless stories were recalled of his happy times in Blaisdon.

On Joe's retirement from the Royal Mail, the people of Blaisdon held a lovely garden party in the village on a beautiful summer's afternoon and they presented him with two comfortable garden loungers and a cheque in appreciation for his devotion to his job and friendship to the villagers over the years. Joe's family were there to enjoy a very special afternoon, one that would never be forgotten.

Joe loved his garden and spent many happy years of retirement producing a beautiful display of colour for passers-by to admire year after year and when the days work was over he would relax on the garden lounger with a cup of tea!"

2 photographs of postman Joe Bailey.
The young helper is believed to be Tim Magee.

Dave East, who has been delivering the post in Longhope for 35 years, has firsthand experience of what life was like for Blaisdon postie, Joe Bailey and imagines what Joe would have told us:

"4am wakes me up. I have a wash, cup of tea, and then it's straight out into the cold air. Yes lots of folk envy me on a summer's morn, but on a freezing November morn it is a different story.

I arrive at Longhope delivery office for 5am to meet the mail from Gloucester and add this to the local mail, which I collected the night before. Mr. Hampton, the postmaster opens up and we get on with the job of sorting the post into rounds then putting my round in order: Blaisdon, Nottwood Hill etc. I put my bundles of letters into my Post Office sack, collect up some tablets left by the doctor, which I take for folk and set off on my trusty bike, down Velthouse Lane. I ride on past Bowketts, Sutridge, as there is no mail for them today, on to Mrs Jones, Dingle, the last house in Longhope. I reach Velt House Farm, the

Daniell's. 'Morn Bert.' I think they put the clock right by me, or the train. It's now 7.00.am. and they are in the middle of milking, so I hand them their mail. On down to the village of Blaisdon as far as Monk Hill Farm, home of Dennis King. The Red Hart is closed, but Elsie shouts 'Good morning Joe.'

I think the hardest part of the round is Nottwood Hill. When I get to that end of the Blaisdon Lane I park my bike by Bill Hatch's hedge and trudge up the footpath along side his property, eventually reaching Nottwood. Then off round the hill, delivering to the cottages scattered around and back down from whence I came to retrieve my bike! It keeps you fit. Back up past Velt House Farm, milking over, the churns are collected by 9.30. Delivery done, it's home for breakfast. I collect 4 or 5 letters on my way back to the Post Office, which folk wait to give me. That's it till 4pm when I go round the post boxes to collect mail for delivery next day, and also do another delivery in the village if required. Six days a week all weather, but I wouldn't change working for the G.P.O. for all the tea in China."

The village Post Office and Blaisdon Hall were the first 2 places in the village to have a telephone. A uniformed telegram delivery boy who rode out from the main office in Gloucester on a motorbike delivered telegrams. **Gerald Savage**, from Minsterworth, was one of these messenger boys and he delivered to the Blaisdon area on a Saturday afternoon and Sunday morning, the rest of the week was covered by one of the Forest offices.

"Before it became common to have a telephone in every house, let alone every handbag or pocket, urgent messages were sent via the GPO Telegram system. Messenger boys delivered the telegrams. People who did have a phone usually had the telegram read to them down the phone and a confirmation copy would be put in the post.

Messengers, often as young as 15 years of age, delivered the telegrams by bicycle mostly in the town and city areas, messengers on motorcycles catered for the countryside villages. From 16 to 18 years of age, parental permission was required before motorcycle training commenced. In the forties some offices had 250cc BSA motorcycles, in the fifties the bikes were 125cc BSA Bantams, towards the end of the service mopeds were used.

Telegrams conveyed good, sad, and business news. Bad news ones (serious illness and death) were marked on the envelope with a sign by the telegraphers so that the messenger would be aware, in which case the house was approached with as much sensitivity as a young lad could muster and we always tried to ensure that the recipient had someone with them before we left. Some telegrams were for happy occasions such as weddings. Saturdays were busy for these and it was not unusual to receive a tip!"

Telephone Box & post box in wall outside Post Office at time of its closure.
(E. Etherington)

The Post Office 1904.
The Parslow Family including a 21 years old Mary.
(J. & P. Higgins)

Above;
Joe Bailey delivering to the Old Mill.

Far Left:
Telegram of congratulations.

Left:
Telegram 'Boy.'

ATER SUPPLY

Blaisdon did not get mains water until 1948. For the half century before this, those without wells on their property would visit 1 of the 4 standpipes with their jugs and buckets to obtain fresh water. The only other source of water would be to collect rainwater. The standpipes were connected by underground pipes to large, underground tanks situated in front of The Lodge. These standpipes were not pumps as the fall of the land kept the water under pressure. There was a handle on the side of the pump and pressing this down released the water.

The picture on the right shows the standpipe opposite the Old Mill. Using the pump is Miss Elsie Lane. She was a niece of Mr & Mrs Lane (Syston Cottage). She sadly died on 4th November 1931 at the age of 18 and is buried in Blaisdon Churchyard.

Tony Brady writes about the water supply prior to 1948:

"Near the village War Memorial is a fresh water well. The late Mr Bill Brewer, the former Blaisdon Hall engineer (1912 -1950) recalled that the men digging the foundations to The Lodge in the 1890s struck a water spring. It was decided to trap the newly discovered spring water: a huge underground tank was created in front of The Lodge. Iron pipes were laid and a gravity supply was now on tap, not only to the Kitchen garden, but the dwellings below The Lodge, via a series of standpipes

Miss Elsie Lane
at the Old Mill Water Standpipe.

164

along the village lane. The Kitchen Garden was a major beneficiary as, prior to this, horse drawn barrels filled in Longhope Brook, met its large water needs. A remote pressure valve opened to replenish the tank and closed when it was full.

Because of the natural sloping ground and the need for a horse trough, an expense the Parish Council baulked at, a ground level well was created close to Spring Cottage. Thus the occupants of the nearby Post Office, School and cottages could draw off water for household use.

Water collection point outside Spring Cottage with grill covering to prevent use of water.

Bertie Buckett recalled the well protected with a wooden cover to prevent animals drinking direct from it. As most carts carried a bucket before the arrival of tractors, water was drawn to refresh thirsty horses. The boys at Blaisdon Hall often drank from it on walks and cross-country runs; they lay flat on the ground and sipped from its limpid surface. I remember drinking there and splashing mud from my legs before running the final lap, under the arch and up the drive to the Hall.

Factors such as the high tadpole count, in the Blaisdon Hall baths, determined the end of the water supply and the call for statutory replacement. In 1948 a ring water

main laid from Hinders Corner was soon linked to all the village properties.

My modest claim to history is that in 1957 I was given the job of back-filling the line of the iron water pipe that runs up Blaisdon Hall Park from the road opposite Buena Vista Cottage. Earlier a man from Taynton, with three fingers missing from his right hand, had spade dug the trench single-handed in 3 weeks!"

Elsie Price standing on the little bridge at the end of the water culvert next to the Red Hart.

In front of the school railings was a little stream of water (enough to get wet feet) which is thought to be surplus water running off from the spring near The Lodge. This water then disappeared across the road only to appear again on the right hand side of the road adjacent to the Red Hart orchard. From here it flowed with more gusto down to the edge of the Pub where it disappeared once more under a little brick bridge upon which many bottoms sat and dangled feet into the cool water. It must be said that watercress from the stream was very much welcomed by the Red Hart occupants (and others!).

After disappearing under the road once more it found its way down through the village diverted by The Forge across the field and then into another stream reappearing through a pipe into a culvert at Bridge Cottage and then into the Longhope Brook!

There were four pumps placed strategically in the village, the first outside Spout Farm, then The Nurseries, The Forge and the last opposite The Old Mill. These standpipes were not pumps as the fall of the land kept the water under pressure. There was a handle on the side of the pump and pressing this down released the water. The villagers shared these pumps, except those who had their own wells in their gardens for the supply of water.

Roger Etherington has more details of the village water supply and Artesian Well at Stanley Corner:

"The borehole at Stanley Farm is 800ft deep and penetrates 600ft under the sandstone. It was sunk in 1906 by E. Timmins of Runcorn. Water in the borehole was artesian and came to just below ground surface level and indeed is said to have over-flowed when the mines at Cinderford closed down. An analysis of the water in 1907 showed it was too hard for domestic purposes."

The Hall was supplied with water from the system linked to tanks and an artificial rainwater catchment lake in the woods above Cinder Hill (known by most of us as "The Reservoir"). It retained the overflow pumped up to tanks from an artesian well sunk below The Pump House at Stanley Corner. Concealed in the Blaisdon Hall Tower, a one thousand gallons capacity tank was gravity fed from the Reservoir sand filtration tanks.

Tony Brady helped run the pump engines at Stanley Farm:

"The surviving Pump House once contained a beam

2 views of the Reservoir with, above, the Smith Children & Vic Mockford.

engine combined with a horizontal ram positioned over a deep bore-hole well. Qualified people such as Mr Bill Brewer, Brothers Alan Garman, Joseph Carter and Jan Orysiuk were responsible for its operation and care. For safety reasons, two persons were involved in starting it. I often assisted Fr Dan, mainly as an observer, and was sometimes trusted with the duty of turning the pump off.

The first action was to open the main stopcock to the exit water pipe. Turning a handle on a flywheel after a heated cartridge was inserted in a tube started the pump. As the flywheel speed increased, a lever was manually thrown and engaged a belt-drive. You had to be quick to remove the winding handle: it could be lethal. It was known to spin off through the pump house window. Simultaneously, the operator moved a sliding electric switch to provide power to the process.

The wheel drive was connected to a long double horizontal piston, which moved twin rods fixed to an overhead iron beam. This plunged a rod down the well-bore causing a loud gasping sound. As the beam rose, emitting a loud whoosh, the second rod sucked the water up meeting the horizontal ram thrusting forward. The motion drove the water into a watertight space, forcing it into the underground pipe leading out of the pump house, to the filtration tanks situated next to the lake up in the woods. Wall mounted gauges showed water pressures.

The machine was stopped after 4 or 6 hours use by manually moving the belt-drive to a neutral sleeve and switching off the electric power; the main stopcock was closed to prevent water backflow. Grease/oil maintenance was scrupulously done readying everything for next time."

Top:
The Pump House at Stanley (2010).

Below:
An example of the type of machine used in the Pump House.

WAR MEMORIAL

Blaisdon War Memorial sits on raised ground above the road overlooking the junction of Blaisdon and Velthouse Lanes. It is made of granite and was dedicated on 1st January 1920. It is inscribed with the names of villagers who lost their lives in the First World War. Since this old photograph was taken, villagers and Blaisdon Salesian School old boys who died in the 2nd World War have been added. The inscription is as follows:

In Memory of the Men from this Parish
who fell in the Great War

1914-1918
John Bullock   Harold Jones
Owen Bullock   Oliver Jones
Edgar Dowding   Frederick Parslow
George Hopkins

"Live thou for England, we for England died."

"Their name liveth for evermore"

1939 – 1945
Edward Dowdall   William McNamara
James Langrell   Ronald Bowkett
Brendan McGurk

War Memorial.
(S. Waters)

John Bullock
The brother of Edith Bullock, who married Edgar Dowding mentioned below. He also had another sister named Sarah and 2 brothers, Bill and Frank. Their home was Cherry Tree Cottage on Nottwood Hill.

Owen Bullock. (A)
Worked on the Blaisdon Estate farms.

Lance Corporal George Hopkins (B)
The Son of George and Rebecca Hopkins of The Mount Nottwood Hill. He served in the 9th Battalion, Worcestershire Regiment and died at the age of 25 on the 10th August 1915. He is remembered with honour on the Helles Memorial in Turkey.

Private Edgar Dowding
The Son of Charles and Leah Dowding, he married Edith and had a daughter, Irene Dorothy and lived at Stanley Cottages in Blaisdon. He served with the 13th Bn Gloucestershire Regiment and died from his wounds on the 31st July 1917 at the age of 36. He is remembered with honour on the Brandhoek New Military Cemetery in Belgium. There is also a memorial on his parents' gravestone in Blaisdon churchyard.

A

B

C

D

Lance Corporal Harold Burcher Jones (C)
The son of Daniel and Martha Jones of Brookside Cottage, Woodgreen, he served in the lst/2nd Bn Monmouthshire Regiment and was killed in action on The Somme on the 28th January 1917, aged 21. He is remembered with honour at the burial ground at Flers Nr the Somme in France where he fell and is also on the gravestone of his sister Margaret in Blaisdon Churchyard.

Private Oliver Jones (D)
The son of Isaac and Elizabeth Jones who lived on Nottwood Hill. He served with the 2nd/6th Bn Gloucestershire Regiment and died on the 19th August 1917 at the age of 26. He is remembered with honour at the Oxford Road Cemetery at Leper in Belgium. The plaque was presented to his family.
(R. Jones)

Lance Corporal Frederick Thomas James Parslow
The Son of David and Elizabeth Parslow of Blaisdon Post Office and brother of Mrs Annie Goddard. He was born in Blaisdon and was a Bell ringer and Chorister at Blaisdon Church. He served in the 10th Bn Gloucestershire Regiment and died on the 18th December 1916 at the age of 39. He is remembered with honour in St Michael and All Angels Churchyard Blaisdon.

ℑT has been said by some that it is superfluous to give an address at a funeral, because the presence of the dead should speak a message more eloquent than can be spoken by the lips of the living. But before we bear the mortal remains of our brother to their last rest, I feel constrained to try and interpret the message which their presence speaks to us.

First of all, they tell us a truth which must impress even the most casual spectator, for they bring home to us in a way new to this parish the reality of the War. Here we have amongst us the body of one who received his death wounds upon the field of battle, and gave his life for his country.

Then there is the lesson of self-sacrifice.

The death of every soldier who falls on active service is a sacrifice; but only those who knew him intimately are able to judge the magnitude of the sacrifice. In the case of Frederick Parslow that sacrifice was great. All who knew him well will agree that he was not by nature fitted for a military life. He had passed that time of life when the adventure and romance of a soldier's life makes its strongest appeal. Having spent the whole of his life in and about the shelter of his home, at the age of 39 he felt little drawn to a life of unrest in foreign countries amidst the turmoil of War. Not only so, but with the strong love of home there was joined the duty of filling the place left vacant by his father's death—a place which none was better fitted to fill than was he. But though the drawings of inclination and affection were strong, that of duty to his country was stronger, and he willingly offered himself while it was still within his power to refuse. As we trace the course of events that have followed, we are struck with the strangeness of the fortunes of War. Called up but six months ago, ordered to France scarcely more than two,

of all that has gone from this place he is, as far as we know certainly, the first to lay down his life. And of those who have gone to serve their country from this parish, I feel sure that upon consideration we shall all agree that none will be more missed from the life of the village than he. Most of our men who have joined the Army were of but a few years' residence amongst us; and of those who had grown up from childhood in our midst none had attained more than twenty years or so.

Frederick Parslow had lived here from his birth, and during the whole of that time his absences from home were few and far between.

But we shall miss him as something more than a neighbour. At the time his father died it was generally recognised that none was more suitable to fill the public positions which fell vacant. Of his work in connection with the Church, I can speak with nothing but praise. He was invariably reliable, painstaking and anxious to please. I, and I have no doubt most of us, were looking forward to many years' service from him, filling the post of sexton and clerk with the same simple devotion to his Church as his father had shewn before him. But God has willed otherwise, and has, as we believe, called His servant to a higher work.

And now we come to the last rites. But in the midst of our sorrow we cannot fail to thank the kind Providence which has permitted him to be brought back to his native place, to lie beside those who have gone before, beneath the shadow of the Church he loved.

And though the familiar form is removed from our sight, we must not think of him as gone wholly beyond our reach.

All who depart in the true faith are still with us members of Christ's Holy Church, and as such still within the reach of our love—still within the reach of our prayers.

For them and for us it is ever true, " The Eternal God is our refuge, and underneath are the Everlasting Arms."

Above:
The Address given by the Rev. G. Ensor
at the funeral service of
Lce-Cpl F. T. J. Parslow
on
Saturday, December 23rd 1916.

Right: Lce-Cpl F. T. J. Parslow's gravestone.

Lieutenant William Arthur McNamara

The son of Revd Arthur Edwin Thomas McNamara and Mrs Myfanwy McNamara of Flaxley Rectory. His father was Rector of Blaisdon from 1923 to 1948. He served in the lst Bn King's Shropshire Light Infantry and died on the 20th April 1944, aged 24. He is remembered with honour at Beach Head War Cemetery Anzio in Italy and on the grave of his parents in Flaxley Churchyard

Sergeant Ronald Herbert George Bowkett

The son of Herbert and Gertrude Bowkett of Stanley Cottages. He served in 76 Sqdn Royal Air Force Volunteer Reserve as a gunner and died on the 8th November 1942 at the age of 22. He is remembered with honour in Oldebroek Cemetery in The Netherlands.

Private Edward Kevin Dowdall

The Foster Son of Mrs S Hicks of Gloucester. He served with the 2nd Bn Gloucestershire Regiment and died of malaria on the 27th October 1943 at the age of 20. He is remembered with honour at the Kirkee War Cemetery in India.

Sergeant James Langrell

A member of 106 Sqdn Royal Air Force Volunteer Reserve where he was a navigator. He died on the 31st January 1943 during a bombing raid. He is remembered with honour at the Becklingen War Cemetery in Germany.

Brendon McGurk

Served in the Gloucestershire Regiment and was killed in France in June 1944. It is believed he came to Blaisdon from St Charles Home, Brentwood, Essex or St Mary's, Hyde.

Lt. William McNamara.　　　Sgt. Ronald Bowkett.

Michael Jones recalls some of the effects the 2nd World War had on Blaisdon:

"As in the rest of Britain, life had to go on in the village in the normal way, with the additional burden of working to defeat the enemy in whatever way we could.

During the blackout all lights were shut off with drawing the curtains and blinds. After boarding the Gloucester train, the guard would walk up and down calling out 'Remember your blackout,' saying either 'Pull your blinds down' or 'Put the lights out!'

We all had to face rationing, but being a close-knit community, housewives knew what others liked, so food swapping often took place. I recall my mum swapping sugar for butter. Again, being in an agricultural area thanks to the generosity of the farmers, eggs, vegetables, milk and rabbits were shared, helping to combat rationing.

Double Summer Time made it much lighter late in the summer and autumn evenings and I remember hay making and harvesting up to 10 o'clock. Also coaches brought workers, mainly women, from nearby places such as Gloucester and Ross, to help on the land.

The Italian POWs, mainly from the big camp at Newent came to work on farms, especially fruit and potato picking. Also many came to support their footballers in matches against the Hall.

The Yanks or Americans were often in the village from 1942 onwards in their tanks, jeeps, and other army vehicles. I am not sure where they were based, but I do know that the administration office was in Southgate Street in Gloucester where we boys called from time to time. Though at the time no one was aware of what was happening, they practised making road tracks driving and exercising army activities in the surrounding woodland and countryside. When they drove down through the village by the school, Mrs Smith used to let us out to go to the fence to wave and cheer them on. In turn, the Yanks would wave back and throw sweets, especially chewing gum, to us in the yard. For many of us, it was the first sight of black people. Once, an army jeep was being slowly driven past, leaking fuel badly, and in the end had to stop by the school. The driver's mate jumped out and plastered the leaking tank with chewing gum to stop the leak!

Up at Blaisdon Hall in the early years of the war, the Brothers and Priests were treated suspiciously as there were lots of Irish, some Italians and a few other nationalities. However, as the war years went on, this feeling disappeared, with the Hall becoming part of the community, especially

as mentioned earlier, providing food products to combat rationing. The Hall also laid on concerts and well-known plays and music. Furthermore, they formed a club for the village boys and nearby parishes, together with their other sports activities for the village, especially cricket and football: all these contributed to a good relationship in the end. Also helping the Hall/village relationships was the fact that several Old Boys had joined the Services, and one priest had become a Major as a Padre in the Army."

The war memorial is the focus for the Act of Remembrance on the Sunday nearest Armistice Day. Villagers and Hall folk have gathered together each year to remember the debt owed to those who lost their lives defending our country. Since the Salesian Order left Blaisdon Hall, this union has continued with the local Catholic congregation joining with the village for this service. In the days when Blaisdon Hall School had a Combined Cadet Force (CCF), they would march down the Hall drive and stand in formation beneath the Lodge's archway. As **Tony Brady** recalls:

"The Sergeant ordered "Present Arms" and Colonel Forde completed inspection. Fr Boyd and Fr Hilton stood to attention each holding a wreath. Fr Docherty led the prayers and sprinkled holy water assisted by the servers dressed in red cassocks and white cotters. Their candles flared briefly in the breeze, guttered and died. The band played 'Abide with me,' as Colonel Forde accepted the wreaths from both Chaplains and laid them at chest height on the Memorial alongside those of the villagers. Through the fresh green laurel leaves entwined with red poppies that formed the wreaths the names of the remembered villagers stood out.

The Last Post was sounded together with a final presenting of arms and general salute. St. Michael's church bell tolled; the Angelus bell rang out from the tower of Blaisdon Hall and the mournful whistle from a goods train passing under the bridge at Blaisdon Halt echoed through the village."

Blaisdon CCF on parade under the Lodge Arch,
for the Armistice Day Service.

**They did not give their lives:
Their lives were taken from them.**

At Blaisdon Hall, in sombre sun,
The boy soldiers formed up in line:
The Sergeant inspected each in turn.
Colonel Forde (Retired)
Took the salute; the cadets'
Drilled colour party moved off.

Towards the village Cenotaph
The troop marched on
And as the band struck
Up the tune 'Blaze away'
Flocks of pigeons
On sloping Cinders Hill
Exploded into flight -
Spreading like shrapnel
To enfilade the distant trees.

Crackling like gunfire
Echoed in the woods
And pheasants beat
From cover plunged
To earth, killed
In fern and bracken
By weekend shooting
Party's fusillade.

At the war memorial wreathes rested
Where villagers' names inscribed on stone
Are listed. St Michael's Church bell
Chimed an end to silent minute. Then a
Bugle call died away and birds sang out an anthem.

Tony Brady

THE CRUCIFIX

The Crucifix stands in the grounds of the Lodge to Blaisdon Hall. There are very few people, if any, who could remember the time that it wasn't there. Villagers have grown up with it and acknowledge its presence with the greatest of respect. The late **Ruth Magee** wrote about it as follows:

"Probably the most impressive and yet the most poignant moment of all my early years was seeing the Union Jack fall as our Village War Memorial was unveiled by Mrs MacIver. Almost twenty years later, a life-sized crucifix was erected, facing that War Memorial, on the opposite bank – another Symbol of Supreme Sacrifice, right in our midst. In this quiet and lovely village it is good, I feel, to have these two Memorials at the centre. Everything comes so easily to us these days and we are so accustomed to our freedom and to peace. It is as well to be reminded that though they cost us nothing, they were bought at a price and a very high price too. We must always be grateful for that in Blaisdon."

The Salesians of Blaisdon Hall erected the Crucifix and the following is a reflection by one of its past pupils, **Tony Brady:**

"The prominent Cross is positioned directly opposite the Blaisdon village War Memorial that commemorates the service and sacrifice of the Blaisdon villagers who went to fight in the two Great Wars, never to return. The Salesians placed the Calvary in its position shortly after their arrival in Blaisdon Hall in 1935 and they erected a similar Calvary in the grounds up at the Hall. The Calvary became an abiding presence in that sanctified place and a lasting image. It was even renovated by the last owner of Blaisdon Hall. More importantly, it matters because as you look up to the present day Cross and, depending upon the angle of vision, you can see St Michael's Church beyond on a rising aspect. In those reflective moments the true purpose of the Calvary is achieved, it inspires thoughts that are not only poetic but spiritual."

THE LODGE

The Lodge. (S. Waters)

The Lodge was built to be the Gatehouse to Blaisdon Hall. Of stone construction, the large integral gateway creates an imposing entrance to Blaisdon Hall. It was built after the Hall, in 1894.

In 1934 Mr and Mrs Will Gleeson were the occupants, Mr Gleeson being the butcher for the Salesians. They lived there until their deaths in the early forties and are buried in Blaisdon Churchyard just inside the top gate. Mrs Magee then lived there while her son, John, was studying at Blaisdon Hall.

In 1945, Mrs Elsie Bertha Grace, known as Betty, came to live at The Lodge with her 3 sons, Peter, Jimmy and Freddy, having lost her husband in the war. Her husband had been billeted at Down Ampney from where he flew on his last and fatal mission.

Mr James Grace was serving in the RAF during the Second World War. He was attached to 271 Squadron C-47 (Dakota) FZ-626 based at Down Ampney, Gloucestershire. In 1944, he was involved in 'Operation Market Garden,' the largest airborne operation of all time. Its purpose was to seize bridges over the River Rhine to allow the Allies to outflank German forces. The Dakota he was flying in was on a mission to drop supplies to the troops on the ground, when it was hit by ground fire. It crashed, killing James and 4 of his comrades, while 3 others survived. The date was 19th September 1944 and James was 28.

L/Cpl. James Grace.

Newly widowed and with 3 small sons to bring up on her own, Mrs Grace came to Blaisdon to work as cook for the Salesians at Blaisdon Hall. Their arrival in Blaisdon coincided with the plum-picking season. Their transport was an army lorry. For some reason they arrived at The Lodge via Velthouse Lane and Freddy remembers he and his brothers reaching out from the back of the lorry and grabbing plums from the overhanging branches of the plum trees as the lorry drove slowly along the narrow Lane.

Freddy Grace continues:

"My brothers and I attended school at the Hall and received a brilliant education where discipline was strict but fair. On one occasion I was not paying attention in class and the teacher, who kept a billiard cue by him, pointed the cue at me and told me to put my pen down and be quiet, the rest of the class were to continue with what they were doing. The bell went for break and everyone in the class got up to leave but I was told to stay at my desk. When the classroom had emptied, the teacher then said, 'Now you can pick up your pen and finish what you were supposed to be doing earlier.' Hence, I missed out on break. But it was a lesson learned, not to mis-behave in class but to pay attention and get on with it. I later transferred to Abenhall School.

Whilst living at the Lodge, water for the house had to be collected in a bucket daily from the spring which was on the opposite side of the road to the Lodge. I well remember my 2 brothers pushing me outside after dark with the water bucket and being told to go and collect water from the well on my own.

Amongst my best memories are the parties I was invited to by Mrs Keating at The Laundry where we would have tinned peaches and ideal milk, but only after 2 slices of bread, which you had to eat otherwise you didn't get anything else! Tinned peaches were a real treat in post war Britain. They are still a favourite of mine to this day.

I remember going rabbitting on a Sunday morning and shouting for the adult to come if a rabbit was in the net. Because meat was rationed and generally in short supply, rabbits provided a good nourishing meal and rabbit stew would be continuously on the hob and added to as a new supply of rabbit was caught.

We would go scrumping walnuts from Bertie Buckett's walnut tree in the field next to the Tan House. We would watch for Bertie to fetch the cows for milking which he fetched from the field via a gate in the Velthouse Lane, we would then jump over the boundary wall on the village side and throw sticks up into the tree to knock the walnuts off. We never got caught and as far as we know Bertie never knew we did it.

Another faint memory is of a big bonfire being lit in front of Blaisdon Hall to commemorate VE Day in Europe. I also remember going to the reservoir in the woods and falling in, lying on the bottom and looking up to see tadpoles swimming above me. Fortunately, I was able to get out to safety.

For Coronation day in June 1953 Brother Jan, one of the Salesian Brothers who lived and worked at the Hall at that time, constructed an illuminated coronation crown which

1. L-R: Jimmy, Freddy & Peter Grace outside the Lodge.
2. Mr & Mrs Gleeson with neice, Frances, who, as Mrs Jones, lived in Vectis.
3. George Austin & dog.
4. Betty Grace & Freddy.
5. Beryl & George Austin With Friends and something for the pot.
The water tanks for the old village supply are buried beneath their feet.
6. Beryl Austin plum picking.
7. Beryl & George Austin plus pig.

he then erected on the top of the tower of Blaisdon Hall. This crown could be seen for miles around and attracted many admirers. Coronation day was also memorable as Sir Lance and Lady Crawley Boevey of Flaxley Abbey opened up their grounds and entertained the whole of the Flaxley and Blaisdon communities. There was a pageant, fancy dress parades and races for the children and later in the afternoon a tea party was laid on in the refectory."

Freddy married Valerie Keyse who lived at Flaxley and 47 years, 2 children and 2 grandchildren later they are still happily married.

Mrs Grace left Blaisdon when she remarried Tom Maskell and went to live at nearby Greenbottom. It is a testament to her popularity whilst living at The Lodge and working at the Hall that when she died old Hall boys came from far and wide to attend her funeral and the following eulogy was given on their behalf by the President of the Old Boys Association, Charlie Springett. It was first published by **Terry O'Neil** in his book 'Recollections of Blaisdon Hall" and is reproduced here with his permission.

"There is so much that can be said about Betty, she was a good friend to so many Blaisdon Old Boys and known as Mrs Grace, and Mum to some, especially to Bernard who is serving at this Mass today. Betty was our great cook at Blaisdon Hall over the years we were there. Even in those days of shortages and food rationing Betty and the Salesians always managed to produce three meals each day for the boys. She would often spoil a boy or two who happened to be helping with the washing up and kitchen duties.

Often Betty would be ready to welcome a boy in the Lodge for a cup of tea and a chat, the first lady the boys ever talked to who would try to understand how they felt, having been put in an orphanage and deprived of a family home from an early age, most from infancy. Blaisdon Hall was their first real home, and to be well treated by the Salesians, with discipline, and Betty, with understanding. I think it goes to show why a number of Blaisdon Old Boys have travelled from Cardiff, Newport, London, Middlesex, Dorset, Sussex, the Isle of Wight and Stoke-on-Trent to be here today. Other members of the 'Blaisdon Brotherhood' wished to be here today, but alas, Age, Time and travelling will not permit it. But they are here in spirit and in our prayers today to say 'Good Bye and thank you to our special friend, Betty.' May she rest in peace."

George Austin came to Blaisdon in July 1940 to learn a trade under the care of the Salesians, leaving for a while in 1951, to return as gardener and groundsman. On marrying in 1957 he lived in the Lodge with his wife and two children. George and his family left Blaisdon during the 1980s.

Deep snow in front of the Lodge.

LAISDON HALL

Blaisdon hall is built of Box stone with Corsham dressings with gables and bay windows. There is an East tower over the entrance. The crowning glory of the Hall is not its construction but its view, which is surely the best of any house in Gloucestershire. From its elevated position above Blaisdon, the vista spreads over the river Severn into the counties beyond, scenery unspoilt by man or machine. A separate school block was built nearby in the 1960s but this has been demolished and the area returned to its original layout.

Blaisdon Hall, looking from the drive towards the main entrance.

Mr & Mrs C MacIver with their children, Isobel, Aline & Helen Ruth.

Blaisdon Hall was built in 1874 by Edwin Crawshay, son of Henry, an ironmaster. The family had bought Blaisdon Estate lands in 1864 though there was no manor house on the estate prior to the building of Blaisdon Hall. The iron industry went into sharp decline during the years Blaisdon Hall was being built and the Estate was aquired by Peter Stubs, a businessman from Warrington, Lancashire,. While at Blaisdon, in 1900, he became High Sheriff of Gloucestershire. After he died, in 1905, his elder daughter, Mary, inherited the estate. She had married Colin MacIver from Lymm, Cheshire and they lived at the Hall until their deaths in 1927 (Colin) and 1928 (Mary). The MacIvers were responsible for replacing many of the older buildings in the village as mentioned earlier. Following their deaths, the estate was sold and in the 1930s, the Hall passed into the hands of the Salesian Society who owned it until the 1980s.

Above:
View of Blaisdon Hall from the croquet lawn showing
the orangery.

Left:
Internal view of main entrance hall of Blaisdon Hall.

180

The Salesian Society was created by Saint Don Bosco in the late 19th century to further his lifetime work to help young poor children. The UK website (www.salesians.org.uk) describes the Salesians as:

"An international Roman Catholic Religious Order of men dedicated to be signs and bearers of the love of God for young people, especially those who are disadvantaged. Wherever we work, the development of the young through education and evangelization is the focus of all our concern because we believe that our total dedication to the young is our best gift to humanity."

In Blaisdon, this charitable work took the form of developing a 'School of Agriculture and Trades' centred on Blaisdon Hall and the neighbouring farms. The Salesians purchased them when Blaisdon Estate was sold in the 1930s. Most of the boys that attended the school were from orphanages such as St Joseph's in Enfield. As the need for agricultural labour reduced with increased mechanisation, they sold the farmland in the early 1960s but Blaisdon Hall continued as a school for vocational training taking socially disadvantaged children from around the country. It finally closed and the Hall was sold in the 1980s.

Sheila Evans writes, "In 1935, Blaisdon Hall became a school and home to boys who had experienced hard and difficult times in their young lives. Many had been living in the very harsh conditions of orphanages at the time and when they first arrived by train at Blaisdon Halt they were often alone. It is impossible to comprehend the feelings of these young lads as they walked to an unknown future through the length of the village up to Blaisdon Hall. The sheer size of the building must have been intimidating.

The boys settled into their home making new friends and eating much better food than they had ever had before. Alongside their general education the boys worked at Stud Farm growing crops and learning animal husbandry and many of them became highly skilled in a large range of trades and crafts.

Most of the boys had no home to return to for holidays, but they grew to love Blaisdon Hall, as it became their new home. The large numbers that still attend regular reunions in Blaisdon as well as the fondness with which they recall their time in Blaisdon best exhibits that the school was of great benefit to many boys."

There are many wonderful memories of Blaisdon Old Boys on their website (www.blaisdonbrotherhood.info) and in their book, 'Recollections of Blaisdon Hall.'

Alastair C Bourne writes from his home in New Zealand:

"I arrived at Blaisdon Halt station in around 1945 and I got a glimpse of the Hall from the bridge and gulped in horror at the old grey building that looked to me like a prison; I was terrified. I was met by a cadaverous giant of a man, a Brother Pat, who turned out in the end to be a real gent and all round nice guy. I soon learned that the Hall was a fabulous place to live and learn. For the first time in my life I was treated with respect and kindness. I say, lets not forget the real and good nosh too, what a joy to be eating good food again. I thoroughly enjoyed my years at the Hall and met some nice people, Salesian Priests and Brothers, who I remember fondly. I am very grateful that I attended the Hall where I learnt so much about many things. Those years are the fondest and happiest memories of my childhood. The standards that have stood me well throughout my life were set by the Salesians at the Hall and are still in place."

Michael McKenna was at Blaisdon Hall between 1938 and 1941 and recalls:

"During the years I am covering, Britain was fighting for her life and her enemies were bombing every major town and city throughout the nation and even Blaisdon did not escape the attention of the enemy. I vividly remember being awakened in the early hours of a moonlit night, to be hurried down from the dormitory to the bomb shelter. In the vicinity somewhere, mobile anti-aircraft guns were putting up an unceasing barrage of gunfire. The din was unbelievable and I fully expected to witness a scene of utter destruction throughout the village on the following morning. To my complete astonishment the only local casualty was a poor cow killed three or four miles away. However a huge crater in a nearby field was diligently searched for shrapnel to keep as a war memento.

Memories of a more pleasant nature reflect a placid and peaceful preparation of the approaching Christmas Day. It would have been either on the 23rd December or on Christmas Eve at around 3 p.m. that we were engaged in bringing large logs into the Hall, to be burnt on the commodious fire situated in one of the larger rooms. I remember snow having settled on the ground outside, and the joy of sitting near the blazing fire before going into the chapel for Midnight Mass. I recall the pleasure on Christmas morning when entering the refectory to see the dining tables covered in tablecloths, and set with plates of mince-pies and bottles of Tizer, Ginger Beer or Lemonade.

Given today's abundance of every possible choice of food and drink, it would be difficult for the modern generation to begin to understand the extent of the joy and happiness we felt. This deep appreciation of small things has stayed with me to this day.

In conclusion I wish to express my sincere appreciation of the help and guidance I received at the hands of the Salesian Fathers and Lay Brothers.

To my dying day I will hold a deep affection for Blaisdon and acknowledge that were it not for the training, both in moral and material sense, I might well have strayed off the narrow path. God bless all who belong to the Salesian organisation, and all who have had the privilege of receiving their tuition and guidance."

The late ***John O'Reilly*** was at Blaisdon from 1943 to 1945. He recalled an amusing incident with a newly acquired pony:

"In 1945 Fr O'Sullivan bought a pony called Nobby from Daniell's Farm, near Longhope, and a rickety old cart. I had charge of Nobby, and would take the milk from Stud Farm up to the Hall. One day something startled him as I was taking the milk churn off the back of the cart. I went flying and so did the milk, while Nobby bolted and set off through the park. The cart hit a bump and turned over, shattering into pieces, and the harness was stripped off the pony, and was in tatters.

The pony raced down to the Lodge gates but fortunately I had shut the gates on my way up and I was able to catch the pony and walk him back to the farm. We were both a

Top: Salesian School band. A young George Austin (The Lodge) is playing the trombone.
Right: Hall & Village boys in the Army Cadet Force on parade, Westbury-on-Severn.
Left: Hall Boys' Band, including;
Father Francis Rogers, Lawrence Stanton (Curly), Freddy Heathcote, Larry Dunbar, Alan Ferry, Ronald Daley.

little shaken as I told Fr O'Sullivan what had happened. His first words were 'How's the pony, is it OK?' I said, 'Yes but what about me?' his reply was, 'You look ok!!! Harness Lofty and take up some more milk!'

He didn't arrive via Blaisdon Halt but was picked up by the house car from Gloucester Central Railway Station. The build up to The Visit was intoxicating. This could have been Don Bosco himself such was the thorough preparation. I was on chapel cleaning duties under a ten times more fussy than usual Brother Gerald Clifton.

The Blaisdon Salesian Community of Priests & Lay Brothers with the Rector Major on the day of his visit to Blaisdon in 1954.

Occasionally, there would be notable visitors to Blaisdon Hall, when the life of Boys and Staff would be turned upside down during the preceding days. **Tony Brady** describes one such visit:

"The high point of 1954, without doubt, was the visit by Don Ziggiotti, the then Rector Major and leader of the Salesian Society, who came all the way from Turin in Italy.

The choir rehearsed a special song of welcome with words and music specially composed by Father Francis Rogers. The school brass band fine-tuned its specialities: Willkommen, Colonel Bogey and Semplice. The first thing we boys noticed on first sight of The Rector Major was that he had 'bombed hair,' Blaisdon parlance for a crew cut.

As the band belted out tunes at once rousing and melodious, Father Henry Wrangham who was Rector of Blaisdon greeted the visitor, whose car had drawn up under the Tower portico cum covered entrance which is open on three sides with the fourth side giving onto the front door. Inside the main doors, Laurence McDonagh, the summoning-bells boy, pulled vigorously on the suspending rope that rang the bell in the tower. The welcoming group paused with the RM in the vestibule where the choir sang a beautiful song in Italian.

The Rector Major then went into the Community dining room for lunch as the band played him in with a rendering of Papa Piccolino, a popular hit of the day. After lunch, Don Ziggiotti was taken on a lightning tour of the school, which ended with a communal farewell in the main entrance hall. The band played O Sole Mio and I managed to get our distinguished visitor's autograph, which he inscribed in my proffered diary. On the way back to Gloucester, the RM and travelling companions, including Father Hall (Provincial), called at Stud Farm where he proudly showed off the largest covered Dutch barn in the whole of Gloucestershire. It was known locally, not in scorn but wonderment, as Father Hall's Folly. We overdosed on the joy and significance of that great and historic occasion for months after."

Eric Nutcher came to Blaisdon in 1941 at the age of 14, having spent most of his life in St Joseph's Orphanage, Middlesex. The Following extracts are taken from his autobiography, 'He Uffed My Dorks,' firstly from the introduction and then he reminisces about an occasion he helped at a service:

"Many years ago, I started to write my autobiography. I managed 1 paragraph, ' I was born on 3rd July 1927. On the 4th July I was tried, judged and sentenced. Four years in the workhouse: 10 years in Borstal; later changed to deportation to Australia for an indefinite period of hard labour.'

Reading it now, it sounds a bit over the top. The Borstal institution I referred to was St Joseph's Orphanage. My crimes were: being born out of wedlock and having a different colour skin, both hanging offences at the time, so I got off lightly. My one regret is not having enough time to get myself a decent lawyer. I don't think I was entirely to blame…."

Eric Nutcher.

Eric continues with his story:

"One September evening in 1943 I was waiting to serve at Benediction as a right marker. At the very last minute Bro. John Madden placed the thurible (a container, suspended from chains, for burning incense) in my hands together with the brass receptacle for holding the topping-up incense. I had no time to argue, so set off towards the altar.

When I got there I placed the receptacle on my left side and started to swing the thurible from left to right. There didn't seem to be enough smoke so I decided to utilise a bigger swing. I swung from L to R back to L when there was an almighty bang. It would appear I had sent the receptacle flying. Gently placing the thurible down I endeavoured to collect as much incense as I could, about a thimble full. It is worth considering I had never handled a thurible before.

Halfway through the hymn 'O Salutaris' it was time to replenish the thurible. I handed the receptacle to the priest prior to lifting the top of it while looking down at the chains thinking which one do I pull? Unfortunately, I pulled the wrong chain and emptied the smoking incense onto the sanctuary carpet. Not much I could do but pick up as much burning incense as I could. When I had finished I could smell the burning flesh. The only good thing to come out of all this was the fact that only the boys in the front row could see what was happening. Most of them were in hysterics. Enough for now. Worse was to follow!

The thurifer, amongst other duties, has to extinguish the candles at the end of the service. So, I walked up the aisle thinking nothing else could go wrong. Not so, I proceeded to the right of the altar and extinguished the candles effortlessly. Moving to the left of the altar, I extinguished each candle except the last one. Being rather small I had a job reaching this last candle, which was the highest one. I must have tried 20 times to extinguish this candle to no avail. The boys in the front row of the church were again in hysterics. Thinking, 'I'll have one more go,' I made a quick sign of the cross then pulled hard down on the extinguisher. Fatal move: the extinguisher got stuck on the end of the candle and I was in no-man's land. I couldn't stay there forever, and if I moved the whole works would come tumbling down. Fortunately, a theologian had seen the trouble I was in and came to the rescue. For some obscure reason, I was never called upon again to be an altar server or thurifer. The sequel to this was when a comedian among the theologians presented me with a candle extinguisher for a Christmas present."

Vincent Faulconbridge, later known as **Vincent Shaw,** worked as Head Gardener at The Hall. **Margaret Hogg**, having known Vincent for over 50 years, writes:

"In November 1944 Vincent Faulconbridge arrived at Blaisdon Hall from St Joseph's Enfield. During his time there he had taken a keen interest in gardening so, on his arrival at Blaisdon he went to work in the gardens under the guidance of Brother Kane. Gardening was to remain one of Vincent's lifelong interests. Vince spent many of his evenings studying gardening and eventually took several gardening exams.

When Brother Kane left Blaisdon the running of the garden was taken over by Brother V. Clarke who, Vince

Top:
2 views of the Chapel at Blaisdon hall.
Left:
Statue of St. Don Bosco, situated in the Chapel.
Above:
Ordination Service at Blaisdon Hall c1947-8.
Servers: Anthony & Philip Jones are seated,
Richard Ashcroft (candle) &Kevin Keating (book).

said, made gardening very interesting to his students. He instigated the planting of apple, pear and plum trees as well as the soft fruits, such as gooseberries, blackcurrants, raspberries and strawberries, and set up 10 bee hives which acted as pollinators for the fruit as well as providing honey for the Hall community.

Blaisdon Hall was a self-sufficient community and any spare produce from the gardens was sold locally and also at Gloucester market. Gooseberries and raspberries from the gardens as well as the apples, pears and plums were canned on the premises to be sold also at the market to provide a useful income. Len Carter, who joined Vincent working in the gardens in 1946 recalls that at plum picking time all boys, whatever their trade, were called upon to help pick the plums and then assist with the canning and they had to reach a total of 1,000 cans before they were allowed to retire for the day. At 14 years old, they would start the canning process at 9 a.m. and often not finish until 9 p.m.

Similarly, at haymaking time down at the Stud Farm it was all hands to the pump, boys from the Hall, the theologians and the farm boys all working together to get the hay cut and harvested. Meals were brought to the field by tractor so no time was wasted travelling back and forth to the Hall. These times were greatly enjoyed by everyone; working together as a team under the supervision of Fr Dan Lucey, Brother Alan Garman and others who worked full time on the farm.

Manure from the Stud Farm was transported to the Hall gardens around Easter time each year to use as a mulch for the fruit trees and fruit bushes. This was transported to the Hall either by means of a tractor and trailer or by 'Sam' the horse who by all accounts could be very temperamental at times and quite difficult for the young lads to control. Always on Good Friday, the early potatoes would be planted.

Vince left the Hall sometime in 1946 and went to work in the gardens of the Oratory School in Reading. He later returned to Blaisdon Hall in 1948 and in 1949 took over the running of the garden. When he left Blaisdon for the last time, the garden was taken over by Alan Ferry.

After his return to Blaisdon in 1948 Vince began delivering the Sunday Newspapers to the villagers and got to know many personally and was a popular figure in the village. He made many lifelong friends here and returned to Blaisdon for the 'Old Boys' reunions each year together with Len Carter when they would 'do the rounds' of their old friends.

When he finally left Blaisdon at the end of the 50s Vince went to work in the building trade with Len Carter and when this came to an end, he eventually moved to Bognor Regis where he joined the Ambulance Service. During this time, Vince met and married his wife Anna and they had 2 daughters.

Vince was always the same. I don't recall ever seeing him lose his temper no matter what was thrown at him. He was always cheerful and had an easy going friendly manner which made you immediately warm to him and feel at ease in his company. Vince fitted in no matter who or what the circumstance.

He and Len continued to visit my mother, Elsie, after we

Above:
Vince Faulconbridge relaxing in Blaisdon.
Above Left:
Vince in Blaisdon gardens taking a swarm of bees.
Left:
Brother Victor Clarke with the Bromford.

Left:
Robert Foley & Vince Faulconbridge working the plough in the gardens.
Below:
Vince attending plants in the greenhouses.
Below left:
Group of Hall boys working in the gardens of Blaisdon Hall.

left the pub and moved to Newnham-on-Severn. After my mother died Vince and Len would visit her grave in Flaxley Churchyard to say 'hello to Elsie and Frank' and they also continued to visit me, their visits were always welcomed and they could both be relied upon to raise your spirits. Vince always liked to look at the garden when he visited and was always interested to see how it was doing and ready to offer any advice if requested. Sadly, I learned that Vince had died on 20th July 2010 and I know he will be greatly missed by his family and all who knew him."

The young Salesian theologians, during their time at Blaisdon Hall, formed a group called 'the Oratory.' This was specifically for the village boys, whom they encouraged to join and take part in football matches against the Hall boys, playing on Harvey's Acre. The boys were also taken on camping trips to Weston-Super-Mare and Cheddar. The village boys also played their part in the shows that were put on for the entertainment of the village and surrounding areas. These gave great entertainment and only involved a walk up the drive to Blaisdon Hall.

1

3

2

1. Outside the Red Hart, L-R:
John Dunbar, Vincent Shaw & Tony Brady.
2. All dressed up for their part in 'Ten Little N*****r boys,' are
(L-R):
Richard Ashcroft, Gerald Wyman, Michael Keyse,
Roger Etherington, Jimmy Grace, John Smith, Peter Grace,
Andrew Ashcroft, Anthony Jones & Freddy Grace.
Their faces were blackened up before going on stage.
3. The Brothers who set up The Oratory, L-R:
Michael Brazel, John Connolly, Martin Daley.

The Oratory (L-R)

Back Row:
Phillip Jones, Kevin Keating, John Keating, Michael Keating, Bro. Martin Daly, Oscar Jones, Barry Davis, Digger Hallem, John Dowding.

Sitting:
Bro. John Connolly, ?, Bro. Michael Brasil.

Kneeling:
Gordon Wyman, Jimmy Grace, Michael Keyse, Gerald Wyman, Richard Ashcroft, Michael Jones, Peter Grace.

Front Row:
John Smith, Anthony Jones, Freddy Grace, Andrew Ashcroft, Roger Etherington.

The Blaisdon Oratory on a day out to Chedder Gorge (August 1948) :
Back Row, L-R: Tony Kibble, Oscar Jones, Bro. ?, Bro. ?, Bro. Bernard Higgins.
Centre Row: Kevin Keating, John Keating, Digger Hallem.
Front Row: Jimmy Grace, Eric Weeks, John Dowding, Mike Jones, Philip Jones.
(M Jones)

Michael Jones writes of the camping trip:

"Campers cycled from Blaisdon to Oldmixon via Gloucester and Bristol, passing under the Avon Gorge suspension bridge. The younger ones were brought on the Salesians' open topped Bedford Lorry."

VECTIS

Turning right after leaving Blaisdon Hall via The Lodge, the road is known as Velthouse Lane, possibly named after Velt House Farm. The name is subject to local variation, sometimes also known as Velt House or Veldt House. Situated next to The Lodge, the first house in Velthouse Lane is Vectis, now known as Blaisdon Court. From 1938 to 1952, Vectis was the home of Mr Percy and Mrs Frances Jones and their children, Philip, Michael and Anthony. Michael and Anthony have written of their time in Blaisdon, first **Anthony Jones**:

Vectis with Mr & Mrs Frank Brown in the doorway.

"My memories of growing up in Blaisdon are a mixture of sad times and happy times, though I am glad to say most are happy. I was born in the Dilke Hospital, though I was a very sick baby as my mother was also ill at that time. The wonderful Mrs Dowding used to walk down through the woods to look after us as well as doing the cleaning at the school and lighting the school fire every morning in the winter. She walked backwards and forwards through the woods three times a day in all weathers; she really was a remarkable lady and such a character. Those woods were incredibly muddy and dark.

My first memory of Blaisdon is starting school with Mrs Smith and Mrs Berry. I ran home and Mrs Smith fetched me back, she was a lovely lady as well as a good teacher I can remember in later years going to listen to classical music with her and her son Arthur.

I was what they called 'a little b....r,' the things we used to do! Gideon Price was landlord of the pub and I remember he used to give a halfpenny for empty bottles. When they were returned I used to go round to the back of the Pub, pinch the empties and then take them round the front! This went on for a long time before Gideon cottoned on!

Then there was Mr Joyce. We used to knock his front door then whiz around the back just to have a look in the house though we never took anything. Today, I expect, we would have been locked up.

My father, Mr Percy Jones, came home from the war in 1946. I did not know who he was but eventually he settled back into village life and he helped to run the football and cricket team in Harvey's sports field. I can remember he had terrible malaria and Dr Pauli used to bandage him up a lot.

I spent a lot of time plum picking, blackberry picking and apple picking. It was good fun. Nobody could pick plums or apples as fast as Brenda Davis! When we picked blackberries we used to take them to Mr Walton ('Ginger'). There again he used to weigh them and I used to go in his shed round the back and help myself to those already picked, hide in the bushes then take them to 'Ginger' the next day.

I was not always bad, I learnt to catch rabbits, skin and sell them to Stephens the butcher or anybody else. I used to catch them with ferrets and nets. One day I was walking home with ferrets in pocket and across my shoulders. I had a stick with half a dozen rabbits hanging from it. I was walking down the hill in the middle of the road by Annie Goddard's (Post Office) when I heard a shout 'look out.' It was Cedric (Mr Etherington to us) on his bike. I jumped one way and he went the same way and hit me for six! I ended up in a big heap covered in blood; Cedric thought he had killed me! He took a long time to be convinced it was rabbits' blood I was covered with, although I was pretty bruised. That night he came round to see me and he asked Dad, my Mother had died by then, if he could take me to the cricket at the Wagon Works Ground to watch

Gloucestershire play. It was there that I had my first ice cream, bless him!

When my mother died, which was very sad, everybody in the village looked after me especially Mrs Ashcroft and family and Mrs Keating and family. I have slept in a lot of different houses in the village.

By this time I had lots of friends but I always seemed to get into trouble with Freddy Grace. He was a great friend and fellow adventurer. We did not burn the barn down, we were there, but I am not telling any secrets! We did borrow bicycles from Longhope Youth Club to get home. P.C. Plod made me take them back the next day and I was on the police radar! We did go to the Hall and get in the kitchen and help ourselves to food, we also got into the walled garden and helped ourselves to strawberries, tomatoes etc.

Mr and Mrs Board used to feed me. She was a big lady and Tom was a small man. They were fabulous with me. One day they sent me down to Birdwood on my bike to Jim Hayward to pick up the 'rickmould.' They convinced me they needed a 'rickmould' to go over the new hayrick to stop it blowing away. Mrs Hayward made me a drink while Jim got the 'rickmould.' He put it on my bike and told me not to undo the sack, but to go round to Mr Sedgebeers for the rest of the 'rickmould,' more orange squash and another sack. It took hours to get back to Board's; I had to walk most of the way, as there was so much weight on my bike. Then they tipped the sacks out; they were full of bricks and rubbish! It took years for me to live that down!"

1. Anthony Jones on the occasion of his 1st Communion at Blaisdon Hall with The Bishop of Clifton c1950.
2. Philip Jones on the ladder with Michael underneath, in the garden of Apple Tree Cottage (Syston Cottage).
3. Philip & Michael Jones.
4. Mr Percy Jones.
5. Philip in pram.
6. Mrs Frances Jones.

Sam, the Horse, with James Revell on the reins, taking the milk churn from The Stud Farm to Blaisdon Hall.
Hitching a free ride are Philip & Michael Jones with a friend behind.
The Lodge is to the left. At this time, in 1930s, the crucifix was yet to be installed.

Michael Jones has his own tales:

"We lived in Vectis, renting it from Mrs Lyon from Cheltenham. It was in this house that my mother died in 1951, and she is buried in Blaisdon churchyard.

We knew Syston Cottage as Apple Tree Cottage when our family lived here for a couple of years before we moved to Vectis in 1938. Mr and Mrs Lane moved into the cottage after we moved up the village. Mrs Lane could, and would, talk for hours standing at her gate, but rarely was anyone let in; she had a vicious-looking dog hunched across her front door! Mr Lane, a former policeman, had a business in Gloucester and died whilst at the cottage. In the early 1990s whilst at a meeting in Newport, somebody asked me where I was from, as I didn't sound local. In reply, I said I had lived in Gloucester itself, as well as in a nearby village, about 10 miles out. He replied he knew a village called Blaisdon, as many years ago, when first starting work, he worked in a small jewellers and watch repairers in St Johns Lane, Gloucester and the person he learned his trade from was Walter Lane!

I became friendly with Mr and Mrs Etherington, at The Forge. This was through sport, especially cricket, and later on during his last working years I used to see him regularly in Gloucester. When we first got to know each other he showed me his cricket memorabilia, especially books, magazines and score cards. He gave me a couple of annuals, one of which '1933 News Chronicle Annual,' contained explicit details of the notorious 'bodyline' tour of Australia by England in 1932/33. Mrs Etherington, I recall, used to potter in the garden, borders especially, and used to take pleasure in showing me her flowers .

Mr Joyce lived at The Tan House. My main recollections were inside the house itself; he had numerous team photos, also school and family photos. He used to sit reading, especially by his window, with the light, albeit not too bright, shining through. Now at home, on the radio, and at school, we had it drummed into us about the blackout; no lights must ever be showing. With my mother, early one wartime dark evening, we went to Mr Joyce's door, passing his windows with the light showing, and she made him aware of this, reminding him of the blackout regulations. He replied politely, apparently, it was not our business, and also that he didn't agree with the blackout anyway, as it achieved nothing. So he continued to display lighted windows with no curtains, and apparently other people too had approached him with the same result!

Mr Harvey of Home Farm remains in my mind because he was, or had been, a keen sports follower, horse racing especially, and he let one of his fields be used by the Hall and village for cricket and football. The other memory of Mr Harvey was for the last month, although it seemed even years, when he was not well, we used to wave to him and chat through his window and later wave to him from the wall by the road. He occasionally used to turn back and wave.

Gideon Price, who, apart from his pub activities, will be remembered for his pigs, his guinea fowls, and the infamous circular saw. This saw, set up in his orchard, facing the school, was used to make logs (and piles of sawdust!). As school kids we used to line up on the fence watching the sawdust and the logs flying everywhere. Then a respite, as he used to access his continuous supply of cider to quench his thirst (and oil the saw?). By hook or by crook, Gid was never hurt on the saw, even though he had his own health and safety regulations!

Two families lived at The Old Rectory, the Smiths and the Allums. The Smiths were a family of five, and had the larger part of the house, with Mrs Allum and her son Jim living upstairs in a couple of rooms. Just after the war when factory sirens were introduced, Jacqui, one of the daughters of Mr and Mrs Smith cried her eyes out, as it apparently reminded her of the blitz noises. Then in later years I met Mr Smith, his wife, Jacqui and their son John at Rank Xerox in Mitcheldean, where I worked for a time. Mrs Allum used to keep herself to herself, but I remember at the end of the war when Jim came home from the Forces, Mrs Allum put a large poster on the house wall to welcome him home. Jim, too, later worked at Rank Xerox.

At the village school, Mrs Smith, assisted by Mrs Berry, taught for many years. Several years, after leaving Blaisdon and after Mrs Smith's retirement, I used to see her at Gloucestershire County Cricket matches, especially the annual festival at Gloucester and occasionally at Cheltenham. This would have been from about 1960 – 1972 inclusive, and occasionally, Arthur, her son, used to accompany her. Mrs Smith lived at Hempsted Way, where Arthur was an assistant vicar. Mrs Smith was well known and well respected by the cricket club officials, being a member for many years.

Next door at The Lodge, my mother's aunt and uncle lived from 1934 until their deaths in 1941 and 1942. Will Gleeson was the butcher for Blaisdon Hall, having moved from another Salesian College at Shrigley, Bolton. As my mother's parents died young, she lived with uncle Will and Auntie Florrie, moving with them to Blaisdon. The Gleesons are buried just inside the top gate at Blaisdon churchyard.

Will Herdman, a retired North Country engineer, lived in Buena Vista with Miss Boyle, a relative. He continued his engineering as a hobby and one of the items he built was an accurate scale working steam train, a model based on an LNER freight train. Occasionally he would light up and when we watched it we were in awe to see the smoke and steam, and to see the train actually move. For the privilege of watching we earned our reward by carrying buckets of drinking water from the spring well in the village to their house.

The Post Office was run by Mrs 'Annie' Goddard, who lived here at one time with her sister-in-law, Mrs Sherrat, who died here in about 1945. She was a typical country postmistress, and had a little shop too. She not only ran her own activities, but made sure she knew other people's business as well! This was assisted by the fact that the only public phone in the village was on her counter, prior to the phone box being built outside her gate in about 1945. Her nephew, Ken Johnson, regularly visited her from Craven Arms, Shropshire. He was about 2 years older than me.

Stud Farm belonged to the Salesians of Blaisdon Hall. The people running it were Lay Brothers i.e. those not studying for priesthood, Old Boys from the Hall and the boys themselves learning the trade from the school at the Hall. A resident Priest, usually Father Dan Lucey, oversaw the farm. Alan Garman, Patrick Flynn and Joe Carter being the best known of the Lay Brothers. However, the best-known character from the Farm itself was Sam, a shire horse drawing his cart for several years. The farm itself was huge, it consisted of many acres, and all aspects of farming took place: cattle, dairy and beef, poultry, grain, orchards, sheep farming, with the largest single aspect being the Dairy. The Hall and the Farm were very good to the villagers with various products shared around from the farm and also a large market garden by the Hall.

Mr and Mrs Buckett and their son Bertie, ran a small farm on land surrounding their house, Stanley Lodge, plus a small field two miles away in Velthouse Lane. Twice-daily they would drive their small herd from their farm to the Velthouse Lane field, originally Mr Buckett was in front with a pony and trap, and then behind the six or so cows, either Bertie or Mrs Gertie Buckett would be walking. When Mr Buckett died Bertie took over the responsibility of cattle driving, usually walking with his bike. Bertie himself was Mr Softy. Historically, his parents made him like this, being very possessive as he had an elder brother killed on a motorbike during the 1930s. He played the accordion and piano and used to sing at the occasional party, usually at the school. Also I remember Bertie 'digging for victory.' A cabbage patch was dug in the corner of one of the fields! He took a lot of teasing, but always in good nature."

Mr & Mrs Percy Jones,
strolling along Westgate,
Gloucester.
(1932)

 Arriving in August 1953, the Evans family, Alfred, known as Ben, and Joyce plus children, Daphne and Susan lived in Vectis for about a year. The village made a lasting impression on **Daphne Martin** (nee Evans):

"We moved to Blaisdon from Worcestershire as my father had found a new job at Rotol based at Staverton. There were four of us when we moved. Our brother, Andrew, was born in December 1953. Moving to the village came as a surprise. We had television and other 'mod cons' but there was no mains water or electricity in the village so we couldn't use them; luckily they came later that year. The electricity was connected close to the cup final as I remember my sister and I being banished to our bedrooms while Dad and other football enthusiasts from the village watched the match on our TV.

The day after we moved in our neighbour's Great Dane, Portia, visited us. My sister and I told Mum and Dad she was as big as a donkey! Another surprise was going to Hinders Corner to catch the bus to East Dean Grammar School in Cinderford. Luckily we were able to buy a bicycle from Mr and Mrs George Beard who delivered the fruit and vegetables. Of course when it snowed we had to walk and once I had to walk what seemed like half way to Cinderford, as the bus could only get through to Longhope. For a child the village life was good. The garden at Vectis had a large area at the side that we used to play in with Mum's old pots and pans, doing some cooking; I cannot remember what we cooked!

It was a treat to go on the train to Gloucester and I can remember being told by Mrs Lane as we passed her house, 'You had better get a move on, I am just going to jump on my bike.' Luckily we always made it in time.

Bertie Buckett had a field along the Velthouse Lane, which passed in front of the house. He used to take great pleasure embarrassing me by prodding the last of his cows as they plodded along in convoy and saying 'Come on Daphne, get a move on.' I am sure it wasn't the same cow each time!

Something, or should I say somebody I found in the village was my husband, John Martin, who lived at the Old Mill. We were both in the church choir and confirmed together at Gloucester Cathedral. He was a dreadful tease and played lots of tricks too. He once took me tobogganing in the snow by the church and when he pushed me down the slope I ended up under the railings at the road up to the Hall in a heap! When we left the village my East Dean uniform was put to good use as it was passed on to Elizabeth Etherington!"

Sue Waldron (nee Evans) was Daphne's younger sister. While Daphne went to senior school, Sue attended the village school. She and her father **Ben Evans** recall:

"Dad can remember running down the village on 16th December 1953, in the middle of the night to use the telephone as the pay phone near Vectis was out of order. It was a very foggy night and the ambulance only just arrived in time for Andrew to be born at Gloucester Hospital.

Dad slipped over on ice spilling 2 buckets of water from the well across the road at Spring Cottage. He had to return for more. As a result of this event, he cleared out a shallow well in the corner of the kitchen. The water was clear enough for washing etc.

Mum took Andrew in a pushchair to Gloucester on the train. One day she missed her train and the next one was not due to stop at Blaisdon. However, the Guard arranged an unscheduled stop just for her and the pram!

I was only 8 that year, so I have fewer memories than my sister and had to wait a while longer before I met my husband, Brian. I do, however, remember the very large spiders that would appear in the bathroom. Also, balancing on the wall along the entrance to Blaisdon Hall, then falling off, luckily on the grass side, so no damage was done. Mrs Pickering would come to baby-sit for mum when she had to go out.

1. Daphne, Andrew & Susan Evans.
2. Joyce with Andrew.
3. Joyce & Ben Evans.

The Brown family moved from Tuffley, Gloucester to Blaisdon in April-May 1954. The family consisted of parents Frank and Doris, plus 10 children, named in order of age, Joyce, Colin, Alan, Janet, Shirley, Eric, David, Peter and Sally. Gillian was born whilst living in Blaisdon.

Janet Brown recalled the family's arrival In Blaisdon:

"On moving day, most of the children came with our Grandmother by bus from Churcham to Hinders Corner at the top of Blaisdon Lane. The walk down to the village felt like a very long trek. We kept asking, 'How much further?' Gran would just say, ' It's only round the corner.' On seeing the house for the first time, most of us made for the garden and the plum trees, eating too many and making ourselves sick!"

Colin Brown, seen below in army uniform, continues:

"Vectis was a large four bedroom house but not modern by today's standards. There were no doors on the rooms so you walked through one room to get to the next with no privacy at all. There was no running water; this had to be carried thirty yards across the road from the village spring. All hot water came from a Rayburn in the kitchen, which was also the only means of cooking.

There was no proper sanitation in those days, so the waste ran into a cesspit, which was sucked out, on a regular basis.

The land with the house was half an acre and was all used and maintained by the family, all of us having jobs to do before and after school. i.e. feeding chickens and pigs, chopping and sawing firewood, getting meals and making sure the Rayburn was stoked up. Being a large family there were very few luxuries and not a lot of time to get bored or fed up. All school holidays were spent working on the land, especially in the summer holidays, blackcurrant and plum picking. It all helped to bring money into the household.

After moving to Blaisdon I started school at Abenhall a secondary modern school in Mitcheldean. After a year I sat an exam to go to Cinderford Technical College to take up mining and engineering. I passed the exam and started at the College, travelling by bus from Hinders Corner, a thirty-minute walk from Vectis. This was my first opportunity to meet other people from the village and make friends with them. In my second year at the College, 6 of my siblings including myself caught yellow jaundice and spent four weeks in Over Hospital. It was unusual to have so many from one family all there at the same time. This meant that I missed a whole term at college. I never caught up, hence it was a waste of time going there.

After leaving the College I started work on a farm in the village owned by the Kings. This I really enjoyed, but my parents decided I was not getting the correct wage so after a few words I was forced to finish work at the farm. I then got a job as a builder's labourer and my first job I was involved in was building an outside swimming pool at Blaisdon Hall.

1. Mr Frank & Mrs Doris Brown.

2. The Brown Children
Back Row: Colin, Gill, Joyce, Alan.
Middle row: David, Eric, Janet. Shirley.
Front Row: Sally & Peter.

3. Janet in the garden at Vectis.

4. Gill & Sally Brown, in front of their dad's car.
Spring Cottage is in the distance.

Most of the youngsters of my age in the village would meet some nights at the local pub, just to get together, not a lot of drinking was done, mainly soft drinks and crisps or chocolate and enjoying ourselves. This is when I started to be attracted to young ladies; my first girlfriend lived in the village. The Public House was run by Mr and Mrs Hogg, but it was not like pubs today, no meals were served and there was always a pleasant atmosphere. Everyone knew everyone in the village and seemed to get along, though my parents never seemed to mix with many people, either in the village or out of it, I don't know why. As time went by I travelled further to work as a labourer often coming home on the train on the Gloucester to Hereford line. I remember being asked if I would like a ride on the train itself one night. This I did, but it did not appeal that much to me as a future job. I was happier sat in the carriage with the young ladies. Another hobby was bell ringing one night a week. This I enjoyed and ringing the bells on a Sunday was always a challenge trying to get the tune correct.

As time went on we all started to get wiser and started growing up. After another row with my parents over money, which always seemed to be a problem, I was told to pay more lodge money or to leave. I decided to leave and went next door and stayed with George and Beryl Austin who lived in the Lodge. I only stayed for two nights and then moved to Flaxley into the Rectory for a couple of weeks. As a result of this experience I changed my life and joined the Army, not returning home for some time and when I did, things weren't the same. Eventually my parents moved from the village to Cinderford and my brothers and sisters all married or moved away.

I often think of my time spent in Blaisdon – it holds special memories for me."

Colin's brother, **David Brown,** seen below in his school days, continues with some of his favourite memories:

"When travelling on the train to or from Blaisdon Halt, I loved leaning out of the window and getting the train smoke blowing in my face.

Once I was old enough to go to the Doctor's on my own, I felt I had accomplished quite a feat. I loved watching the horse and cart arriving with a delivery of coal. One of my favourite jobs was to go to the shop in Little London for bread and milk. We would walk through the woods, though never on our own, as it was quite scary.

As a young boy, many happy hours were spent down at the Stud Farm under the watchful eye of Brother Joe, who would let me ride the tractor with him, and watching the cows being milked by Pat Tobin. These were definitely my favourite times. Bertie Buckett would walk his cows down to Stud Farm to be 'introduced' to the bull and Tom Board also brought his cows down for the same reason.

Even as young children we all had our 'jobs' to do but once they were finished, I was allowed to go and play with my school friends in the village, sometimes not arriving home until it was dark. In those days, everybody seemed to know where you were, so it was quite safe. When it came to hair washing, as children, we were never allowed to use tap water. Water was collected from outside Spring Cottage and heated on the Rayburn and that was then used for hair washing. After Sunday lunch, all the family would go for a 2-hour walk, through the woods and lanes, no matter what the weather.

I remember on a Friday afternoon, Miss Reece, our head teacher would make us clean our desks. On one occasion she looked at me and told me 'to put some elbow grease into it.' Looking around, I thought it was some sort of polish!

Once, when I was about 10, I began going to Flaxley School Room where, on a Friday night, we had a youth club that was well attended by children from Popes Hill, Nottwood Hill, Flaxley and Blaisdon. We played snooker, table-tennis and music so loud that the vicar, David Bick, said 'it tested his patience.'

Following a trip to London with my father to see Buckingham Palace and the usual sights, my twin brother, Eric, and I stood guard with our toy guns outside Vectis for the next 3 days. The guards in London didn't move so we were not going to move either, much to the amusement of the villagers as they passed by.

Living where my family and I do now, in Stanley Lodge, I often think of Bertie Buckett standing by the Oak Tree at the bottom of the drive and how, if he walked along the lane, he had a habit of snapping back bits of branches on

the hedges as he went. You could always tell where Bertie had been."

Mr and Mrs Brown lived in Blaisdon until 1972 when they left to live in Cinderford. Mr Brown died in January 1993 followed by Mrs Brown in May 1996. They are buried in the churchyard along with their son Alan who died in January 2008.

The Brown Children enjoying a tractor ride.

Beryl Austin in charge with Gill, Eric, Peter, David, Sally & Alan, just behind The Lodge.

PARKSIDE

Parkside from the garden of Buena Vista opposite.

Parkside is next door to Vectis. It was originally two semi detached cottages and rebuilt after a fire in 1863 as one cottage. The original plaque on the cottage was uncovered by the present owner, Mr Barnard, during renovations. It bears the initials 'T H' and the date 1849. In 1912 it belonged to the Blaisdon Estate.

Mr Alfred Holder lived here from 1935 to 1953 after which it became the home of Mr and Mrs Day and their sons Roger and Billy. Unfortunately, it has not been possible to trace any member of this family, but Tony Brady recalls life at the Hall without a Matron and then the arrival of Mrs Day, who was their first Matron.

"During the 1940s and 1950s, Blaisdon Hall doubled as a Salesian School and a Seminary: more precisely, a Theologate, where men preparing for ordination to the priesthood lived and studied Philosophy and Theology. These men practiced celibacy as a requirement for acceptance into the priesthood, so the presence of women was not encouraged; married women were regarded as less likely to deflect a cleric from his vocation. When I went as a schoolboy to Blaisdon in 1952, there were just

three women employees: Mrs Jones, whose husband Ivor, worked on local road maintenance for the District Council and Mrs Grace, a widow, who had lost her husband during World War 2. Both women worked in the kitchen. Mrs Grace (later Maskell) was Cook and Mrs Jones a general kitchen help. Mrs Allen was a daily cleaner.

When boys became ill they were cared for by the 'Infirmarian,' Father Hugh Drumm. He managed a six bed Ward and liaised with the Doctor who came in when called from Mitcheldean. Before coming to Blaisdon, Father Hugh ministered to a dispersed flock of Catholics on the Falkland Islands for over 25 years. After evening tea, he conducted a daily clinic which coincided with his violin practise and any boy calling on him would wait until he had completed whatever piece he was playing before describing their symptoms: 'Father, I've got a headache,' 'Father, I've got a boil,' 'Father, the House-Master sent me' and so on. He was avuncular in his manner, kindly and popular with the boys. The school Confessor, he said Mass faster than all among his fellow-priests, was a comical preacher and had no disciplinary role. Once a year, the Doctor and a female nurse came and every boy had a medical examination.

Following the changes brought about by the Education Act 1948, Blaisdon began to be visited and assessed by the Education Board Inspectors. They approved the school on most measures, but noted the paucity of female influences and particularly recommended that the boys' health and hygiene be put in the care and supervision of a Matron. Sometime in 1953, Blaisdon Hall's first Matron arrived from Wales. For some months Mrs Day worked alongside Father Drumm and, when her probationary period was completed, took over his responsibilities. The Matron also organized the Linen Room. This meant she saw every boy regularly as she operated the issue of fresh weekly laundry. Her duties also extended to controlling the boys' dietary needs and assisting the school Burser, Father Cyril Fairclough.

Matron was a qualified, registered Nurse. She was married to Jim who travelled daily to work in Gloucester and they had two children, Roger and Billy. From her appointment onwards and for many years, Matron and her family lived at Parkside until 1970. In due course, more women, some unattached, came to work at Blaisdon Hall and, eventually, were engaged in the general management and care of the schoolboys alongside the Priests and Lay Brothers."

Blaisdon Salesian School Annual Sports Day 1957.
Left to Right:
Mrs Day & her mother, Father John Connolly (Headmaster), Mrs Embling, A Guest, Billy Day. Mrs Embling's confectionary business supplied the Hall tuck shop and she was a Salesian benefactor. In the background, Brother Allen is up the ladder, adjusting the Papal flag.
(T. Brady)

Another view of Parkside with the cottage painted white.

Presentation of Sports Prizes c1957.
Father Henry Mullaney (Rector) is presenting prizes and the small boy watching is Billy Day.
(T. Brady)

CHERRY RISE

Cherry Rise is the third property on the right hand side of Velthouse Lane. It was built on the site of the land used by the village school for the pupils to grow vegetables etc. At one time, the land was rented to the occupiers of Parkside. Mr Ronald Smith, who was a Fire Officer with Gloucester Fire and Rescue, built the bungalow for his wife Cynthia and their four children, Peter, Martyn, Elaine and Sharon. The bungalow was built in 1957 and the family lived there for the next ten years.

Elaine Smith shares her memories with us:

"My family came to Blaisdon 1957-1958 when I was 3-4 yrs old. My dad built Cherry Rise, a bungalow in Velthouse Lane just below Blaisdon Hall. The bungalow was named Cherry Rise because of all the wild cherry trees, which used to grow in the woods above the bungalow.

I remember my first day at Blaisdon School. I was four years old and started in the springtime. I remember crying because I didn't want to leave my little sister Sharon as she clung onto me. The school closed down when I was 10 or 11, because there were only 18 children and we were bussed to Westbury primary school. There were threats of the school building being sold but the whole village clubbed together to buy the building for the use of the village and it still belongs to the village today.

Sports days were held on the cricket field where the pavilion is. We went to it past Capt. Back's house, the Old Rectory. I remember winning one race and being given a magic colouring book. I didn't have a paintbrush, so I was thinking I would have to make one from my hair, but I felt really proud to win.

Village fetes were very important and quite a big event in the village. My mum used to make endless amounts of coconut ice and cakes. My sister and I won a few 'firsts' in the fancy dress competitions. In one we were dressed as 'cave girls' with dahlias in our hair, sacks for skins and teddy bears tied to sticks for our 'caught food.' We were called 'Big Ug' and 'Little Ug.' I remember my mum winning the hat made from a colander competition. My brothers, Peter and Martyn, collected feathers from in the woods and they made a bird, a Jay, from a potato with bright blue feathers. Mum covered the colander with ivy and foliage. My mum was a member of the W.I. and they had a poem competition. She wrote about the woods and the meandering River Severn. If anyone has a copy I would love to see it. She won first prize.

Mrs Goddard was the local Post Mistress. The Post Office was situated on the hill before the Church. I would often sit with Mrs Goddard behind the counter, sticking pictures of flowers I had cut out into old ledgers.

In the summer holidays we used to pick baskets of blackberries for 6d a punnet. We used to take them to Blaisdon Halt, where they were transported by train to London for jam. We also used to pick Blaisdon Plums and pears for Bertie Buckett, who was a real character. He had a name for all of his cows and, when he called them, they would come to their own name. I remember Bluebell, Buttercup, Cowslip and Poppy.

I made a great friendship with Brother Joe Carter from the age of about six years old which would last until he died. He was a wonderful man. When we had the big freeze with snowdrifts as high as hedges he dug the village out. I think we were snowed in for a fortnight. My Dad put chains on his Austin A35 and managed to get coal and bread for the Village. Brother Joe used to keep chickens for food for the Hall. They were kept in a shed with lights on to keep the birds warm. He would let me help him feed and water them.

I used to go everywhere with Brother Joe. When the top

Elaine Smith with
Brother Joe Carter.

playground was being built I remember going to look for Brother Joe following the noise of his tractor. The wood had been cleared of silver birch trees and there were mountains of gravel. Brother Joe welded a seat on his Massey Ferguson tractor, I used to hang on when he was ploughing the fields around Blaisdon and he used to say, 'Hold on tight were rolling on.' We would sing our hearts out, 'We'll be coming round the mountain when she comes' as he flattened the gravel! He gave us a dog which would have been got rid of because it wasn't wanted. Our family called him Joey in honour of dear Brother Joe!

Blaisdon Hall Bonfire Nights were special! With toffee apples and lots of families would camp and stay for days. Blaisdon Hall pantos were quite spectacular. I remember going to see one called, I think, 'The Mandarin.'

My Dad used to take me to Blaisdon brook near Flaxley and he taught me to tickle brown trout. I only ever caught one but Dad caught three. We took them home and fried them for tea, Lush! When I was about eight I went on the train from Blaisdon Halt to Gloucester with my Mum. I had to have drops in my eyes and mum bought me some chocolate for being good. We caught the train back to Blaisdon, but for some reason the train didn't stop. Mum pulled the emergency cord, the train ground to a halt and we got off at Longhope and trudged home in the hot sun. When we got home my chocolate was all melted!

The fathers from Blaisdon Hall used to walk down by our bungalow quite often with the schoolboys. My Mum used to shake apples down from our Newton Wonder tree and give them to the boys. I remember one lad; he was an albino with very striking white hair and pink eyes. It must have been difficult for him, being different from all the other boys!

The Days lived next door to us as Mrs Day worked at Blaisdon Hall. My brother Martyn used to play with Billy Day the son. Martyn remembers Billy's Dad coming round to our house. They made three fishing rods from scratch for Billy, Martyn and Peter. Martyn holds the record for the most fish caught from the lake in the woods behind Blaisdon Hall of 76 Roach and Tench!

My two brothers rang the bells at Blaisdon Church, taught by Rev. Bick. My sister Sharon and I sang in the choir at the Church with Rev. Bick. Funnily, we used to call him Mr Bick even though his title was Reverend Bick.

I remember one Nativity Play at Blaisdon Church. I played Angel Gabriel and Mr Etherington made sure I didn't fall from a rickety pair of steps. He always said I was the loveliest Angel he had ever seen! My mum made the wings from coat hangers and old tights sprayed gold. They looked like donkey's wings. On Mothering Sunday we were asked to collect primroses and wild violets and make them into bunches, then we took them to Church where they were blessed and given to our mums.

We used to carol sing, going to Flaxley Abbey. We had hot mince pies and orange squash. Also we went to Nottwood Hill to the Howard Williams's carol singing. I remember their Xmas tree covered in real lit candles was the biggest I had ever seen!

My time spent growing up in Blaisdon with my family will always be with me. I feel part of my soul still remains there and it is a great joy for me to still see Blaisdon Hall from my home now, here in Westbury, and to recall those memorable times shared with Brother Joe."

Brother Joe on the tractor with Elaine, Antonino D'Ambrogio & his father, Leno (1987).

1

2

3

4

1. Programme for Aladdin showing cast.
2. Mrs Cynthia Smith holding Sharon with Peter, Elaine & Martyn
in front.
3. The cast for a Blaisdon Salesian School Christmas production of
Aladdin.
4. Mr Ronald Smith with Elaine and Sharon.

BUENA VISTA

Buena Vista: 1959.
Hilary, left, & Marion with Nanny Luker and Sally, the dog.

Buena Vista sits on the left of Velthouse Lane opposite the preceding 3 houses. It was originally known as Coity but is now known as Little Garth.

A series of owners lived in the property, including Mr Will Herdman and Miss Boyle, Mrs Lindsay and Mr and Mrs Garrod. Mrs Lindsay is particularly remembered because of her Great Dane. To the children of the village, it seemed to be the size of a donkey. Each morning she would get on her bike with her cat sitting in the basket at the front and the Great Dane running beside her. Off she would go down Velthouse Lane and back again, both benefiting from this exercise! In the late fifties it became the home of Mr and Mrs Jayne and their daughters Marion and Hilary.

Hilary Jayne recalls her early days in Blaisdon:

"One Sunday evening in August in the late 1950s my uncle's car led us from Longhope along a narrow lane, Velthouse Lane, until we came to the Blaisdon Fault rocks above the railway line. My three cousins, uncle, aunt, my sister, mum and dad strolled to the Woodgreen waterfall and I discovered my first taste of heaven, a leafy green-arched lane, the Blaisdon brook's cascade over a weir and beyond a timber bridge, a sunlit field of birdsong and silence.

It gave my mother itchy feet and she wanted a taste of the rural life for her family. We trundled at weekends round various country properties for sale until The Citizen advertised a house in Blaisdon. On a foggy November afternoon we descended into the village to a bungalow behind the Red Hart, Buena Vista. Previously it had been called Coity then in the 1970s it became Lilla Smith's Little Garth.

Clockwise from top:
Walking to church through the Gate.
Hilary's wedding day to Roger Etherington. She is being given away
by her uncle, Mr Walter Jayne. Sister, Marion, is bridesmaid and
Mrs Edna Jayne is behind them.
Marion Jayne, bridesmaid.
(both: 18th July 1964).
Mr George Jayne in the garden at Buena Vista (1959).
Mrs Edna Jayne at Buena Vista (1959).
Hilary Jayne by an Anderson Shelter in the back garden (1959).

My parents looked around while we wandered away for half an hour; the War Memorial's names were read, the spring steps were investigated on the opposite corner. No cars came or went, the place seemed deserted. We regarded Jesus on the cross at the Lodge and followed the road down past the school, on past a Rectory with a tree growing from the roof above crumbling renderings of grey cement, then dawdled down to the silent Red Hart where the spring's waters met up with us again, channelled through a deep ditch before they vanished behind the pub to cool the beer.

No sounds came that afternoon; all was still, no traffic, no distant tractor, no church bell, no train at Woodgreen whistling an arrival at Blaisdon Halt, nothing but the cawing now and then of a crow or a bell in the distant tower out of sight at the Hall. Suddenly from the mist a figure in black appeared passing the school. It raised a tattered hat and muttered a grumpy, 'Hello.' We were astonished; no one spoke to strangers where we came from. On reflection it must have been Cyril Baggett who lived in a henhouse on Nottwood Hill. We turned back, half an hour would be up by now.

Outside the high wooden gates of Buena Vista we heard the front door open, then some protracted goodbyes in a woman's deep booming voice from the owner, Mrs Garrard who added a friendly slap across my parents' shoulders for good measure. It didn't put my mother off. We had to have that house, that view, but it took much persuasion. Yes, it was further to work at Dowty Rotol, but there was a bus for Dad up at Hinders Corner and a train at least five times a day to Gloucester or Ross or Hereford, and we could grow our vegetables just as well here as Churchdown and there would be plums for jam and a baker and butcher

and fishman called twice a week AND the phone box was handy next to the Post Office and the country air would be a tonic, etc etc….

Four months later we moved in. I learnt bell ringing from Joe Martin, how to raise my feet above my bicycle pedals when dodging the geese at Spout Farm, how to square dance in the schoolroom at a village social together with scrubbing the bells in the belfry (why?), sweeping up vast armies of blowflies assembled in the cupboards beneath the bungalow's eaves, how to sing in the church choir and to cycle without lights along the lane from Longhope after Young Farmers and how to deal with bats flitting from one window to another in our bedroom.

And how we loved our view: a garden of undiggable clay, Davis's orchard, the village houses nestling before Rabbit Hill then Westbury spire and the Severn's silver unwinding beneath a line of Cotswold blue. A paradise for six summery months, a taste of heaven before, one heavy hot August night, my dad died and everything changed."

Hilary Jayne with Sally, the dog.

WOODGREEN

After the cluster of houses at the start, Velthouse Lane runs away from Blaisdon, passing below Blaisdon Hall and providing a spectacular view of the building. At the far end of the Hall's land the road turns and dips into a woody dell. At this point, the road forks with Velthouse Lane continuing towards Longhope, while the small lane to the left crosses the path of the old railway line before going down to the small hamlet of three houses known as Woodgreen and then on to Gaulett Farm. There is some variety of spelling between Woodgreen and Wood Green, earlier OS maps using the former while more recently, the latter has come into use. Gaulett too has a variation of Gaulet on the earlier documents. The farm is just inside Flaxley parish but the story of its inhabitants impacted on Blaisdon and is therefore included.

Above: The turning to Woodgreen on the left with Velthouse Lane continuing towards Longhope on the right.
Below: Climbing towards Woodgreen, 16th November 1963. (B. Ashworth)

Train approaching Woodgreen Crossing, 25th January 1962.
(B. Ashworth)

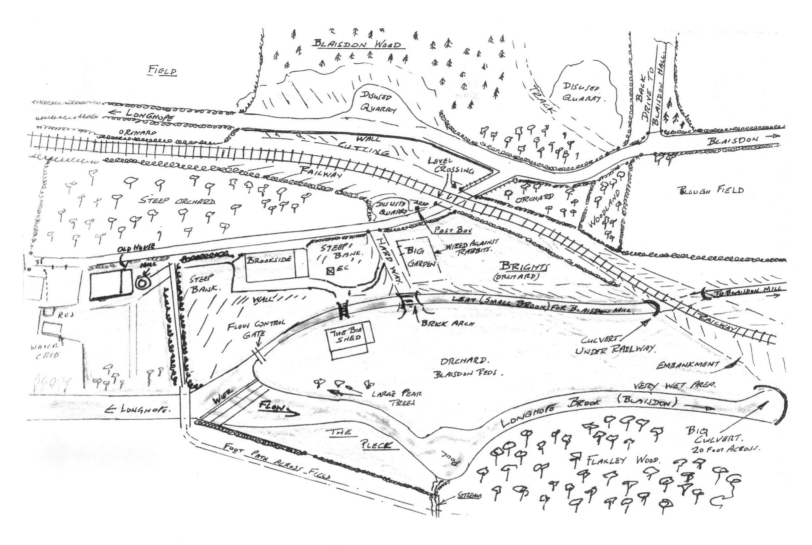

Sketch of Woodgreen (Not to scale).
(B. Jones)

BROOKSIDE

The first house reached after taking the Woodgreen turning, is Brookside, now known as Weir Cottage. Much enlarged in recent times, it was originally a classic 2 up 2 down stone cottage. Brookside was the home of Daniel and Martha Jones and their nine children for many years. **Brian Jones** continues:

Sketch of Brookside before latter additions.
(B. Jones)

Brookside or Weir Cottage from the weir.

"Daniel Jones was a gamekeeper on the Blaisdon Estate. After which, he worked for Flaxley Abbey as a woodman and following January 1927 when the Abbey reduced its staff he did whatever casual farm work he could find including mole catching and rabbit control.

Daniel lived at Brookside until shortly before he died, spending his last year with his son Arthur in Shrewsbury. He died on the 12th December 1945 at the age of 85 years. His wife died ten years earlier on the 20th April 1935, aged 71. They are buried in Blaisdon Churchyard.

Daniel and Martha had two daughters. Nellie was a

church organist and teacher at Blaisdon School, prior to marrying Mr Frank Price and moving to Caldicot. She died on September 11th 1961 at the age of 73. Their other daughter Margaret died, aged 7 months and is buried in Blaisdon churchyard.

All the sons of Daniel and Martha Jones joined the Railways. Railway staff counted their luck to be so employed. Loyalty to the railway was strong throughout the system, but always greatest in country districts. The rates of pay were comparatively more attractive here where few other employment possibilities existed. Getting a job as a Lad Porter or Engine Cleaner was to be set up for life.

Cyril Jones, their youngest son was killed in a railway accident whilst employed as a railway porter at Stonehouse on 26th January 1928. He was 23 and is buried in Blaisdon.

Three of the brothers fought in the 1914-1918 war. Harold was killed on The Somme in January 1917 at the age of 21 and his name is on the Blaisdon War Memorial. George Jones saw action in Eygpt, Palestine and Burma and was awarded a commission in the field.

William joined the Royal Artillery and trained as a signaller in Plymouth before going to France in October 1917 for the duration of the War. After the War he returned to the Great Western Railway. He retired as the signalman at Grange Court after 54 years service. From 1957, he and wife, Evelyn, lived at Western View in Blaisdon."

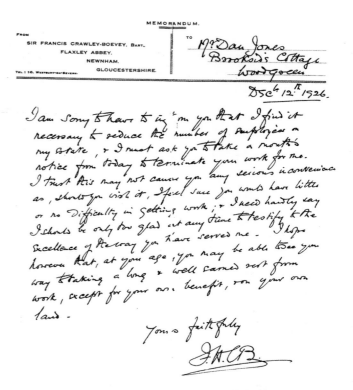

Notice of dismissal from Sir Francis Crawley-Boevey to Mr Dan Jones :

I am sorry to have to inform you that I find it necessary to reduce the number of employees on my estate, and I must ask you to take a month's notice from today to terminate your work for me.

I trust this may not cause you any serious inconvenience as, should you wish it, I feel sure you would have little or no difficulty in getting work, and I need hardly say I should be only too glad at any time to testify to the excellence of the way you have served me. I hope however that, at your age, you may be able to see your way to taking a long and well earned rest from work, except for your own benefit, and on your own land.

Yours faithfully,
F.H.CB.

The Jones family c1910.
Back Row: George, Arthur, Nell, Bob, Harold.
Front Row: Fred, Dan, Cyril, Martha, William plus dog, Flo.

Clockwise from top right:
Nell and William.
Nell Jones.
Funeral of Cyril H Jones. Evelyn & Bill Jones in centre, George Jones, 2nd from right.
Cyril Jones.

Norman Penny was born in Camberwell in London in 1938 and together with his parents, George and Ethel, came to live at Brookside or, as it was then known, Weir Cottage at Woodgreen in the1940s. His memories include:

"I attended Blaisdon C of E School and took my turn at pumping the organ at Church and rang the bells. I remember my mother used to walk along the line back to Woodgreen after getting off at Blaisdon Halt. She also attended church and was a member of the Mothers Union.

My father started work as a night watchman at Grange Court where the telegraph poles were processed. Later, he became a shunter at the Gloucester depot of the GWR Railway.

On leaving school I started work as an engine cleaner at the Gloucester Depot of GWR and after twelve months, progressed to a fireman on the steam trains. I was the fireman on the trains passing through Blaisdon during the last week of it running on the Hereford to Gloucester Line. I remained a fireman until 1984 when I became a driver on the Diesel locomotives. I finally retired from the railways in 1998.

The family left Blaisdon in 1953 and went to live in Matson. My father died in 1955 and Mother, Ethel, died in the 1970s. They are both buried in Tredworth cemetery, Gloucester. I have lived in Matson for the last 57 years."

Top: Mr George Penny & Mrs Ethel Penny.
Centre & Bottom Right: Norman Penny.
Lower Left: Christie Vesey works at Grange Court

Top:
The Pendennis Castle with Norman 5th from right.
Left:
Fireman Norman Penny, left, with Driver, John Cole.
Above:
Norman at the controls of a diesel Locomotive.

STREAMWAYS

Streamways is the middle of the 3 houses alongside Longhope Brook at Woodgreen. It is a 17th century timber framed building.

Mr and Mrs Little lived at Streamways in the thirties before Mr and Mrs Ivor Jones and their family moved there in 1938.

Mr Percy Little was an Air Raid Precaution Warden. There is little else known about them except the terrible death

Woodgreen railway crossing.
(B. Ashworth)

that befell Percy as he set off on his motorbike and sidecar to ride to Newnham and collect his weekly money. His wife used to go to the crossing and open the gate so he could ride across without dismounting. This particular morning she wasn't there to open the gate and Percy was struggling with his bike on the crossing when a train hit him. The bike was carried along the line and finished up wrapped around a telegraph pole. Mr Little's remains were taken to Woodgreen Cottage, home of Mr and Mrs Harry Lewis and put in the incubator house.

The Inquest was held in the front room of Velt House Farm, the home of Mr and Mrs Daniell and family. Bert Daniell remembers coming home from school and seeing at least nineteen men in the front room. He also remembers that after the Inquest a collection was taken amongst the men for Mrs Little and on presenting her with the grand total of 37 shillings she said, "Is that all my poor Percy was worth?"

Mary Goulding (nee Jones) remembers life at Streamways:

"When I was 3, I came to live at Streamways in 1938 with my parents, Ivor and Enid Jones and baby sister, Margery. My other 2 sisters, Doreen and Vera were born whilst we lived there.

Streamways was the second cottage across the railway line at Woodgreen. The Blaisdon brook was at the bottom of our garden and Dad helped to build the bridge which crossed over the brook into the Gaulett farm fields.

I remember the occasions when the brook was in flood, watching all the trees and debris floating past and the terrific noise like thunder when the water passed over the weir. If we needed the toilet we had to put our coats and Wellingtons on as the toilet was outside and being on lower ground than the house, the flood water covered the floor. What made it worse we had a watercress bed and the water from there ran behind the toilet and into the stream.

The Weir and Bridge over the brook at Woodgreen.

Father used to catch trout and eels in the brook. He used to put some line on a bean stick for us girls to try our luck. Sometimes we'd put a worm on the end of the line and leave it overnight. We would run down the next morning to see what we had caught, sometimes an eel, never a trout, but the worm was always missing!

We all went to Blaisdon School and I particularly remember being in the schoolyard the day a plane came over on fire, someone had parachuted out onto the Stud Farm, but the pilot stayed in the plane which was heading towards Stanley Cottages and he just managed to keep it above the roofs before crashing into the field behind, where it burst into flames.

We had a Club at the school on Friday nights with the mothers doing refreshments. Mother was well known for her custard slices. One night, we were walking home from the Club, when a line of 'black' confronted us. It was the Brothers and Fathers from Blaisdon Hall in their long black cassocks, five or six in a row, stretching the width of the lane. They used to walk down the back drive of the Hall and back up the main drive before retiring to bed!

Walking back from school along the Velthouse Lane many a time Mr Griffiths from Gaulett Farm would come along in his old car and give us a lift. He would wind down his window and we would jump on the running board and hold on tight!

I will always remember seeing the red squirrels and hearing the nightingale singing between the back drive to the Hall and the railway line gates. We would find glowworms and birds' nests and see so many different kinds of birds. The water dipper always nested under the waterfall. I remember finding where the badgers had rooted out wasps' nests in the banks. We loved picking the primroses and violets to take to church to be blessed for Mothering Sunday. We used to find snakes curled up in the grass as we picked the flowers.

Father worked for the Council, cycling everywhere. During the war they had to cut down the cow parsley from the verges before they flowered, all by hand, because in the moonlight the white flowers showed up where the roads were and the planes could follow the roads to the cities. He had to guard the bridge when the bomb dropped until it was repaired.

Father kept us fed during the war with rabbits and pheasants. The farmer thought someone had a double-barrelled 4 ten but it was father quick on the draw! He would shoot a brace of pheasants with his single barrelled 4 ten.

We used to travel to Gloucester on the train. If we were running late, instead of going all the way round the village to get to the station, we used to hurry down the line to get there before the train arrived. If a goods train came along we would hide behind the bushes. They always knew we were there and they would toot and wave! Margery remembers mother buying a carpet and when arriving at Blaisdon Halt the Guard asked how far did she have to carry it. She explained where we lived, so he said, 'leave it on board and I will drop it out by the crossing gates.' Reluctantly she did leave it on the train for it was very heavy, and when she got to the crossing, there it was leaning up against the gate!

A little old lady lived at Gaulett Farm. She wore a fox fur with beady eyes and we called her Granny Lewis. She was

From the left:
Ivor Jones with his shotgun and
digging in the garden.
Ivor & Enid Jones in the doorway
of Streamways.

Left: Mary, Margery, Doreen & Vera Jones.
Above: Mrs Enid Jones with Doreen & Vera.

tiny with white hair, which was always curled. She also wore long black clothes and black plimsolls. She also used to walk the line in time to catch the train, even though she was in her 70s.

We used to look forward to the Sunday School and Choir outings where we all travelled on coaches. Then came the party every Christmas at Flaxley Abbey, where we would get our book prize from Lady Crawley-Boevey for attendance plus a present.

Every Saturday I used to cycle to Little London to take the shopping list to the shop for the goods to be delivered in the following week.

In the autumn we would pick blackberries and take them to Mr Walton at Hinders Lane on my cycle. He paid us 6d for a lb. That was our spending money when father took us to Barton Fair, in Gloucester.

When the plums were ripe we all had to work. As soon as we were old enough, father would put the ladder in the tree for us to pick the plums. He always warned us that if the ladder moved, always hang onto the ladder and not the tree. Mother did not do this one year and injured her shoulder, but he always put it safe for us girls. I sometimes had to cycle over to the Red Hart for a bottle of cider. Father needed a drink after working till dark, for the plums always came first!

Being the eldest of the four girls I had to help father a lot. When he cut down old plum trees I had to get on the end of a crosscut saw. It was hard work but I enjoyed it. I remember the lovely fires when he burnt up the twiggy bits, especially if it was cold and frosty!

Father died in January 1960 and Mother left Streamways in the spring of 1969 to live in the village at The Cottage."

WOODGREEN COTTAGE

The final house in Woodgreen is Woodgreen Cottage. This was owned by the Lewis family of Gaulett Farm. In the 1930s, Robert Lewis, his wife Dorothy and their daughter, Mary lived in the cottage. They moved into the farmhouse on the death of his father in 1938.

The cottage had remained unused for some years and, by 1970 was derelict. It was bought at auction when Gaulett Farm was sold in 1971. ***Gerald and Megan Kear*** recall:

"We bought the house for £1,200 and, as the pictures show, it was in a completely dilapidated state. We spent the next few years, restoring the original house and extending it to hold our young family. It was very hard work but the family enjoyed the experience. At least that is what Gerald tells them!"

Top and above:
Woodgreen Cottage prior to renovations.

Left:
Megan Kear examines the internal structure, which shows the wattle & daub structure of the internal walls.

AULETT FARM

Looking up the valley towards Gaulett from Woodgreen.
(S. Waters)

Gaulett, or Gaulet and occasionally Gawlett, Farm is recorded as early as the mid 16th century. It is part of the Woodgreen Hamlet, nestling into the valley on the far side of Longhope Brook. It is in the parish of Flaxley, though land to the north of the farm was at one time in Blaisdon Parish.

In the 1930s, Mr Robert and Mrs Annie Lewis, who lived there with their children Robert Harry Lewis and Mary Nancy Lewis, were farming Gaulett.

In 1932, tragedy fell upon the Lewis family at Gaulett when Phil Lewis, nephew of Robert Merrett Lewis was taking the milk from Gaulett to Blaisdon Halt. He had just opened the railway-crossing gate at Woodgreen when a train appeared and struck the cart. The horse was cut in two and Phil died instantly. His remains were taken to Velt House Farm and remained there until an inquest was held. The sadness of the death is compounded by the fact that it is believed that he was due to get married on that day.

Mr Lewis senior also had an unfortunate accident one night as he returned to Gaulett from a night at the Red Hart. It appears he was rather the worse for wear when the horse and trap that he was driving tipped him into the brook at Woodgreen. Unfortunately this experience had a lasting effect on his general health and it is thought led to his death at the age of 62 on the 3rd September 1938.

Robert Harry Lewis had married Miss Dorothy Annie Stephens and they had a daughter named Mary. Prior to his father's death, they had lived at Woodgreen Cottage. When Robert senior died, they moved into Gaulett Farm, living with his mother Annie and Sister Mary.

Only two years after moving to the farm, on February 4th 1940, Robert arrived home to find his wife dead in her bed. Within minutes of finding his wife's body he collapsed onto the bed and died. This great tragedy shocked the village and was widely reported. Attendance at the funeral was high and many sent flowers including Sir Lance and Lady Crawley-Boevey of nearby Flaxley Abbey. Their daughter Mary was 16 at the time of her parents' deaths. Mary Lewis, Annie's daughter, was married to John William Griffiths and on the death of her brother and his wife they moved to Gaulett and lived there with her mother. Annie died on the 17th December 1965 at the grand age of 96. Mary's husband John died on the 1st February 1971 and soon after Gaulett Farm was sold and Mary moved into the Old Post Office in Blaisdon village, renaming it Hillcrest. Mary died on the 5th February 1983 and is buried with her husband John in Flaxley Churchyard.

Double Funeral At Flaxley

Mr & Mrs R. H. Lewis
Of Blaisdon.

As the bell of Flaxley Church tolled through the woodlands on Friday a farm cart, pulled by a horse, wound its way along the country lanes bearing the coffins of Mr and Mrs R. H. Lewis of Gawlett Farm, Blaisdon, whose deaths occurred under poignant circumstances.

Finding his 38-year-old wife dead, Mr Lewis, who was 37, collapsed across the bed and died himself.

A crowd of villagers and schoolchildren watched the horse and cart stop at the church entrance gate and eight bearers lift the coffins.

Mr and Mrs Lewis were particularly well known in the district, in which they had lived for some years. They were found dead by Mr Lewis's mother.

The service at the church and graveside were conducted by the Rev. A. E. McNamara, Rector of Flaxley, while the organ voluntaries were played by Mr T. C. Mayo.

Above:
Extract from unidentified newspaper report of funerals of Robert & Dorothy Lewis. Note the spelling of Gaulett.
Top Left:
R. H. Lewis outside the Red Hart.
Centre:
Dorothy Lewis.
Bottom Left:
R. H. Lewis with A. Holder (seated) & D. Price.

ELT HOUSE FARM

Velt House Farm,
Showing the Daniells' later addition on the right.

The final house along Velthouse Lane in Blaisdon parish is Velt House Farm, situated on the right a little after the Woodgreen turning. In 1934, Velt House Farm was the home of Mr Frederick and Mrs Winifred Daniell and their 4 children. Bert was the eldest, followed by Kathleen, Iris and Sheila. ***Bert and Sheila Daniell*** recall life on the farm:

"We children attended Blaisdon Village School when Mrs Berry and Mrs Smith were the teachers. After school, Bert, aged 10, would arrive home just in time to milk the cows, by hand. Life was made a little easier when a milking machine was installed in 1941.

Bert was also the organ blower at Blaisdon Church. The pump was situated in a very cramped position behind the organ. In 1936, when Bert started this, aged 10, the organist, Mr Mayo, from the Forge at Flaxley, paid him £1 a year from his own wages. However, when his sister, Kathleen, took over the job she asked for a rise and got £2 per year. Iris and Sheila also had spells on the pump. Bert remembers one Easter Sunday when he had already pumped for 2 services that the Vicar called for a hymn after his sermon, only to be met by silence from the organ. Miss Ruth Brewer set off to investigate and found Bert fast asleep. A quick prod soon revived him and the music swiftly followed.

After school was over for the day, all the children would return home and set to work on the farm. After Kathleen and Iris left the farm to be married, Bert and Sheila carried on working the farm till they retired. Following retirement, the farm was sold and they started to enjoy what were their first real holidays. They have travelled around the world. Whilst in New Zealand, Bert showed his skills at hand milking and was awarded a 'Certificate of Udderance' for his efforts."

Their mother, Winifred died in 1960, aged 60, and their father, Frederick in 1984, aged 83.

Bert Daniell handmilking a cow in New Zealand (2000).

230

1. Fred & Winifred Daniell with Bert.
2. Kath Daniell.
3. Iris Daniell.
4. Sheila Daniell.
5. From left: Shirley & June Warren, Sheila, Bert, Iris & Mrs Daniell.
6. Doreen Teackle holding the doll, Clarice Finch & Bert Daniell.

ST. MICHAEL'S COTTAGE

St Michael's Cottage was formerly the laundry for Blaisdon Hall estate. The house was originally known as 'Whitehall'. Built on high ground situated between the Church and Blaisdon Wood it has a panoramic view across the Severn. Mr Jim Keating and his wife Margaret moved into St Michael's Cottage with their 3 young sons, Michael, John and Kevin in 1941. Their daughter, Rosemary, known as Biddy, was born there in 1943. ***Michael Keating*** recalls his memories:

"Mum and Dad were married in 1928 at the procathedral in Bristol and for a time rented a flat. In the early thirties they bought a new house on a development at the edge of Bristol; a house with at that time all modern amenities. However, the war and the blitz in Bristol, which included a direct hit on a house of a cousin led them to a decision to leave sometime in May 1941. They thought it would be better if we could move to the country away from the bombing in Bristol.

At some stage we had visited a Mrs Roberts who at that time lived at Grange Court about six or seven miles west of Gloucester. Dad borrowed a car and we set off to Grange Court early one morning. We found the house, but the family had moved some years before to Minsterworth about 3 miles away. We eventually found them and the outcome was that our family rented half a farmhouse across the road from where they lived. Mum went back to Bristol with Dad that night leaving the three of us with the Frost Family. Mrs Roberts was Mrs Frost's mother and there was a husband and six younger Frosts. I guess we were bewildered. John cried for his mother most of the night, much to Kevin's disgust. We were all in the same bed. Next morning, again to our disgust, we were sent to school at Walmore Hill. I gather mum arrived back that day with clothes etc and as far as I remember we moved in with farmer John Browning. Dad was working at Filton, 24 hours on 24 off, and used to come up and have every other night with us.

Just down the road was the River Severn with a pub on the bank called the 'Bird in Hand.' Across the road was a flat field and about the time we got there it was being cut for the hay crop. All the local children seemed to be helping after school, so we joined in, something we had never been involved with before. Incidentally, if you were thirsty there were stone jars of cider in the hedgerow, my first taste of 'scrumpy.' When the haymaking was over the field became the local cricket pitch and we were there every evening. At that time there was double British summertime, two hours ahead of GMT so in May and June it didn't get dark until nearly midnight. The other standout memory was the inter school sports day between Walmore Hill and Westbury Schools.

We found the nearest Catholic Church was at Blaisdon and we used to cycle there for Sunday Mass, five miles each way. The Salesians had an empty house on the estate and offered to rent it to us. I believe the rent was 4/6 a week. We moved into St. Michael's Cottage in July 1941, about ten days before the end of the school year. I had to cycle to school at Walmore Hill every day for the last week of the year; I was nine.

The mother and younger brother of one of the priests, Father Grace, had temporarily occupied the house but I believe only for a short time. It hadn't been regularly occupied for some considerable time. It had been built

Mr & Mrs Keating with Biddy.

as the laundry for the estate when it was privately owned. We rented the house and had use of the remaining copper boiler and sink. The rest of the laundry and drying rooms had been given a wooden floor, and fitted with a wood stove, and a billiard and table tennis tables to be used as a 'clubroom' for any of the 'old boys' who were working in the area.

The house had, at a later stage to being built, been fitted with a septic tank sewerage system, to replace the earth closet that was still the norm in the rest of the village. We had an outside WC toilet, and the middle bedroom was being converted to a bathroom. It had a washbasin and toilet but no bath. Subsequently a bath was brought down from the hall but it was huge. It wouldn't go through the front door, let alone go up the stairs. Undaunted, the two lay brothers, Tom Gallagher and Tom Doherty, put it in the lean-to log shed in the small yard, built a wall and fitted a door, then connected it to the cold water supply that was connected to the toilet next door, et voila we had a bathroom. To put hot water in it we filled the wash boiler and lit the fire, boiled it twice, and we had about six inches of warm water.

The house had originally had a living room, kitchen and a reasonably sized pantry, but when we moved in, the pantry had been converted to a smallish kitchen and the kitchen to a living/dining room. The kitchen had an old 'Ideal' coal stove but it was past its prime and the hot water boiler was cracked. The cooking was done on a bottled gas ring and a primus stove. It also had a sink, with cold drinking water tap, a small table and four built-in shelves. There was a gas light in the kitchen run from the gas bottle, but it was never used. We relied on paraffin (kerosene) lamps for all our lighting.

The water for the toilet, the bath and the laundry sink was piped from a small reservoir up in the woods. It was terribly 'hard' water, and we didn't use it for drinking as it was supposed to be boiled first. Because it was so hard it didn't lather and you would get a thick scum on the top if you used soap. We mainly used rainwater from the tanks in the yard for washing.

For drinking we had a well in the garden. It was eighty feet deep and had a large hand pump to get the water up. You could either fill buckets from the tap, or you could fill a tank at the top of the laundry by turning off the tap and pumping. It took about three hundred strokes for the tank to fill from empty, or if you were efficient, about sixty strokes a day to keep it topped up. This supplied the tap at the kitchen sink.

According to the locals the garden hadn't been touched since the First World War and it was obviously completely overgrown. When we opened the kitchen window the stinging nettles outside were so tall they fell into the kitchen and touched the opposite wall. It had one old apple tree, a cooker, and three Perry pear trees, and a fair number of Blaisdon Red plum trees. The plum trees had put out so many suckers that we didn't get any fruit the

first year. It took several weeks just to hack a path to the top of the plot and when we got there we found another quarter acre plot. We called that piece 'rabbit field' as it was full of rabbit holes.

At the start of the school year we started at Blaisdon School. This was a far cry from the school in Bristol. Blaisdon was a C of E run village school with two teachers, and I think twenty-nine pupils, from 'babies' to Standard six. We were in two rooms. Mrs Smith was head teacher and taught standards 2 – 6 in the big room and Mrs Berry taught babies to standard 1 in the small room. The children came from three villages, Blaisdon, Flaxley and Northwood Green. Children as young as four and a half walked to and from school in all weathers. The Blaisdon children went home for lunch. The children from Flaxley and Northwood Green brought packed lunch.

The facilities at the school were primitive to the extreme. The two senior boys fetched two buckets of water, one for the Boys' cloakroom and one for the Girls'. This was the total water supply for the school. The toilets were earth closets emptied every night. The heating was two open coal fires and the lighting paraffin lamps. The schoolyard surface was packed dirt. There was no facility for organized sport.

The school had religious instruction every morning from 9 till 9.40. On Fridays it was catechism so, as Catholics, at first we didn't go to school on Fridays until 9.45. Shortly after we started school one of the brothers, Brother Corcoran, started giving us religious instruction in the evening. Originally it was held in the lounge room of the Lodge, where Mrs Gleason lived. At a later stage it moved to somewhere in the main house every morning from 9 - 9.30 and we went to school at 9.45 every day. At that time there were six Catholics at the school, the three of us, plus Mike and Phillip Jones, and Jo Milanta. Jo was an evacuee from Gibraltar who lived at Stanley farm. One of the things that I still remember was one morning we dawdled on the way down from the hall to the school and we didn't get to school till about 9.50. Mrs Smith decided that as we had arrived after the 9.45 deadline we couldn't be marked present so she sent us all home. She knew that Mum was away for a couple of days in Bristol and that Grace Cue was looking after us. Grace however had a part time job and didn't get home until nearly four.

All the children in either their last or, depending on their birth date, their penultimate year took the Scholarship exam. This was the forerunner of the eleven plus and my birthday allowed me to take the exam in the last but one year. I passed the entrance exam but didn't get a full scholarship, only a half, but because Dad earned more than £3 a week we had to pay full fees which were £3 a term. I took the exam again the following year when I was in first form at East Dean Grammar School and passed the full scholarship, but still had to pay full fees. When John came to the school he only

passed the entrance exam, but he got a discount in fees as there were two of us there. By the time Kevin passed it had become the eleven plus exam, and fees had been abolished.

Mr & Mrs Keating with their 4 children.

When I started East Dean the school bus only came as far as Longhope. We cycled up the Velthouse Lane to catch it. We used to leave our bikes in the front garden of Mr Smith who at that time owned the grocers store in Longhope. As well as us from Blaisdon all the children from Little London also had to get to Longhope to catch the bus. There were four girls from Little London who started the same year as me, including Margaret Beard, June Green, and Kathleen Stevens. Kath's father was the local butcher. Sometime later, Mum got the school bus route extended to Hinders Corner. She went round and got signatures from all the families of children living beyond Longhope and the route was extended.

The School at Blaisdon also served as the village hall and social centre. A 'Social Club' was established which was on a Friday night and the school was also used for whist drives and occasional amateur dramatics. There were outings to Weston and other places but the first one to London was organised by Gwen Dowding."

Centre:
Mrs Margaret Keating.
Clockwise from Top Left:
Mrs Keating with John & Biddy (late 1940s).
Mr Keating with Biddy, Kevin & John at St
Michael's Cottage.
The Keating family with Catholic priests.
(John Keating)

Recollections of **Kevin Keating**:

"In the early forties Blaisdon village school was frequently a very scary place on Monday mornings. Village elders/ busy-bodies/landowners complaining about the weekend behaviour were allowed into the school to have their 'sixpenneth of terror.' The culprits were, in their view, the newcomers in the village. We did, of course, get up to a fair bit of nonsense, but how on earth were these people ever allowed into the school? The toilet buckets were only emptied on Saturday mornings. The contents making their smelly way down the village. Incidentally, the toilet paper was on a string hanging in the main schoolroom. 'Can I do paper?' was the terminology used to request a piece of paper and needless to say, it was very rarely used!

A highlight of the school year was Country Dancing! I was a first reserve for the Rufty Tufty country dance team at a fete at Westbury Court. As an 8 year-old I cycled there but sadly never made the team. I think they came third! I have many, many happy memories of Christmas parties. We were allowed to stand next to our desks and tell jokes and riddles. e.g. Why did the chicken cross the road? We would sing from the National Song Book. My favourites were Minstrel Boy, British Grenadiers and North Country Maid. The school was also used for social activities such as Ballroom Dancing classes run by Miss Whittard and to welcome home the WW2 heroes. Banners were displayed: 'Welcome Home Bert/Frank/Percy' etc.

In the summer of 1946 I was one of the 4 boys who passed the eleven plus. Quite an achievement for the school; an 80% success rate! The head teacher, Mrs Ethel May Smith, gave us all 6d. We stayed friends with Mrs Smith long after we left the village school. On Saturday mornings in the winter we carried flasks of hot water to her garage in Velthouse Lane. The hot water was for the car radiator as it had been drained. There was no antifreeze available and she only used the car once a week for shopping.

Mike and I were once chased and caught by the police constable for riding home from Westbury Army Cadets without lights after dark. We received a severe telling off!

The Salesian Community at Blaisdon played a major part in our lives. The extensive facilities at Blaisdon Hall were freely available through the Oratory Club which was first established by Father John Connelly. The range of activities was really extraordinary; football and cricket, which tended to dominate, camping, boxing, cycling and dramatics. We also managed to include Army Cadets and loads of school football. Sam Cottner told me rabbits became pigeons to escape the reaper and binder and I believed him! As a student after National Service (1956-1959) I often worked at Stud Farm (£6. 14s per week). Many Salesians helped us in so many ways and Father W. Boyd (still going strong in 2009) was outstanding."

Recollections of **Biddy Keating**:

"One of my earliest memories is of starting school at Blaisdon, where I spent a happy 18 -24 months, before changing schools and, aged six, travelling by train to St Peter's in Gloucester each day. Outside the playground was unforgiving, rough, uneven and stony. I still have a scar on my knee to prove it. Inside the school two classrooms. The small room was for the 'babies' as we were known; a dark room with a high window, low stools and tables and rag rugs to sit on for stories; chalk and slates to write on, and a high fire guard, but I don't remember a fire. Our teacher was a tall lady with dark hair, rather scary. She was firm but not unkind, I think she cycled to school at first from Westbury.

In the adjoining room, the big room for the 'Big children' (six plus), a large sunny room with desks and inks wells, a black board, a piano and a Coke stove. Presiding over it all seated at a high desk on which lay a cane and bell, was the head teacher, Mrs Smith, a formidable lady with a voice to match and a steely determination that we would all learn and achieve. She WAS the school. In appearance a toned down Edna Everidge smartly dressed with large glasses and bright lipstick AND she played the piano, loudly! There was lots of singing and music, hymns, National Song Book and country dancing, Eat your heart out "Strictly" my Strip the Willow, Rufty Tufty, and Gathering Pease Cods would bring tears to your eyes.

And ah, the lasting memories of nature walks, country dancing, learning to sew and of pungent smells. The dusty wooden floors, the acrid coke stove, appetising smells of home cooked school dinners created by Mrs Cox (I can still smell the lemon curd tart). Sour milk bottles awaiting collection AND the elephant in the room or, more correctly, 'out the back,' the toilets, the pong of Jeyes fluid and effluent! I had a horror of slipping into the abyss and tried to avoid using them!

I started school with Liz Etherington, Jenny Smith, Margaret Green, Valerie Keyse, Tricia Angove, John Blake and later Maureen, John Watts, Doreen Jones, and later still Anita Martin and Heather. The big ones, Susan Cox, Susan Young, Jackie Smith, John Martin, Anthony Jones, John Smith, Roger Etherington. Other families: Dowdings, Harveys, Howells, Graces, Ashcrofts and later, the Hoggs and Days.

Birthday parties and Christmas parties, fireworks, all shared with some of the above; one year our Christmas tree was floodlit. We had a generator and dad fixed up a floodlamp and old car headlight. The same year all the parents were invited as well afterwards for a drink and pressies from the tree. Dad's sense of humour slightly got the better of him. Mrs Jack Smith's surprise present was a chicken claw, uncooked, wrapped in tissue!

The schoolroom provided a social life, the social club with Joe Ricketts on the Piano. Outings to the seaside, and picnics and swimming in the woods in what was euphemistically called the lake, it had a diving board and raft! We learnt to swim there. There were cricket matches and football matches at Harvey's field in 1942. In the first football match the team was Phil and Mike Jones, Barry Davies, John Dowding, Digger Hellum, Eric Weeks, John, Mike and Kevin Keating and Barry's two cousins from Popes hill. Mum had to get a permit to buy a football; there was a raffle to raise the money, it punctured the first time out on the barbed wire but Bro. Anthony Gorton sewed it up and repaired it.

I went to Miss Whittard's ballet and tap classes in Gloucester on Saturdays and in the week I went with my brothers and many other young people and learnt the Palais Glide, St Bernard waltz amongst others and danced with the 'lovely' Edie Daniell. My brother John also thought her lovely!

Our life also revolved around the Salesian parish; Blaisdon Hall film shows on Sunday nights. On occasions Father O'Neill would cover the projector and say don't look! Talented playing and singing from the theologians. Pantomimes and plays with the Oratory. There were large Corpus Christi processions with packed coaches arriving from Gloucester and the surrounding area. Beth Ashcroft and I would strew flowers each year with Beth Ashcroft. Life on the Stud Farm was fun, collecting eggs with Bro. John and riding on the tractor with Bro. Joe, ploughing the fields and singing, mostly hymns I think.

Then there were the train adventures, such as going to school with Freddy Grace and after missed trains having the trains reversing to take you on. My brother John taking a light for his cigarette from the signal lamp at Woodgreen one night walking down the line from Longhope and putting the signal lamp out!

It may not have been swallows and amazons but it was a happy time."

Left:
Biddy Keating & Beth Ashcroft,
flower strewers for Corpus Christi
procession.
Above:
Biddy Keating.
Right:
Biddy c1958.

ST. MICHAEL & ALL ANGELS, BLAISDON

Blaisdon parish church, dedicated to St. Michael and All Angels, sits on a tump overlooking the present village. From its elevated position it is possible to see the River Severn winding its way towards the Bristol Channel and the Cotswold escarpment in the distance. The church is believed to date back to the 13th century, though it may have suffered damage in the village fire of 1699. It was certainly rebuilt in 1869, as it had become very dilapidated. Only the original tower was left untouched; a new nave and chancel were built and a north aisle was added. The cost of the rebuilding was £2000 and Henry Crawshay Esq. of Oaklands Park, Newnham-on-Severn, met this. The architect was Mr F.R.Kempson of Hereford and the Bishop of Gloucester led the service of consecration.

One hundred years later, in 1969, a service was held in the church to celebrate its centenary. The Bishop of Gloucester, the Rt. Rev. Basil Guy, was the preacher, and the Rector, the Rev. D.J.Bick, conducted the service. The Bishop dedicated a new processional cross that had been bought following a collection in the parish.

Among the congregation present were representatives from the firm that rebuilt the church, together with Miss I.

Crawshay, a relative of H. Crawshay, and members of the Hart family, whose ancestor was one of the churchwardens in 1867. Mr J.N. Griffiths acted as cross-bearer. Miss Judith Pickering and Mr C. Etherington read the lessons. The organists were Mr H. Buckett and Mrs C. Manners. At an elegant luncheon after the service, in a marquee, the ishop pointed out that Mr Crawshay had erected his own monument in his lifetime.

Few items have survived from before the rebuilding of the church, though there is a plaque recording the fire of 1699 that destroyed much of the village, the age of which is uncertain. There is also an old chest dated 1708 and plaques to earlier Lords of the Manor. More recent memorials, especially the stained glass windows, record the families who lived at Blaisdon Hall and Rectors of Blaisdon.

In This Village

On Friday about four of the Clock in the afternoon of the 7ᵗʰ day of July 1699 From a Smith's Shop, happened a Fire, which in the space of Two hours Burnt down and Consumed Dwelling Houses Barns, Stables and outhouses containing 135 Bays of Building, which loss sustained by Estimate on Oath amounted to the sum of 4210. 18. 9.

A Wholesome Tongue is a Tree of life, but Perverseness therein is a breach of the Spirit. Prov. XV. Ver. 4. And the tongue is a fire, a world of Iniquity. So is the tongue amongst our members, that it defalth the whole body, and setteth on fire the course of nature – and it is set on fire of Hell James III. Ver. 6.

1

2

4

3

1. The record of the village fire in 1699.
2. Painting by Joe Martin, given to Evelyn Burgin,
Mr Bate's housekeeper, when she left the village.
3. Internal view of the church.
4. View of original path to church past Far View.

Above:
Stained Glass windows depicting the Nativity scene.
Placed in memory of Colin & Mary Helen MacIver by their children.

Above: Windows next to the pulpit, dedicated to the memory of Rev. Edward Jones (d.1911).

Right:
Window above altar, dedicated to Peter & Isabella Stubs by their daughter, Isabella Waters.

Centre Right:
Section of window depicting St Michael &, below, 1 of the bells.

Top Right:
Font at Blaisdon.

Far Right:
Former Blaisdon font, now at St Mary's Church, Kempley.

The font was replaced at this time, the original being used as a roller. In 1913, it was given to the Saxon Church at Kempley where it remains.

In 1912, Mary Helen MacIver paid for the tower to be repaired, the 5 bells recast and a sixth one added, dedicating the works to the memory of her parents, Peter and Isabella Stubs of Blaisdon Hall. Her husband, Colin MacIver, paid for a clock to be put in the tower.

Until the union of Blaisdon and Flaxley parishes in 1922, the Rectors lived at Blaisdon Rectory. Following the union, they lived at Flaxley Rectory, serving both parishes from there. The Reverend McNamara was Rector from 1923 to 1948 and the Reverend Dennis Lane who spent six years with the parishes followed him. Together with his wife Mary, Rev. Lane often invited the parishioners to the Vicarage to enjoy their hospitality with fetes and events in the Vicarage gardens. In 1955 the Reverend Coleman came to the Parish, followed by the Reverend Fooks in 1959. Rev. Marchant arrived in 1961, leaving in 1963.

1

2

3

4

5

6

7

8

9

1. Rev. Lane.
2. Rev. McNamara, his wife, sister-in-law, & son Bill.
3. Rev. Lane.
4. Rev. McNamara.
5. Rev. Marchant.
6. Rev. McNamara, wife, sister-in-law & son Bill. Flaxley Rector early 1920s.
7. Induction of Rev. Coleman 1955 outside Flaxley Abbey.
Bishop Askwith of Gloucester is in the centre.
Churchwardens on left are Mr B. Buckett & Mr G. Beard (Blaisdon).
Churchwardens on right are Sir L Crawley-Boevey & Mr Teague (Flaxley).
Rev. Coleman is on the Bishop's right.
8. Rev. Coleman.
9. Rev. Fooks.

St Michael & All Angels Church Choir 1951.
Back Row:
Mary Jones, Catherine Jones, Cedric Etherington, Bertie Buckett, Rev. Dennis Lane, Joe Martin, Oscar Jones,
Ursula Howells, Honor Larner.
Front Row:
Jackie Smith, Marjorie Jones, John Martin, John Smith, Eric Weeks, Terry Keyse, Norman Penny (Organ Blower),
Norma Davis, Katherine Eagles.

Left:
Elizabeth Etherington in Choir uniform 1951.

Through the years, many other people have played their part in the life of Blaisdon Church. The churchwardens for much of this period were Mr George Beard from Nottwood Hill and Mr Bertie Buckett from the Village. Mr Joe Martin was the Tower Captain and was responsible for teaching the young people the art of bell ringing. They also learnt to ring the hand bells and accompanied the choir when they went carol singing at Christmastide.

The Choir consisted of a mixture of young and old and was watched over by Mr Etherington the Choirmaster. The Organists during this period were Mr Mayo from The Forge at Flaxley followed by Mr Roberts from Northwood Green and then Mr Bertie Buckett. In those days the organ had to be pumped and most of the children in the village had a go at this job with a very small remuneration involved as an incentive. They had to sit in a very confined space behind the organ and when required, pump away to enable the organ to produce the music. Mrs Gwen Dowding cleaned the Church every week ready for Sunday Services and the men took turns at lighting the old boiler to, hopefully, combat the winter chill.

Sunday in the past meant church for all the family and at least two services if not three. All the members of the family trudged up and down through the village to attend the services, whatever the weather, though some went rather reluctantly and everybody would dress smartly for the occasion.

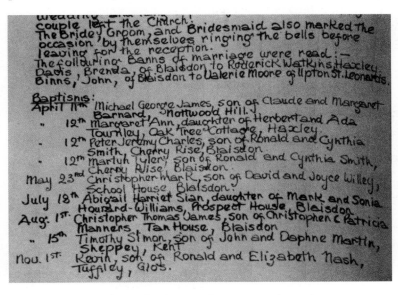

A Page from Blaisdon Parish register in the 1960s.

Sunday School took place every Sunday in the Village School. All the children went; attendance being compulsory. Mrs Smith took Sunday School as part of her teaching responsibilities though nobody seems to remember much about it, except the stamps given each week to stick into a little book to note attendance. However, the Catechism was taught so that it could be recited by heart along with the Lord's Prayer.

Everybody does remember the lovely outings with the bell ringers and choir. The main destinations were Weston-Super-Mare, Barry Island, Porthcawl and Clevedon. One special trip took everyone to London and another to Stonehenge. The Rev. Dennis Lane always came along as he appears in a lot of the photos. There was great excitement when the sea was first seen and the smell of it coming through the windows! Of course there were always buckets being handed round for those of a sickly nature along with the words, "Can't you hang on, its not far to go?"

As the photos show, the whole village turned out for these outings. For some, it was their only chance to see the sea, as very few had their own transport in those days.

Elsie Price, aged 14, described one such outing that took place on 10th August 1926. It shows that these trips were a village highlight for many years, only ceasing when car transport became universal. The spelling of Quoir rather than Choir is hers:

My Quoir Outing Visit to Cheltenham Yesterday

"During the winter months the quoir collected money by raising up Whist Drives and Concerts. When it was divided out we had 7s 2d each and we decided to go to Cheltenham for the day. The elder members went to see the Australian cricketers play and the younger ones went about Cheltenham.

We started off on the 9:27 train from Grange Court. Our tickets were very cheap, only 1s 8d return but of course it was an excursion. The carriage we were in was very comfortable and I did not want to get out when our journey was reached. However we were very lucky because we did not have to change at Gloucester.

It was drizzling with rain when we got out of the train so we made our ways up the street to the 'Museum.' The things there were very numerous, a wonderful collection of many coloured butterflies were pasted on a large card. I cannot say everything that was in here because it would take too long to describe but what I will say and that is this, 'If at anytime you are visiting Cheltenham it is worth the time to go in and have a look around.' You are not charged a halfpenny unless of course you wish to buy any cards. (There was a man just as we went inside the door selling cards of different views).

After seeing all we wanted to we went out and had a look at the fountain in the Promenade. Fortunately for us it was playing and it looked very pretty. Passing on we had a look round a few different shops. We visited Woolworth's and bought a few presents to take back home with us. Then we had a sit down in a lovely large park where there was a Band playing. In this park I had my lunch or dinner. We did not all bring lunch with us so Miss Mayo and the rest of the girls etc went into a Restaurant and had Dinner.

At one o'clock we got on a bus (No: 62) and went to Bishops Cleeve. We had a jolly time there and going down the Shoots was lovely fun. At four o'clock we had tea out on the tennis lawn. We had bread and butter, brown bread and currant bread and a pot of tea and a large plate of different kinds of cakes.

We had not long to stop after tea so we had a rest and then we went and obtained our tickets and back to Cheltenham by train. Now we had about ¾ of an hour to look at the shops. Then we made a happy return journey home very tired. The next morning I stayed in bed until about half past nine. We had a happy time and we are very sorry Quoir Outings aren't every week."

Above:
Blaisdon Church Choir & Bell Ringers.
An outing to Malvern & Worcester 1928.
Ruth Brewer & Elsie Price among others on board.
Left:
Standing: Elsie Price & Ruth Brewer.
Sitting: Miss Mayo & Gertie Savage.
(M. Hogg)

1. Sunday School Outing, late 1940s:

John Martin, Pauline Hayward, Peter Hayward, Brian Hayward, Mr John Hayward, Gran. Hayward, Mrs Hayward & Mrs Martin.

In front: Anita Martin, Lesley Hayward, Rachel Hayward, Jane Martin (in pram).

2. John Keating, Oscar Jones, Burt Nelmes, Pepe Milanta, Ursula Howells, Jean ?, Margaret Beard, Melvin Middlecote (in Front).

3. Back Row: John Martin & Brian Hayward.

Middle Row: Anita Martin, Sally Brown, Rachel Hayward, Lesley Hayward, Christine Bayliss, Pauline Hayward.

Seated: Mrs Brown, Mrs Hayward with Jane Martin, Mrs Martin, Heather Martin.

4. Oscar Jones, Ursula Howells, Margaret Beard, Barry Davis.

5. Josephine Warlow, Rev. Lane, Mrs Blake, Roger Keyse.

6. Porthcawl 1949: Elizabeth Etherington, Rosemary Keating, Jenny Smith, John Smith (behind).

7. John Martin, ?, Heather, Jane & Anita Martin.

8. Ursula Howells, Tom Green, John Dowding, Oscar Jones.

Outing to Stonehenge in the 1950s. The party includes:
Roger Etherington, John Martin, Rev. Dennis Lane, Mrs Etherington, Michael
Keyse, Mrs O. Jones, Mrs Nellie Marshall, Brenda Davis, Grace Davis, Cedric
Etherington, Mr Penny, Peter Hayward, Bertie Buckett, Brian Hayward, Mrs
Bowkett, Tom Board, Mary Jones, Cath. Jones, Mrs Martin, Anita Martin,
Norman Penny, Marjorie Jones, Pauline Hayward, Norma Davis, Jane Martin,
Elizabeth Etherington, Doris Bowkett, Terry Keyse.
Right:
Front: Mrs Grace, Mrs Keating, Mrs Etherington, Mrs Smith.
Back: ?, Cedric Etherington, Mrs Mockford.
Below: Half the Village!

AR VIEW

Far View sits just below the Church and is bounded on one side by the Churchyard. The original pathway to the church runs through its garden.

It was originally used as a Poor House, which had been opened under the authority of an Act passed by King William IV in the sixth year of his reign. The villagers were levied a Poor Law tax to support it.

Far View from the Gate showing the church in the distance.

In 1847 the house became the village school at the cost of £60 and the school and site was vested in the Rector of the Parish and two other trustees. There was room for 103 children in a parish of 241 people. The school served the parish but space was somewhat restricted and there was only a small yard. A series of poor inspection reports led to the building of the new school in 1896 as previously described.

The old School then became a recreation room for the tenants of the Blaisdon Estate. The Church Verger occupied the teachers' old quarters and the other part became a clubroom. Nancy Bate remembers the women used it in the afternoons and the men in the evenings but not on Sundays. It was a kind of social sewing meeting and no doubt a gossip shop. Nancy remembers her mother taking her there once when she was very young. The billiard table was covered with white cloth and women were helping each other with sewing and fitting. The men would chat, play cards, crib and billiards.

When the Estate sold the house it became the home of Mr. Mrs & Miss Whittard. Miss Whittard was a very distinguished looking lady, remembered for her hair. She was never seen without two plaits made into Catherine wheels and placed perfectly over each ear. She was a beautiful lady and taught ballet and dance to the children in the village. Michael Turnball, a young man from Blaisdon Hall, used to play the piano for her lessons.

Later, Mr and Mrs Brown and their daughter Sally came to live at live at Far View in the fifties followed by Mr and Mrs Pitt and their Son Mark.

3 photographs of Mark Pitt.
Above : At Far View showing the gates behind and Stud farm in the distance.
Left: At Stud Farm.
(L. Stanton)

SHARON

A short distance along the lane and on the opposite side to Far View is Sharon, originally known as New Cottage. It replaced a much earlier timber framed building and, like others around the village was built by the MacIver family. Mr and Mrs Brewer, their daughter Ruth and son William lived here. Later it became home to Ruth and her husband, John Magee together with their son John, who was known as Tim.

Sharon in 1953. Mr Brewer & Grandson, Tim.
The house has been decorated for the coronation of Queen Elizabeth II.

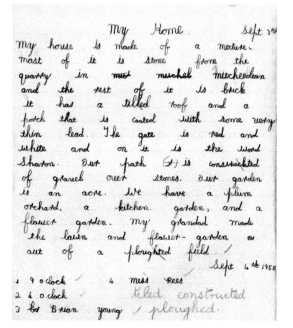

Tim Magee's description of his house, aged 8.

Sharon, then known as New Cottage, 1931.

Aerial view of Sharon.

Mr Brewer was the Electrician and Estate Engineer for Blaisdon Estate when Mr MacIver was Squire. He was in charge of the large generators that supplied the Hall with electricity before the village was connected to the National Grid. Being very handy with his hands, he even made the church collection box from some old packaging boxes.

John Magee taught in local schools. He also became an Ordained Church of England Priest. As a result, he officiated in many services in the local churches but especially in Blaisdon. Tim, John and Ruth's only child, was born in 1949 and tragically died in 1986, before either of his parents, John dying in 1995, aged 76 and Ruth in 2005, aged 93.

1

With Care.

In the event of my death
Please return these photos
with wallet and other effects
found on my person
to Mrs Brewer
Blaisdon Longhope
Per Wm Brewer   Date Glos.

From Ol W Brewer
20971 b MT A.S.C.

STAMP
HERE

2

3

4

6

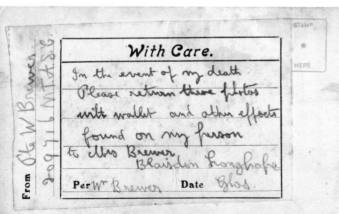

5

7

8

9

10

1. William Brewer in 1st World War uniform with Alice Brewer and their children, Ruth & William, outside New Cottage.
2. Card carried by William Brewer in case of death during active service.
3. Generator room at Blaisdon Hall.
4. 5. 6. William & Alice in their garden.
7. Ruth Brewer age 3 in 1915.
8. Ruth with her brother William in 1919.
9. 10. William & Alice Brewer.

Gilly Wells shares some of her family photographs and recalls the life and times of her Aunt Ruth:

"Ruth Louisa Magee was born on 18.6.1912 at Cheveley, Cambridgeshire to Alice and William Brewer.

In 1912 her father moved to Blaisdon to become an electrician at Blaisdon Hall and in November 1913, Ruth and her mother followed. Initially they lived at Thackwell, Longhope and when New Cottage in Blaisdon became vacant, they moved in and Ruth remained there until shortly before she died, a total of 91 years.

In 1915 her father, William, volunteered to serve his country and in his absence his wife, Alice, and the young Ruth moved into Blaisdon Hall and their son, also William, was born in 1916. Ruth always felt responsible for her brother and was a wonderful sister to him for the whole of his life.

When the war was over her father returned home and Ruth and her brother remembered running across the fields to meet him as he came home by foot from Grange Court Station.

Life returned to normal and Ruth attended the village school. She was a hard worker and a clever girl and tried always to please her parents and make them proud of her. At the age of 10 she passed the exams to go to East Dean Grammar School at Cinderford.

The journeys to and from school were something of an adventure as Ruth had to cycle to Westbury where she caught the bus to Cinderford. She said often there were tramps in the lanes looking either for work at the farms or for the Workhouse at Westbury. She was frightened and rode her bike very quickly to pass them. At 17 she left school and went as a pupil teacher to the school at Westbury.

In 1930 she attended a Theological College at Fishponds in Bristol leaving 2 years later with the Archbishop of York's Certificate, having passed with Distinction. She then began teaching at Steam Mills School where she remained for 5 years. She loved the children but did not enjoy working for a less than agreeable Headmaster. The County Council, who wanted repayment of Ruth's college grant, had appointed her. Times haven't changed where money is concerned!

In 1938 Ruth volunteered to go to Filton to teach children of the employees at the airfield who had removed there from the North of England for the duration of World War II. She had 60 children in her class and during the air raids the teachers took their pupils into the caves at Avon Gorge, keeping them singing whilst the bombs dropped from above!

When the dangers increased at Bristol, the children were evacuated to Redbrook and Ruth came with them. She and they enjoyed their time immensely. Most of the children had never been into the country and were thrilled to see trees and flowers, the river and animals and birds and to discover where milk and eggs came from. One day after school Ruth took some of the older children into Monmouth to see a film about Nelson and then walked them back to Redbrook in the dark, singing again. She seems to have done a lot of singing in her time.

Above:
Mrs Marcus, Fred Merriman, Mrs A. Brewer, John & Ruth Magee, Mr
W. Brewer, Joy Pratt (19th August 1948).
Right: Wedding Announcement from unknown newspaper.

Unfortunately, the children's parents were not so thrilled with the evacuation; 'fancy bathing my child in a tub in front of the fire, and having to go outside to the lavatory, and eating vegetables dug out of the ground' etc. Some even took their children back to war torn Bristol or so called civilisation.

When the war ended, Ruth went to teach at Norton Park School in Cheltenham. She used to travel by train from Blaisdon Halt, with a newcomer to the village, a Mrs Magee. One day she told Ruth that her son, John, would be coming to Blaisdon to live, he had been teaching evacuees in the Peak District.

Magee - Brewer.

Nuptial Mass, with Papal Blessing, was celebrated at the wedding of Mr John Magee, son of the late Mr & Mrs Magee of Cheltenham, and Miss Ruth Brewer, daughter of Mr & Mrs William Brewer of New Cottage, Blaisdon at St Peter's R C Church, Gloucester on Thursday.

The Rev. William Daly, SDB of Blaisdon Hall, Longhope, officiated, and the Rev. Charles Grace ARCO, also of Blaisdon Hall was at the organ.

The bride wore a dress of white silk with small floral sprays stencilled in luminous paint, with a long veil and feathered head-dress. She also wore white shoes and embroidered silk gloves. Her bouquet consisted of scarlet and white carnations.

The bride was given away by her father and Mr Fred Merriman, of Birmingham, was the best man.

Miss Joy Pratt, a friend of the bride, was bridesmaid. She wore a powdered blue dress with embroidered veil to match and a silver head-dress. She carried a bouquet of mixed roses and fern arranged in a silver holder.

During the Mass, Motets were sung by the choir of Blaisdon Hall.

A reception was held at the Cadena Cafe, Gloucester, and the future address of Mr & Mrs Magee will be 17 Sydenham Villas road, Cheltenham.

About this time a flu epidemic took place and John went to school as a relief teacher with Ruth. They were both in lodgings in Cheltenham and in 1948 Ruth became Mrs Magee. Meanwhile, Ruth's mother's health was deteriorating and so they returned to Blaisdon each weekend to help with her care.

In October 1949 Tim was born making their happiness complete. When he was about a year old Ruth's mother was becoming very frail and so Ruth and Tim returned to live at Blaisdon full time and John continued to come home at weekends, although by now he was working in Cirencester. Eventually, John found a teaching post in Mitcheldean and the family were reunited in Blaisdon.

Ruth was kept busy with both a small child and an ailing parent to care for, but was very cheerful and conscious of her duty and worked hard. In January 1951 her mother died and Ruth and John remained at 'Sharon,' so named by Ruth as the house was situated between the hill and the plain, a biblical reference. Her father lived another 12 years by which time Tim had grown into a young man full of promise. He attended the same school as his mother in Cinderford. John had now moved to a teaching post at Double View School in Cinderford where he remained for the rest of his working life.

When Tim left school he went to Leicester University to read Geography and having gained his degree he took a teaching job in Gloucester at Oxstalls School. After a while he felt the need of a more practical career and started his own central heating business. However, he eventually returned to teaching, obtaining a post in London's Tower Hamlets. After all, teaching was in his blood.

John, having retired from school decided to take Holy Orders and in 1978 he was ordained as a non-stipendiary priest working in his local church, which besides Blaisdon and Flaxley included Westbury, Northwood Green and Rodley.

Meanwhile, Ruth became involved in other activities away from the classroom, amongst them she provided lunches at Quakers Friends Meeting House and was a Guide at Gloucester Cathedral. Later, she preached at several non-conformist Chapels in the Royal Forest of Dean. Her life was full and she and John were thrilled when Tim announced that he was to marry Jane in 1986 but their world was later shattered by the devastating news that Tim had drowned in the River Thames only three weeks before his wedding. She and John never recovered from their sad loss but somehow managed to pick up the pieces and continued doing the Lord's work locally.

In 1994 John died and Ruth was left on her own for the first time in her life, apart from her brother who was now in a Nursing Home in Gloucester.

She missed John dreadfully and could never accept that he, being several years her junior, had died before her. She found solace in her pet cats and her many friends and family, conversing at length with anybody and everyone!

For 10 years she was able to remain in her own home but sadly when her personal safety became an issue she had to remove to Longhope Manor Nursing Home where she spent the last four months of her life receiving loving care and kindness.

Throughout her life she retained a sense of duty and obligation. She was a very caring and kind lady who was always looking for connections with other people's lives. She kept in touch by letter and latterly telephone with many people including former pupils, college friends and contemporaries of John and Tim. She idolised her parents

Tim Magee with:
Ruth Magee (top left)
William Brewer (Top centre &
far left)
Toby (Top right).

and was always grateful to her father's uncle who had raised him as a child when he and his brother Daniel were orphaned at a very young age. A sense of gratitude to her great uncle's family remained all through her life.

Her love of the family, children and the Royal Forest of Dean have always been passions of Ruth and although not born a Forester she certainly earned her right to be an adopted one. She even spoke the dialect on occasion much to the disapproval of some of her peers. She was always seeking to find out what makes people tick and had a phenomenal memory, there was no such thing as a five minute call to Ruth.

She truly knew the value of everything but the price of nothing."

Tony Brady was a friend of John, Ruth and Tim for many years and recalls them:

"William Brewer bought New Cottage from the former owners of Blaisdon Hall. He was employed as the electrical engineer before the Salesian Fathers acquired the property and was responsible for the generating equipment that powered the electricity throughout the hall and outbuildings. In the five years period that Blaisdon Hall had stood empty, he maintained the equipment and was an unpaid watchman. When the Salesians arrived he was re-engaged to his former duties, eventually retiring when Brother Jan Orysuik took over and in due course the Hall was connected to the National Grid.

Bill Brewer was a widower. He was a staunch Protestant, as was Ruth. John Magee was a theologian one year away from ordination as a Salesian priest in the late 1940s. Ruth would sometimes accompany her father to the hall where she came into contact with John: an attraction formed which led to John abandoning his vocation and marrying Ruth. A couple of years later their only son was christened Timothy, in nearby St Michael's Church.

Bill lived to be 90 and had died in the 1960s. He was a gruff, grumpy sort who came down to Stud Farm most days for fresh milk accompanied by Toby, his faithful long-lived dog. The Salesian Fathers were always referred to as "the monks". When Toby died I helped a bereft Tim, aged 8, bury it near The Gully.

I was friendly with John in the years 1955-1961 and he talked to me occasionally about the trauma of his departure from his Community. Many of his former students continued to visit him at his home. Ruth longed for her husband to continue his studies with the Protestant ministry but John would have had to renounce his Catholic faith. To ensure an income he studied by correspondence course and qualified as a teacher. This led to a teaching post at Abenhall Secondary Modern School in Mitcheldean and finally at Double View School in Cinderford from where he retired as Head of his Department.

As a child Timothy, always Timmy to his parents, was often brought by his father down to the farm and as he grew was very much a part of the Stud Farm extended local circle. John came to the farm chapel regularly to attend Sunday Mass. His son became a teacher and taught in London's East End but died tragically in an accident there aged 36.

After retirement, John studied Divinity and became a Church of England Minister to the great joy and pride of Ruth. The last time I was with them together was when I attended the morning service in St Michael's Church led by John and later had breakfast in their home.

My last abiding memory of Sharon is when I visited Ruth briefly a couple of years before she died. She recalled my happy attachment to John and Timmy and in a most poignant gesture took me for the first time ever upstairs and from a vantage point on the landing, Ruth led my gaze towards St Michael's Church and pointed out the visible graves of her beloved John and Timmy. I am glad that she appreciated me saying that her husband was a true Salesian in his vocation as an educator and that I was edified by his sincere beliefs and permanently influenced by his spiritual example and friendship. John had taught me to understand and respect other people's feelings, values, beliefs and culture, attributes no less relevant today than in those distant Blaisdon times."

SHARON
"Sharon will be a fold of flocks."   Isaiah 65:10

1. The Magee family at home.
2. Ruth Magee.
3. Tim Magee & Piglets.
4. John Magee.

STUD FARM

Stud Farm During the Salesian Ownership.

Sitting at the end of a long drive but visible from the road is Stud Farm. It was originally called New House Farm and has existed for 3-400 years. At the beginning of 1900 it was owned by Mr Peter Stubs who renamed it due to his breeding of Shire Horses. The Stud became well known and its horses won many awards as well as being sold widely. Perhaps the most renowned was Blaisdon Conqueror, whose skeleton now resides in the British Museum. Mr and Mrs MacIver became the owners following the death of Mr Peter Stubs. The farm stayed in the family until it was sold to the Salesian Order.

The Salesian Order ran the Stud Farm as part of its Salesian School of Agriculture and Trades based in and around Blaisdon Hall. The farm was in the charge of Father Dan Lucey an expert stockbreeder who kept cows, pigs and chickens and grew vegetables. Father Lucey is remembered wearing his clerical dress and black homburg hat whilst driving his tractor and working on the farm each day.

Life at the Stud Farm is described by Lawrence Stanton (known by everyone as "Curly"), Tony Brady who obviously enjoyed every minute of his time at the Farm and also John Dunbar who started life in Blaisdon as a Hall Boy at the Farm and finished his time in the village as the Landlord of the Red Hart.

One other much loved member of the Stud Farm brotherhood was Brother Joe and Tony provides a lovely tribute to him. Of all the people from the Stud Farm, Brother Joe was the most well known amongst the villagers especially as he would help out anyone if they needed it.

In 1963 the herd was dispersed and the farm sold to Mr Knight of Huntley, who only stayed for two years after which it was sold to Mr R. Hawker, who still lives in the village with his wife Hilary. The present owners of the Stud Farm are Mr and Mrs Don Rich and their family.

Blaisdon Conqueror.
From a print by
E. B. Stanley Montefiore.
(G. Sterry)

Foaled	14thJune 1884.
Breeder	Peter Stubs Esq.
Address	Stud Farm, Blaisdon, Glos.
Stud No.	15989.
Sire	Hitchin Conqueror.
Dam	Welcome.
Dam Sire	Garnet.
Height	17 hands, 2 inches.
Died	Saturday 22nd October 1904.

Prizes won:

Commended, Shire Horse Society Show, Islington.
2nd Shire Horse Society Show of England, Manchester.
2nd Shire Horse Society Show, Islington.
1st Class 6 Shire Horse Society Show, Islington.
£20 Cup for best stallion in classes 45,46,47.
Reserve for Champion, £10 Gold Medal.
2nd Class 6. Shire Horse Society Show, London.
1st & Silver Medal, Shire Horse Society Show, Cheltenham.
1st in Class 6 & Reserve for Champion Cup at Shire Horse Society Show, London.
2nd Class 54 Royal Agricultural Society's Show, Preston & Reserve for Derby Cup.
2nd Class 6, Shire Horse Society Show, Islington.
1st Class 7, Reserve to Gold Cup & Gold Medal at Shire Horse Society Show, Islington.

Lawrence Stanton, known as Curly, writes of life in Blaisdon and on the Stud Farm in particular:

"On January 8th 1952 I, together with five other boys, Alan Ferry, Lawrence McDonagh, Michael "Fanelli" Smith, David Randall and John King, stepped off the train at Blaisdon Halt to commence a completely new chapter in our lives. We had been sent to Blaisdon from St Joseph's Home in Enfield Middlesex. St Joseph's was an orphanage run by the Sisters of Charity and my friend Alan Ferry and I had been there for about nine years. To say we had not been happy there is an understatement, but times were hard for everybody during that period.

Blaisdon Hall was run by a religious order called The Salesians of Don Bosco and comprised a community of Priests and Lay Brothers dedicated to the care and education of boys like us who had no families to rely on.

There were about seventy boys in residence at this time. We were divided into two dormitories and supervised by two lay brothers and one Priest. During the next few weeks we came to realise how fortunate we were to be sent here to Blaisdon. We learned that there was a farm owned by the community in addition to many acres of woodland. We soon settled into the daily routine of our new life. We were woken at 7am and after washing and dressing made

Opposite.
Top:
The Salesian 'Family' on Stud Farm.
Left:
A rear view of Stud Farm.
Centre: Chapel Window monogram MHM.
Right:
The Chapel built at Stud farm by the Salesians.

our way to the chapel for Mass during which we recited our morning prayers. After this we had breakfast followed by recreation until 9 o'clock when assembly took place followed by lessons in the school block. Lunch was about 12 o'clock and was followed by the choice of football or a walk, then back to school until teatime.

After tea the boys would spend time attending to whatever hobbies they had chosen, e.g. band practice, Irish dancing, boxing, cross country running or reading in the library There was always a play or a pantomime in the offing and there would be practice for these events. After supper there was about an hour of recreation consisting of table tennis, billiards or a game of football in the yard, then it was back to chapel for night prayers. I cannot praise too highly the dedication of the Priests and Brothers at Blaisdon. They were always cheerful and were all firm but fair, we knew where we stood with them. If you ever received a clip around the ear you knew it was deserved.

On Tuesday afternoons there was army cadet training for those who had joined. Alan Ferry and I preferred to go down to the farm to help Brother John Wrigley who looked after hundreds of chickens. Bro. John was always chuckling away and we always thought he sounded just like his chickens! We helped collect the eggs and clean out the numerous henhouses, put fresh straw in the nests, and fed the chickens with corn and meal. There were lots of different breeds of chickens such as Rhode Island Reds, Light Sussex, Black Leghorns and others. They were all kept in separate pens because they laid different coloured eggs. This was the start of my interest in farm working and as often as I was allowed I would go to help on the farm. The person in charge of the farm was Father Dan Lucey.

When it was time to leave school I was offered a job on the farm, which I was pleased to accept. I moved down to the farm to live and work and found life hard but enjoyable.

Things were very primitive in the early days, there was no mains electricity then and we had to use Tilley lamps for lighting. My first wage packet consisted of the magnificent sum of one pound seventeen shillings and sixpence, I was rich indeed!

Every morning Father Dan would knock on the doors to wake everybody. My first job was to prepare the cows for milking by washing their udders and checking that they had no mastitis, by squeezing each teat into a special cup. When I first started on the farm I struggled to get any milk out at all but before too long I had the hang of it. Whilst Head Cowman, Pat Tobin, and his deputy, Johnny Dunbar, milked the cows, my job was to carry the milk into the dairy and pour it through a filter and cooler and fill the ten-gallon churns. When this was done the milk was labelled and recorded ,then loaded onto a trailer and taken to the top of the farm drive and placed upon a wooden platform for collection by the milk lorry. After this we went into the kitchen for breakfast. There being no mains electricity, all the cooking was done upon the open fire. There was a large tureen of porridge which had been made by Fr Dan

Lawrence Stanton (Curly).

or Bro.Joe and we could have boiled eggs or toast. The kitchen fire was a focal point for us on the farm. There was always a kettle boiling away on the fire and, during the cold winter months, we would place house bricks near the grate which, when they were hot, we would wrap in newspaper and place in our beds for warmth. Of course when we eventually had mains electricity, electric blankets were an early investment. After breakfast, the clean up began. The byre had to be cleaned and hosed down, the milking equipment had to be washed and sterilised and made ready for evening milking. There was always plenty to do to keep us busy. For our main meal of the day we would all climb aboard the milk trailer for a lift up to Blaisdon Hall for a cooked dinner. During this trip we would carry the milk, eggs and potatoes for the school. The busiest times on the farm were haymaking and harvest when we were required to work long hours. It was hard but enjoyable.

The big change for me when I went to work on the farm was the realisation that, after my working day I was, for the first time in my life, free to do as I wished and go where I liked and I relished this new-found freedom. John Boden, who was the one who looked after the pigs on the farm, was a chap who almost lived in the woods. He kept ferrets and would often take me on his walks and show me the many nests he had found, including a wild duck sitting on her eggs. I spent many hours roaming the countryside around the village and beyond. I also got to know many of the local people.

One of the first people I got to know was Mrs Goddard who ran the little Post Office. I think her first name was Annie, but we all called her Fanny. I only popped in for a postage stamp, but was still in there half an hour later! She would peer over the top of her spectacles and talk about everything and everybody. She was a lovely lady but after a few visits I decided that if I was in a hurry it was quicker to jump on my bicycle and go to Longhope Post Office for it. I believe she was awarded the BEM years later and I am sure it was well deserved.

Father Dan Lucey.

When I was seventeen and a half I joined the Army for 3 years. Under National Service which was compulsory, the period of service was two years, but the wage was so low that many signed on the extra year to receive a better wage. During my service, most of which was in Germany I would come home to Blaisdon on leave. Fr Dan had promised that my job on the farm was waiting when I finished in the army. Sure enough when I was demobbed I was welcomed back. My new job was mainly tractor work and I soon settled back

into the routine. This was the time I got to know the many characters of Blaisdon. Bertie Buckett had a smallholding adjacent to the Stud Farm. He lived with his mother across the fields and I would often see his mother sitting at the foot of the ancient oak at the bottom of his drive waiting to be picked up by Bertie in the pony and trap. She reminded me of granny in a Giles cartoon!

Bertie was a gentle man who was often teased by the regulars down at the Red Hart, but he took it all in his stride. During haymaking time a contractor would come with his baler and would charge so much a bale. Father Dan would get the contractor to produce enormous bales for the Stud Farm but Bertie, to everybody's amusement, would ask the contractor to make his bales nice and small, which the contractor would be happy to oblige!

Cyril Baggot was another character who lived in a wooden shack on Nottwood Hill. He was a very quiet man who seemed to me to have been through some hard times. He would walk down from his shack to the Red Hart for a pint most days and he too was the subject of much good-natured teasing by Albert Pithouse and his mates. I think he collected his bread from the Red Hart and the story was told that one day Albert and friends took his loaf out of his bag and replaced it with a house brick. Cyril took most of the teasing in his stride but sometimes it went too far and he would lay about them with his stick and they would scatter into the road outside laughing like schoolboys. Afterwards one of them would buy Cyril a drink and they would all be the best of friends. My favourite Blaisdon character was Albert Pithouse. He was always the life and soul of the goings on at the pub. He would arrive at the pub at opening time and stay until closing time, then he would be there again in the evening and again still be there when time was called. Albert was landlady Elsie Hogg's favourite customer. She and her husband Frank were a lovely couple. Albert would always tease Elsie who would often scream with laughter, while Frank would often scowl and snap back at Albert! Although Albert enjoyed a drink I never saw him drunk, but one summer's afternoon I was walking down past Blaisdon Church when I spotted a pair of feet on the grassy bank. As I came closer I could see it was Albert with his cap over his eyes sleeping like a baby. He had obviously decided it was hardly worth walking back up to Nottwood Hill only to come back down for evening opening!

On our days off on the farm we would often go to Gloucester to the cinema. Sometimes we would go by bus but we preferred the train. When we went on the bus we would cycle to Hinders Corner and leave our bikes in a shed owned by Mr Nelmes. He was a forbidding character and most of the younger people were a little afraid of him. Pat Tobin had said to us that Mr Nelmes had two left feet, I don't know how true that was but we were always grateful to use his shed knowing that our bikes would still be there when we came back on the bus. When we went on the train it was a much more enjoyable experience. The

carriages had no corridors and stretched from one side of the train to the other. The seats were padded and there were pictures on the walls and once the train moved off you were in your own little world. The downside was that during the winter on the return trip you had to be aware of when your station was approaching. The windows were usually steamed up and if you opened them to look out you often ended up with an eyeful of soot. Blaisdon Halt was only lit with two gas lamps so it was easy to miss. One Blaisdon resident named Mr Snow had a nasty experience one night. Apparently he had dozed off and awoke in a panic as he realised the train was about to pull off, he rushed to the door and stepped out but unfortunately he had chosen the wrong side of the train and he landed on the side of the track. He was badly shaken but luckily no bones broken.

Often on the farm men of the road would call in for a meal. Father Dan would always feed them and sometimes give them clothes before they went on their way. There were a couple of regular callers who would do a few weeks work for their keep before moving on. Our favourite visitor was a chap called Harold who originated from Liverpool. He was a good worker and was a wonderful storyteller, and would keep us amused for hours with his tales. He would often stay for a couple of months before getting itchy feet and moving on. Before Harold left Father Dan would kit him out with tidy clothes and new boots and some money. Once when Harold called in, Father Dan noticed that he was wearing an old pair of Wellingtons and Father Dan asked him what happened to the new boots he had been given. Harold was a little embarrassed and admitted that he hadn't gone very far before he took them off and lobbed them over the nearest hedge. When asked why, he said that nobody would give a tramp a meal if he was wearing new boots! Father Dan roared with laughter as did we all when we heard about it.

One day Tony Brady went into the kitchen and told Father Dan that there was a tramp outside who wanted to see him. When the man had gone Father Dan asked Tony why he thought the man was a tramp and Tony said that the man had told him that he knew every hedge from here to Gloucester. Father Dan laughed and told Tony that the man was a pest control officer!

I will always have fond memories of life on Stud Farm and of the friendliness of the Blaisdon villagers."

Above:
Feedtime for the chickens with Warag Field in the background.
Right from top:
Bringing in the harvest.
Father Dan Lucey & Brother Joe Carter.
Harold, the vagrant.

271

Tony Brady, Allan Ferry & Lawrence Stanton
on top of a Bulldozer.

In keeping with the traditional practice of abbeys and monasteries, the farm managers, Father Dan Lucey and Brother Joe Carter, kept open house and I got to know many wayfarers and wandering migrants who took up our hospitality and lived among us for varying lengths of time. Thus, in a time of my most impressionable development I learned to love and serve the poor while a philosophy was encouraged to better myself so I might be an effective instrument in influencing their conditions and be a force for social justice."

Extracted from 'Scenes from an Examined Life, Blaisdon Made Me,' **Tony Brady** continues with stories about the social life of those working on the Stud Farm:

Tony Brady worked on the Stud Farm. He describes his early life and the effects that the Salesian Order have had on his life:

"I was abandoned as a baby in Westminster Cathedral in London and brought up by an organisation called The Crusade of Rescue. My personality was shaped by Sisters of Charity in a variety of orphanages in Hounslow and Enfield and my character formed by priests and brothers in a school situated in the Forest of Dean, Gloucestershire, run by the Salesians who were founded by an Italian priest called Don Bosco. He set up training schools for destitute boys in Turin in the 1860s and was a sort of Lord Shaftesbury, William Booth and Dr Barnardo combined.

When I left school at 15 I had no home to go to but this problem was happily solved by my being placed on a farm where I worked as a pig stockman in an idyllic adolescence.

"In the years up to 1957, the farm workers were more than content to have two-wheeled transport to get about. Up and down the road and drive between the Stud Farm and the Salesian School at Blaisdon Hall; along the main thoroughfare to the Red Hart; on down through the village to Blaisdon Halt to catch a steam train. Then onward and around the local villages; Westbury-on-Severn, Flaxley, Popes Hill, Little London, Longhope and Huntley. Further afield to distant Gloucester City. I refer of course to the humble pushbike. Most of the incoming farm workers possessed a bicycle, as the former owner gifted or sold it on as they left to join the armed forces. In my case there was none available as Johnny Dunbar (Senior Dairy Stockman) had taken over departing leading tractor driver Gerry Williams' racy dropped handlebars Raleigh.

Even so, I was able to resort to the very convenient arrangement at the time; the slogan in Gloucester's top cycle shop read: 'Hire Purchase - It takes the Waiting out of Wanting!' Very soon after starting work as Junior Pig Man in June 1955, and although Fr William Boyd (Bursar) would have kindly loaned me the full price, I made a down-payment deposit of £2 and signed the Agreement to pay the balance of £12 off at 2 shillings a week. I was now the owner of a brand new Raleigh Roadster with dynamo driven front and rear lights; 5 speed Sturmey-Archer gearing; cable, not rod operated brakes and a spring-down stand. A particularly practical and new feature was the metal guard, which completely enclosed the chain. Fr Dan had acted as my Guarantor and his self-presumed bonus was use of the bike, as and when!

Now about this time Ronnie O'Connor, a Liverpool born former Salesian School pupil, returned to Blaisdon Hall after completing National Service in the British Army and was employed as a painter and decorator under the direction of Brother Thomas Palmer. His room was in the former stables. Ronnie, who often looked, and regularly expressed himself, as 'feeling like death warmed up,' soon declared that he would not be seen dead on a bike! That included the mechanized transport of George Austin, Head Landscape Gardener, who zipped about on his whispering all aluminium Italian LE Velocette motorbike.

Obviously nicknamed 'Scouser,' I prefer to remember Ronnie as 'Two Fags Ron' due to his habit of rolling two cigarettes at a time, one to puff on and another to perch on his right ear. When that second one was smoked, it was time to stop whatever he was doing to roll another pair and so on. He was afflicted with a tic, which caused

Tony Brady.

his face to twitch involuntarily. Ronnie put this down to harsh childhood chastisements in a Cheshire children's home, which he dismissed as 'over enthusiastic correction!'

Proud of his achievement in completing his trade Apprenticeship, which allowed no streaks or variation of tones in his painting, nor could the seams be seen in his wall papering, Ronnie indulged himself amply in the leisure pursuits of drinking, betting, darts and shove-halfpenny. Such pleasures were not confined to the Red Hart but a wide range of Public Houses in the surrounding villages. All these pastimes combined fully with this passion for second-hand cars.

As Ronnie had spent his military service in a motorised Corps, he was demobbed with a most prized Golden Goodbye of that time, a full driving licence. He soon bought his first second-hand car, which was quickly replaced. This in turn went back whence it came, to the scrap yard in Gloucester, to be followed at short intervals through further trade-ins, by a range of vehicles steadily improving in style and standard. There were exceptions. Roger Allen remembers accepting a lift from Ronnie at Hinders Corner and having to keep his feet on the central drive shaft casing, as there was no floor in the vehicle! The highpoint was Ronnie's purchase of a Lanchester, to which I will return later.

Down at Stud Farm, we soon became used to Ronnie seeking help for his latest breakdown. No problem if the car failed to start at Blaisdon Hall as it was downhill on the drive all the way to the Lodge. If it hadn't started by then, there was no point turning left for Stud Farm, as there was a steady upward climb from the Post Office to the next downhill run by Blaisdon Church leading to the sloping farm drive. Might as well roll on through The Lodge gates and glide downhill past The Rectory and come to a stop at The Red Hart. From there, Ronnie, after a few pints of Frank and Elsie's best bitter, would telephone Stud Farm and eventually, after getting permission from Father Dan or Brother Joe Carter, I or a farm chum, would take a tractor and tow him in for repairs.

These regular rescue forays and the subsequent under the bonnet repairs experience in the tractor shed, led Lawrence (Curly) Stanton, Alan Ferry, Roger Allen and myself to pool some spare cash with which we bought an Austin 7. Lawrence was principal shareholder as he held a full driving licence, having done his army service in the REME (Royal Electrical Mechanical Engineering) where he had driven and maintained Centurion tanks. Under his guidance, we all learned to drive using the field paths and open spaces that the meadows afforded, once the silage had been cut and lifted.

One evening, we all spun into Gloucester where we went to the pictures. After the show, we got separated and I found our car, which was parked up next to the Bon Marché, the City's Harrods (well, Selfridges!) As the doors were unlocked, a neither unusual nor worrying oversight, I got in and settled in the back seat to wait for the others. Presently, what we would have called a 'Cheltenham type' wearing a trilby hat and smoothing his moustache, walked towards our car and inserting a key opened the door and got in. I sat still. Then he took off his hat. As he turned to

place it behind him he saw me. 'What the .....! Who the devil are you?' he shouted in a posh voice. 'I'm waiting for my mates' I said. 'Get out immediately!' he ordered, 'I'm calling a policeman!'

I realised, as I looked past the irate gent through the windscreen that I was in the wrong car for, two cars ahead in the line of parked cars, I could see my chums standing next to our Austin 7 and looking around. I had got into an identical vehicle. I jumped out mumbling apologies as the man started his car and drove off. If laughter was a fuel in the Austin 7 petrol tank, it lasted long after the ten miles we needed to get back to Blaisdon. Remembering the incident still tickles me to this day.

Ronnie's Lanchester, bought second-hand, introduced us to the luxury end of 1950s motoring. This *marque* was out of the Rolls Royce, Daimler and Bentley stable and when seen in its natural milieu was invariably driven by a chauffeur. What a motor! Four lavishly lined doors, beautifully appointed wooden and leather interior, crafted tasselled rope handgrips and deep pile carpets. Four passengers fitted comfortably in the back seat, two drop-down hinged seats facing them while three passengers could occupy the front seat. All this and built like a tank. A loud throaty klaxon hooted with a press on the foot control.

One evening, returning from watching professional wrestling in Gloucester Baths, we were bowling along downhill and approaching Birdwood village. Ronnie was at the controls and six passengers were on board. Suddenly, there was an almighty bang and the car's rear tilted down and to the right. In the headlights we saw a wheel running perfectly straight ahead, keeping dead in line with the white marking in the middle of the road, and then disappear. 'We're on fire!' shouted Roger Allen, and looking out the rear window we could see sparks were flying up as the axle scraped along the road. The scraping noise was combined with an ear splitting squeal, 'Everyone shift over to the left side!' Ronnie shouted. Five of us complied. The sparks and squealing stopped as we careered on - now on three wheels!

Ahead, at Birdwood, drinkers piled out of the pub as a tyred wheel from nowhere thumped into the side of the bar wall, bounced off and landed in a nearby tree. Then, out of the darkness, the Lanchester loomed as Ronnie managed to bring it to a wobbling, screeching stop. With the willing drinkers' help, we eased the stricken vehicle off the road. Luckily, as everyone in the pub seemed to know Ronnie, the 'Last Rounds' bell had sounded so thirsty Ronnie and me set off to Huntley Police Station. He knocked up the Sergeant, who lent him an oil lamp to position by the car until next morning. Next day Brother Joe, having diagnosed a broken half shaft, towed the amazingly undamaged car back to Stud Farm. It wasn't long before Ronnie had the Lanchester back on the road fully taxed and insured. For some considerable time after that we kept to our Austin 7. A lucky number perhaps!

1

2

4

3

1. The Austin 7, BAD 311, purchased by Tony Brady & friends. Tony Brady (standing), Marcus Pitt (on bonnet), Curly Stanton (in car) & Henry Mullaney (on running board). Henry is the nephew of Rev. Mullaney, Rector of Blaisdon Hall (1956-61).
2. Tony Brady, Jim Meenagham (Tractors), Johnny Dunbar (Dairy Herd), Lawrence Stanton (calves, hens).
3. Tony Brady with piglets, Christmas Day 1956.
4. Ronnie O'Connor in the Red Hart bar.

John Dunbar came to Blaisdon Hall in 1951 and writes of his time there and working on Stud Farm:

"On the 5th June 1951 my brother, Lawrence, and myself arrived in Blaisdon. We got off the train at Blaisdon Halt and immediately I was struck by the quietness of the whole area, and also the lack of traffic and houses. This was in complete contrast to the towns and cities that we had lived in previously.

Compared with other 'Homes' and places that we'd lived in, this was so different. Most of the boys were orphans (like me and my brother) due to the bombings during the war. Some of the boys had lost a parent or parents killed in action. Our time was filled in from morning to night. 'Reveille' was 6.45am and we would be down in the chapel for morning Mass and prayers at 7.30am then breakfast after which we all had our 'housework' to do. My particular job was to clean the sinks and baths in the bathroom.

Once we had finished our 'jobs' we were then able to relax or play until school time. School time was run the same as ordinary schools and activities were much the same. We were put into 'Houses' - 'Alban', A'Becket', 'Fisher' and 'More' named after the saints or martyrs. Inter-house competition was quite keen, and it included all sport, football, cricket, boxing and cross country running as well as the annual sports day which was held on 'Harvey's Field' situated behind the Rectory.

When I turned 15 I was then given the title of 'Trainee,' which meant that I worked down on the Stud Farm during the day but I was still under the care of the Hall and this

John Dunbar,
Working at The Stud Farm.
(1955)

meant that I had to still be housed and adhere to the rules of the Hall. It also meant there was no pay for me during this time. Quite a few months passed by before I finally got on to the 'pay roll'. What a thrill! I finally had my own money. I thought 'I'm a man at last!' School was finally behind me and my working life was now spread out in front of me.

When I first started work, there was no electricity in the village. The only electric was at Blaisdon Hall where they had a huge engine that produced enough energy for the lighting. Down on the farm, we used Tilley lamps for the lighting, and they also provided warmth in our rooms on winter evenings, as there was no central heating. When the electric arrived in around 1955 it was such a luxury that it took us some time to get used to it. But it did make life easier. The other thing that made life easier was the arrival of mains water. Up until then we had to use a pump handle on the well down on the farm. Water up at the Hall was pumped from the Pump Station (a deep well) at Stanley Corner and washing down water was collected from the lake in the wood. How things changed in a couple of years. The only thing Blaisdon didn't have was street lighting. The only outside light in the village at the time was the light on the sign of 'The Red Hart Inn'. It was like a beacon. Well, it was to me.

The farm had a few workers but the 'boss' was Father Dan Lucey, ably assisted by Brother Joe Carter (mainly tractor man), and Brother John Wrigley who was in charge of the poultry section. For my first few months at work, I was usually helping Father Dan going around the farm doing the odd jobs, things like mending gaps in fences or hedges, moving stock from one field to another, hoeing the beet

by hand. It was interesting work and it was also a good grounding for my working life. I then had a few months working with John Boden on the pig section. I think at this time of my life that I had more baths than ever before. This was another chore because we had to go up to the Hall for a bath, as there were no baths on the farm. It also meant that we had to take a change of clothes with us as our working clothes had picked up the smells of the pigs, etc!!

Milking the cows at this time was usually done by Brother Joe, Father Dan and one of the lads. Then one day we had a new herdsman arrive on the farm, a man by the name of Pat Tobin who was going to take over the whole of the milking operation. Pat was a Blaisdon Old Boy. He was among the first intake when the Salesians arrived at Blaisdon Hall in the late thirties. When the war broke out he had served in the Navy as a gunner and saw action in the Atlantic and the Indian Ocean. He had been working for a farmer at Tibberton as the main cowman. When Pat took over the dairy section, Father Dan then put me alongside Pat as second cowman. This was a partnership that was to last until 1957 when I joined the Army to do my National Service.

Even though Pat was a cowman, he was well skilled in other jobs. When all the milking and the dairy jobs were finished, Pat and myself would then be given other jobs, which we did until the afternoon milking. Things like hedge cutting which we did with billhooks, fencing if it was needed, and tractor work such as ploughing, hoeing, seeding, manure spreading, harvesting wheat, barley, oats, beans and even potatoes, which were picked up by the boys. The corn and the beans were stored until the winter when they were milled to produce meal to give to the dairy cows to replace energy and minerals that were needed after milking.

Boys working on the farm whilst I was there were John Boden, Sean McCrossah, Jerry Williams, Paul Studd who was killed whilst on Military Service in Malaya, Peter Manning, then Tony Brady, Jim Meenaghan and Terry O'Neill.

In 1954, at the age of 17½, I received my 'call up' papers for National Service but I was approached by Father Dan to apply for a 'deferment' of service, which I did. I was quite happy with this arrangement and so was Father Dan, as he had seen six of the above names leave to do their National Service leaving labour a bit thin on the ground. This also gave me a bit of leverage, ably backed by Pat, to go and see about having a pay rise, which, in the circumstances, was granted, and I was paid well above the usual agricultural rate.

When I first started work, one or two of the lads who were older than me used to frequent the Red Hart in the village and, now and again, I would go with them! At the time Mrs Price ran it. This was before the electric and it would be lit by calor gas or oil lamps on the bar. Looking back now this lighting gave the bar an atmosphere that it never had once the electric arrived. In those days, the fact that one day I would be the 'Landlord' never entered my head. But then, that was in the future.

All the pints of beer in those days were drawn straight from the 'wood' by hand, the days of top pressure gas and taps on the bar were still a long way off, and then carried from the cellar to the bar. Compared to today's dispensing, it was a lot more work. I used to drink bottled cider which was made by the Gloucestershire Cider Company based at Wickwar and most customers asked for a pint of Wickwar rather than say cider. Wednesday and Saturday nights used to be known as 'Farmers Night'. This was when six or seven of the local farmers would meet to have a drink and a 'natter and chatter' and make a real social evening along with the other customers, playing crib and then 'Tippet' the loser usually paying for the drinks (usually whisky) and keeping their hand in on the quoit board (pre drink and drive days!).

In 1957 I finally decided to do my National Service, this was more a personal choice than a patriotic one, due to the fact that if I had left the farm up to the age of 26 I could still be roped in for National Service and a man of 26 among men of 17 or 18 is at that age an older man in lots of ways. So it was with a little foreboding that I gave Father Dan the news that I would be doing my army time. So it was, on the 4th April 1957, that I left Blaisdon for Lincoln to begin my Army Training, having left behind some of the best years of my life!"

After National Service, John returned to Blaisdon in 1962, initially working for Bovis and lodging at the Red Hart. He married Iris Hogg in1963 and they had a son, Neil. For many years, John was the landlord of the Red Hart.

Opposite:
1. John Dunbar at Stud farm.
2. John & Pigs.
3. John cleaning the milking parlour.
4. John & Jim Meenagham.

Tony Brady fondly remembers Brother Joe Carter:

"I lived and worked with the late Brother Joe Carter during the years 1955-1961. He was responsible for all things mechanical that operated at Stud Farm, a brilliant mechanical engineer, machine-fixer and a driver who could achieve the most amazing feats of skill on an agricultural tractor. At one time silage was drawn from the fields on buck-rakes and deposited in pits alongside what was once the largest covered barn in the West Country. Bro. Joe's *tour de force* was to make the tractor stand upright on its back wheels in the pit as he balanced the loaded buck-rake before releasing its trip handle. It was a spectacular and daring operation and if miscalculated the tractor would have toppled backwards and certainly fatally crushed him. The cutter/blower forage harvester made the buck-rake less used and I remember Father Rector saying that it reduced greatly the likelihood of Bro. Joe being killed.

He was at his peak when I knew him even though he suffered greatly with his back and stomach and despite spells in hospital continued to work all hours. There were up to 10 men living in the farmhouse in those days and there was nobody to care for us when sick. When he took to his bed, which was rare, I tended him as best I could, assisting Father Dan. Fortunately Bro. Joe was a great reader. As a break from spiritual reading he loved the Readers Digest and I used to buy him Time Magazine and Life, which kept him abreast of all things American and International. He fostered my literary interest too and honed my verbal dexterity.

Part of our relationship was the cultivation of a mutual witheringly sarcastic, caustic, vitriolic and vocally inventive, yet good-natured antagonism. As a pig-man, I was lowest in the farm's pecking order and the butt of everyone's scorn; the tractor drivers were of the elite. Even so Bro. Joe's endless repartee and wisecracks benefited me greatly in later life as I eventually broke out of a crippling shyness to achieve articulacy and literary competence. Bro. Joe had a capacity for quoting poetry at length and I read and memorised much in order to keep up with him.

I was in charge of the pig herd at the Salesian farm attached to Blaisdon Hall; 40 sows, each with its own name, two boars and about 300 piglets, weaners, gilts for breeding, porkers and baconers. It was a first class piggery; excellent clean and warm housing, with the sows and their litters allowed to free range in the orchard and their own meadow. We always got 3 As at Nailsworth from the Pig Marketing Board. I used to go to the slaughterhouse in the haulier's lorry, Marfell's from Ruardean, to accompany my lovingly nurtured pigs and ease their parting into the irrevocable process and preparation for the butchers' shops. Stud Farm was a model of good agricultural practice in its time and the Young Farmers Club members used to spend study days there advised by Fr Dan and Bro. Joe.

The farm was a haven for homeless people and Fr Dan and Bro. Joe Carter used to give their own clothes and footwear to the destitute. The farmhouse provided shelter, recuperation and work in season to wayfarers. We had no television and the best entertainment in the long evenings about the fire was provided by our guests who told us all about their travels and escapades. There was a chapel attached to the farmhouse and Fr Dan said Mass every day at 6.30 a.m. Both Bro. Joe and Bro. John Wrigley were up at 5.30 a.m. to perform their spiritual duties; reading and meditation and, in Fr Dan's case, the first of the 4 hour long readings of the office of the Breviary. I often served his morning Mass and if Fr Dan had recently given away his shoes or boots he would be wearing Wellingtons under his cassock as he set off to hear 7.30 a.m. confessions at the boy's Mass in Blaisdon Hall.

The Salesian community life did not come easy to Bro. Joe. He was by temperament a natural member of the 'awkward squad.' Indeed, his superiors in my time were often desperately concerned about his health and excessive working hours and used various ploys to get him to participate in more relaxing aspects of community life. One of the best was putting him in charge of the Tuck Shop where he was able to deeply endear himself to boys in the wider scheme of their development and relax a little in the company of his community. He was certainly one of the most admired Lay Brothers in his time and an enduring Salesian model and mentor.

Bro. Joe was loved and respected by the Blaisdon villagers and was consulted by a wide range of local farmers and our rural neighbours. For those struggling to get by, Bro. Joe would often drop off the couple of hundredweight of potatoes, link box of manure for necessary garden grown vegetables or a trailer load of logs. In the depths of snow bound early winter mornings he was out and about clearing the roads with a combined scraper and brush, which he had devised and attached to his tractor. Once in a high rainfall Spring he saved two village cottages from flooding; one was 'Ma Lane's' next to the Old Mill House. He and Bro. Allen attached a pump, they had modified themselves from ex Army kit, to the power take-off of a tractor and worked through a deluge.

One day Fr Dan dropped off a couple of bags of spuds to Mrs Eggleton at the Tan House, which led to Bro. Joe delivering a trailer load of logs some time later. She came out of the house wearing a fur coat and spoke very poshly and miffed Bro. Joe when she indicated that he was supposed to stack them in an outhouse. He said: 'We only tip them off lady!' which he did. 'This is the way we always do it madam,' I said deferentially, wishing to support Bro. Joe. Mrs Eggleton said: 'As all you do is just tip them I will have to tip a labourer to do the job properly.' She directed the remark at me. This annoyed Bro. Joe even more as in situations like this one, he liked to be on top if it came to a play on words. He tore out of the drive at full speed with the tractor revving as loudly as possible and me almost swaying off the mudguard. Later that evening I earned a handy ten shillings for stacking the logs as she wished.

I last saw Bro. Joe at his Golden Jubilee celebration in Blaisdon and he had become very frail. He was one of the dozen or so men and women of whom I think lovingly each day. I shall remember him so long as I live. It is a precious privilege to have known him and to have been influenced by him."

1

2

3

1. Bro. Joe, Mark Pitt (age 4), Lawrence Stanton (1956).
2. Harvest Time with Father Dan Lucey & Brother Joe Carter.
3. Henry Mullaney taking milk churns to the top of the drive for collection.
4. Lawrence Stanton & Tony Brady feeding the pigs. Roger Allen is on the right with a visiting vagrant in Father Dan's old clothes.

6

5

7

5. Brother Joe Carter watching.
6. Stud Farm from the top of the drive.
7. Lionel Williams, an ex Stud Farm worker with a new born calf in 'Our Lady's Field.' The field behind is known as 'The Tinnings' and Blaisdon Church is visible in the distance.

STANLEY LODGE

Stanley Lodge sits high above Blaisdon Lane at the end of a long drive. It was built by the MacIvers in1908 to be the home of the Estate's Head Gamekeeper, the previous Gamekeeper's Cottage being on the slopes of Nottwood Hill.

In 1897, Mr George Rutter became the new Head Gamekeeper and in 1910, he took up residence in Stanley Lodge with his wife, Alice, and their children, May, the eldest and twins, William and Anne. They had previously lived on Nottwood Hill and the children were all born there. Anne later married David Warren and with son Leslie, lived at Belmont.

Top: Stanley Lodge. (L. Warren)
Above: George & Anne Rutter & son, William c1917. (D. Brown)
Left: William, Anne, George, Alice Rutter c 1925. (L. Warren)

When Mr Rutter retired, Mr William Buckett became the Estate Gamekeeper and moved into Stanley Lodge with his wife, Sarah, and sons, William (Jack) and Herbert (Bertie). When the Estate was sold in 1933, the Buckett family bought the house.

William was killed in a motorcycle accident, aged 24 years, in 1936. George, his father died on 23rd June 1947, aged 64, and Sarah, his mother, on 27th November 1973, aged 87.

Hilary Hawker recalls Bertie and his mother:

"Mrs Buckett had a dominant personality and Bertie always asked her advice before making decisions. He worked as an Insurance Agent for a few years. He became a small farmer, milking about 6 or 7 cows in a small cowshed. He never seemed to milk them all at once. He would maybe milk two or three in the afternoon and then take a walk down to the Red Hart. He would order himself a drink and pay for it, buy a bottle of Guinness for mother, pay for it, then buy a packet of crisps and pay for it. He never paid all at once in case Elsie Hogg, the Landlady, or whoever was on duty when he came in, didn't add his order up correctly and did him out of a few pence. He always drained his glass of beer 3 or 4 times saying the last drop was the sweetest.

He was an extrovert, singing and playing the piano in local Village Halls. He quite liked to be the centre of attention and enjoyed acting. He also played the organ in church, sometimes keeping us all waiting. During wet weather he would wear Wellingtons, as there was no road or pathway from his house down to the road.

Across the road from the top of the Stud Farm drive was a patch of land known as "Bertie's War Effort" where he grew vegetables and talked to the passers-by. He had a lonely life and craved attention but lacked confidence.

After his mother's death, Bertie had continued to live at Stanley Lodge until he could no longer look after himself. He became a resident at Westbury Court residential home and died in Gloucester Royal Hospital in 1987 aged 78 years."

Bertie Buckett dressed up in a village play.

Tony Brady also has memories of Bertie and his mother:

"Mrs Buckett regularly attended Sunday Worship. In summer she drove her pony, Crimson, and trap to St Michael and All Angels church, where Bertie was a Church Warden. Crimson was not a keen churchgoer and evaded Bertie's efforts to catch, bridle and harness her. He would run down to Stud Farm in a state of fluster and exasperation concerned that 'Mother will be late for church!' Father Dan Lucey sent me off to help him and that's how I first got to know him. A practical solution to the Sunday morning pre-church shenanigans was proposed by Father Dan; Crimson was stabled on Saturday evenings.

Bertie's main activity was managing the grazing and the general care of five milking cows. Reared by him from calves, they were complete pets. Bertie never drove his cows; they listened to his soft endearments and followed him about. One of them, named Buttercup, should have been called 'Buttock-Up' due to her habit of coming up behind you and lifting you off your feet.

During the winter, Bertie kept the cows in his byre, which stands to this day near the driveway to Stanley Lodge. Next to it, a handy tarpaulin covered haystack gradually got smaller as fodder was cut daily with a hay knife. The drinking water was taken from the Hall main pipe, running beneath the byre. Come Spring, the cows were turned out to the plum orchard that ran alongside the road and ended opposite the drive leading to Stud Farm. A familiar sight was Bertie riding his bicycle. Wearing his flat cap and long brown overall coat, his cows followed him in line to grazing he rented in meadows along Velthouse Lane below Blaisdon Hall and next to The Tan House.

For recreation he enjoyed Whist Drives and Vincent Shaw, Johnny Dunbar and I squeezed into his two door Austin car for trips to local village halls. Bertie was in his element and charmed all the women present with his amusing manner and banter. A regular prize-winner, 'Mother will be pleased,' was his inevitable acceptance response.

A close neighbour was Cyril Baggott who invariably took a short cut across Bertie's fields to a wooden shack where he lived alone on Nottwood Hill. Cyril could turn his hand to all the farming skills and milked Bertie's cows on the rare occasions that Bertie was laid up. Skeletal in appearance, he was the village Gravedigger. Once I remarked to Bertie that Cyril's face was like parchment. Bertie assured me it was as 'soft as shammy leather!' When I asked him how he knew that, he replied that he tended to Cyril's cuts and bruises. Cyril set snares in difficult thorny gaps, brambly covers and dense scratchy thickets. Trapped rabbits hung limp from his belt and ferrets wriggled in his pockets.

One scorching hot day, Bertie and I were discovered in each others arms by Albert Pithouse, Ted Walker and Cyril Baggott. Stripped to the waist, I was down a deep pit close to Bertie's byre digging to expose a leak Cyril had located by dousing. While Bertie was peering in to check on progress Buttercup came up behind him and nudged him in on top of me. Hanging on to each other in rising water, we were shouting for help. Bertie's cries for, 'Mother! Mother!' and his concern that he, 'will be late for tea,' went unheard. By chance, the tipsy trio came on the scene, having spotted Bertie's brown coat, which I was waving above ground like a flag on an upraised spade. No sooner was he freed, than Bertie bolted with Buttercup following him, leaving me to explain the embarrassing situation."

1. Bertie Buckett with his byre and haystack in the background.
(S. Waters)
2. Haymaking at Stanley Lodge.
L-R: Oscar Jones, ?, Bertie Buckett, Mr Bowkett.
(S. Jones)
3. Bertie Buckett & Daisy Price.
4. Bertie Buckett & friend on the banks of the River Severn.
5. Friesian Cow, name unknown.
6. The Cattle Byre near Stanley Lodge.
(E. Etherington)

ERTIE'S OAK

Where Blaisdon Lane passes the drive to Stanley Lodge, there is an old Oak Tree. **David Brown**, who lives at Stanley Lodge, says:

"Bertie would often stand under the Oak Tree watching the people and vehicles passing by. It is still known locally as Bertie Buckett's oak tree.

As there was no access up to Stanley Lodge the tree actually became a famous post-box! All Bertie's mail and papers were left in a box in the tree. The hole in the tree is still there to be seen.

This tree has been classed as a 'tree of significant interest.' It is not the oldest Oak in the Forest, but it is said to be one of the best crowns for a tree of that age. It appears in a book of the trees of the Forest and many people stop to photograph it when passing by."

STANLEY FIELDS

Stanley Fields with X marking approximate site of crash.
Stanley Cottages are visible through the trees in the distance.

On the 25th June 1945 an Oxford Plane No.NJ3117 was flying towards Blaisdon with two occupants on board. Flight Sgt E.M.G Howlett was the passenger and as it became apparent that the plane was coming down Flight Sergeant Howlett baled out over Ley Park and escaped with shock. He was taken to Blaisdon Hall and later picked up by the RAF uninjured.

The pilot of the plane was Flying Officer Kenneth Edmund Sutton Brown No.167177 Royal Air Force Volunteer Reserve. In an act of great bravery he stayed with the plane, it is believed to avoid Stanley Cottages which lay in its path. Flying with feet to spare over the cottages he crash landed in the field beyond. It was 10.10. in the morning and Flying Officer K.E.Sutton Brown died on impact. He was aged 21 and the son of John and Kathleen Marion Sutton Brown of Halfway Tree Jamaica. Flying Officer Kenneth Edmund Sutton Brown's funeral took place in Haresfield Parish Church on Friday June 29th 1945, as this was the nearest church to his base at Morton Valence Airfield.

The pending crash was witnessed by the children in the playground of the village school and Doris Bowkett and neighbour Frank Bullock were in their gardens at Stanley Cottages at the time of impact.

The word that a plane had crashed soon went round and the villagers rushed to the scene of the devastation. Among them Brian and Peter Hayward from "Iona" who came down the lane on their bikes. Those that were there at the scene will never forget the smell of the burning oil.

Officials from the M.O.D. were sent to the scene to keep guard over the wreckage. An officer took statements from the witnesses. It was whilst Mrs Edie Dowding was giving a statement that Mrs Buckett, who owned the field, which at the time had been full of corn, ran to the scene with arms waving and stamped her feet demanding compensation for the destruction of her corn, which she said was grown for the country. The Officer taking the statements asked her to wait her turn and he would speak to her when he had dealt with the other witnesses, at which point she stormed off! Mrs Dowding from Stanley Cottages supplied drinks and refreshment for the guards who had to stay at the site for a number of days to guard the wreckage.

On the Friday following the accident the two guards watching over the crash site were Rex ? from Coleford near Bath and Gladstone Sparks who was from Jamaica. Much to the delight of the village girls they accepted an invitation to the Friday night Social at the Village School. Mr Rickett, as usual, was on the piano and Rex and Gladstone were on the dance floor showing the locals the art of the Jitterbug. Gladstone possibly had his Wellingtons on! Needless to say the girls were vying for a dance with these two handsome visitors. The young men appreciated the kindness of Mrs Dowding and she received a letter from the parents of Gladstone Sparks to that effect.

This was wartime and life went on regardless of the fact that someone had given up his life to save others in our village. Those involved at the time will never forget this young man's bravery.

During the war another plane came down along the Flaxley Road, this was thought to be a Hurricane. The Pilot baled out and came down in Flaxley Wood. Another plane came down near Zion Chapel in Little London. Mr Copner Senior was working there at the time mending an engine. The pilot was a South African, he baled out and landed in a tree near Flaxley Abbey.

Grave of Flying Officer K.E.Sutton Brown in Haresfield Churchyard.

The stone reads:

Flying Officer
K.E.Sutton Brown
Pilot
Royal Air Force
25th June 1945
Age 21

Until the daybreak
And the shadows flee away.

Airspeed Oxford 1,
type of plane involved in the crash.

1 Stanley Cottages

Two adjoining cottages lie above the road, opposite the entrance to Ley Park. They were built in 1913 and were originally part of the Blaisdon Estate. No.1, on the left, was home to Mr and Mrs Edgar Dowding and their daughter Dolly (born 1910) and niece Margaret. Sadly Edgar died in the First World War and is remembered on the village War Memorial.

Dolly married Tom Green at Blaisdon Church on the 30th November 1940 and continued to live at No 1 Stanley Cottages. Tom came from the hamlet of Greenbottom, near Flaxley, where he was brought up by his adoptive parents, the Gardners. They had five children, Irene, Edgar, Shirley, Margaret & Ashley. All the children went to Blaisdon School. The family would often be seen on most Sundays as Mr and Mrs Green would bring their children on a walk through the village.

Tragically, Edgar was killed on his motorbike on the 22nd September 1966 at the age of 17 years. He is buried in Blaisdon Churchyard. Dolly's health failed and ***Ashley Green*** says that his mother died in 1965 when he was 12 years old.

> 1. No1 Stanley Cottages. (S. Waters)
> 2. Tom & Dolly Green.
> 3. The Green children.
> 4. Lt-Rt: Irene, Margaret, Edgar, Ashley, Shirley Green.
> 5. Edgar Green in Front Garden of 1 Stanley Cottages.

2 STANLEY COTTAGES

Elizabeth Etherington had the privilege of visiting Fred Matthews and his wife Margaret in their home in Gloucester shortly before Fred died.

Fred Matthews recalled life in Blaisdon:

"In 1928, Charles Matthews, my father, was a farmhand who came to live at No.2 Stanley Cottages with his wife Lucy, me and my siblings Doris, Eric and Edna.

Farmhands only had work contracts for four years at a time. They would meet at Barton Fair in Gloucester Market to get other employment when they had completed their four years. Together with my brother and sisters, I attended Blaisdon School. Each year we would walk down to the Halt to catch a train to Grange Court where a special carriage was reserved for us on a train to Barry Island for our annual outing. I thoroughly enjoyed the Christmas, Easter and especially the Harvest Festival, which was the highlight of the year, when we all took vegetables and supplies to the church. The Sunday School outing would be a day trip to Nottwood Hill for a picnic.

I remember fishing in the stream, which runs by Hinders Corner, it was full of trout. The way to catch such trout was to fill a Gupsill Brown 2 cwt sack with house bricks and the trout would then swim straight into the sack, after which I would take them home for supper!"

Above:
No 2 Stanley Cottages. (S. Waters)
Opposite:
1. Charles Matthews with son, Eric & grandson, Robin.
2. Fred Matthews, age 7.
3. Charles & Lucy Matthews c1960s.
4. Charles & Lucy Matthews with members of their family c1949.
5. Wedding of Fred & Margaret Matthews, 24th June 1944.
Charles & Lucy Matthews are back left.
Fred's sister, Edna (Girlie) was Bridesmaid.

1

2

3

4

5

In 1932 Mr and Mrs Matthews and their children moved on to a farm in Boddington, having spent four happy years in Blaisdon. Doris Married Frank Brown and they lived at Vectis during the 1950s and 60s.

The visit to see Fred and Margaret was prompted by a newspaper cutting sent by a member of the MacIver Family regarding 'Primrose Day.' It featured a photo of a family of four children from Blaisdon picking primroses. Fred remembered the occasion well and where the photo was taken, just past Hinders Lane.

When Benjamin Disraeli died on 19th April 1881, Queen Victoria sent floral wreaths of primroses, his favourite flowers, to be placed on his coffin. Following this, each year children would collect primroses and, on 19th April, they would be worn as Beaconsfield Buttonholes, named

Top: Edna, Doris, Fred & Eric Matthews gathering primroses.
Above: Primrose League brooch worn by
Mrs Dinah Etherington.

after the Lordship that Disraeli held from 1876. In 1883, the Primrose League was formed to foster Disraeli's conservative approach and fight for the right of women to vote. Colin MacIver was instrumental in the formation of a Local branch of the League and was appointed its Ruling Councillor. The League existed until 2004.

In 1931, Eliza Rees moved to Stanley Cottages with her family. Her daughter, **Barbara Taylor** (nee Rees) tells of their time in Blaisdon:

"My mother, Eliza Rees, having lost her husband, arrived in Blaisdon with four children to stay with her sister and brother-in-law at Stanley Cottages. My Aunt and Uncle's name was Millen. I was a baby and there was my sister Mary and brothers William and John.

Being so young I remember very little of the early years. I do remember the people next door were Mr and Mrs Savage and their son Arthur. They left and we moved into the cottage. This was before I started school aged four. My Aunt and Uncle moved to Adsett around this time as Uncle Chris was moved at work.

We went to school in Blaisdon where children came from Flaxley and Northwood Green to attend this school. We all also went to Sunday School and Church every Sunday. My brother William pumped the Church organ for a time and my brother John took over from him until he left school. My mother also cleaned the church and school.

My brother John had a truck made from a wooden box on wheels pulled by rope which he loved to take to Ley Park to collect wood for the fire.

I must have been about five or six when the Catholic Brothers came to Blaisdon. They lived at Blaisdon Hall and they also bought Stud Farm which had been run by Mr Nash. This was where we got our milk from and Stanley Farm was where we got drinking water for the family. The pump still stands there to this day. I believe the name of the people who ran Stanley Farm was 'House' or 'Howse'. Mr Howells and his family came when the Catholics took over Stanley Farm. We spent a lot of time together as children playing in the barns and sailing a raft that Brian Howells made, on the pond which was opposite the farm house. The pond is filled in now. Our mothers became great friends.

As my mother was a widow the Brothers from the Hall were very kind to us, often leaving a rabbit or fruit and vegetables for us on the doorstep. Also, in return for a cheaper rent, my mother washed the Brothers shirts and starched their white collars.

Mr Philips from Huntley brought our bread in a horse drawn covered wagon.

Mr Roberts worked in the wood in Ley Park. He was the charcoal burner. He built a wigwam of timber logs covered with turf to keep the fire in and burnt logs inside, slowly so it became charcoal. He had to stay to watch the fire so he built a smaller wigwam of logs for a shelter for himself.

I also remember the roadmen, Mr Bishop and his colleague who would walk over from Northwood Green and spend their day tidying up the verges using a billhook for the grass edges and a long stick with a crook for the hedges. They would sit down on the verge and eat their packed

Herbert & Gertrude Bowkett with dog, Tessa, outside No 2 Stanley Cottages.

lunches at the appropriate time!

When I was 9, we moved to Longhope. My brothers both went to London to work when they left school."

Herbert and Gertrude Bowkett and their children moved to No.2 Stanley Cottages during the winter of 1937/38. **Rosa and Doris Bowkett** recollect their time in Blaisdon:

"Our mother, Gertrude, was the sister of Mr Ivor and Oscar Jones, who have featured in the book. Our parents had 4 children, Ivy, Ronald, Rosa and Doris. Sadly, we lost our brother, Ronald, in 1942, when he was killed in the Second World War, when he was shot down over Dunkirk. He is remembered on the Village War Memorial. In June

1945 the family saw another horrific plane crash, which brought back the recent loss of Ronald. The plane missing the chimneys on the house only by feet came crashing down in the field behind, killing the pilot.

We remember the winter of 1947 when the snow lay deep all around. Mr Bowkett set off with old tennis rackets tied to his feet to climb over Nottwood and into Little London in order to collect the bread for his family and neighbours from Mr Bradley, the baker. He had a sack full of hot crusty bread and started on the return trip. Unfortunately the ascent back over Nottwood proved too much and he fell into a drift of snow, losing his rackets in the process! There was no help at hand so Mr Bowkett lay there for several hours until he was able to crawl home with his load of bread! As a result of this unfortunate episode he developed pneumonia and was off work for several weeks.

The family used to enjoy a walk along the Velthouse Lane on a Sunday evening to The Plough Inn in Longhope where they would meet other family members to have a drink. However, on the return journey home, after dark, along the lane they would collect glowworms and despatch them into the rim of Dad's trilby, thus providing light along the dark lane to Stanley Cottage.

Our Parents both died in the seventies and are buried together in Blaisdon Churchyard."

Top:
Gertrude, Herbert, Rosa Bowkett &, sitting, Katherine Jones
(Gertrude's mother).
Right:
Herbert & Gertrude Bowkett with daughters, Rosa & Doris.

STANLEY FARM

Above: Stanley Farm C1950.
Below: Original Water Pump.

Ursula Howells' family lived at Stanley Farm:

"My father, Charles Howells brought us to Stanley Farm in January 1935 to work for the Salesian School of Agriculture at Blaisdon Hall. The family consisted of my mother, Elizabeth, children James, Evelyn (Maidie), Brian, Ursula (me) and granddad Parsons.

In 1938, while at RAF Cranwell, James died, aged 18 with complications following a mastoid operation and Mum died in 1940 a few weeks after giving

birth to Elizabeth (Betty). Her best friend, Mrs Rees took Betty and looked after her. This became a permanent arrangement so she grew up with two families, foster in Longhope and natural in Blaisdon, but fully aware of the circumstances. Maidie looked after the rest of us, though in poor health herself. She married in 1948. My brother, Brian, left farming to join the Life Guards.

For a while, during the war, Mrs Gatt and Mrs Milanta from Gibraltar, lived in the end part of the house with their children. I believe they returned to London.

Stanley was allied to Stud Farm but had milking cows, sheep, pigs and two working carthorses. We were surrounded by orchards plus hay and cornfields where we local children would help with the harvesting. I remember Bro. Pat O'Connor teaching a couple of us to drive the tractor but, sadly, my harvesting ceased when Dad decided that the Hall boys were becoming aware that I was a girl!

If Dad brought the cows in for early morning milking with his cap off, we knew that there were mushrooms for breakfast.

The Infants room at school had little canvas beds for children to have an afternoon nap and small bottles of milk were warmed in the hearth. In the big room, as well as the Three Rs etc, we learnt to knit balaclavas, socks and gloves for soldiers (on 4 needles!).

We had such freedom then. Out all day making dens from woven hazel sticks, climbing and swinging on fallen trees, ball games etc and in winter, skating on the frozen shallow pool behind Blaisdon Halt. Mrs Sharkey was the station-mistress and was near our home one day picking blackberries for market. She left two full baskets one side of the hedge whilst picking on the other, obviously forgetting how inquisitive cows are and in this case, destructive!!

The Friday evening social club at the school with Mr Ricketts playing dance music on the piano and occasionally, Bertie Buckett singing 'Seven years with the wrong woman' and 'The little shirt my mother made for me.' We enjoyed dance lessons there on Thursday evening when Miss Whittard, a dance teacher, retired to the village. I remember excellent concerts at Blaisdon Hall with Gilbert & Sullivan operas, Irish dancing & brass music.

A plane crash behind Stanley Cottages caused much excitement. Sadly, the pilot did not survive. One of the men guarding the wreckage found time to amaze us children with his pencil and paper puzzles. The things one remembers.

The tramp, who walked the three counties with his pram, would call occasionally for a bunch of mint. He'd already received his new potatoes etc. elsewhere. I believe he had regular 'supply points' along the way.

In 1953, Dad died, I left and I believe the house was sold. Later, following the subsidy paid to farmers for ploughed land, I noticed that the orchards were no more. Trees had been felled, hedges grubbed up and ponds filled in. It resembled a prairie, soon to be covered with blackcurrant bushes to supply 'Ribena.' I wondered what had become of all the birds and other wildlife abundant there and felt a great sense of loss. However, I guess it was done in the interest of progress."

Above:
A pair of child's shoes found hidden in a fireplace, by Jill Rodgett, who lives at Stanley Farm. It was common practice to hide shoes when building houses, for good luck.
(E. Etherington)

Opposite:
1. Charles & Elizabeth Howells, 1919.
Charles served in the Gloucestershire Regiment.
2. Lft-Rt: Evelyn, Ursula, Brian & Betty (October 1981).
3. James Henry Howells (2nd from Right) at RAF Cranwell.
4. James Howells at RAF Cranwell.
5. Grandad Parsons (Elizabeth Howells' father).

1

2

3

4

5

LEY PARK

The track opposite Stanley Cottages passes across fields before entering the expanse of Ley Park Woods. Many generations of Blaisdon folk have enjoyed walks through these woods and, in springtime, bunches of wild daffodils would be taken home to appreciative mothers.

The more enterprising youngsters were known to sell bunches at the side of the main road, though this practice has ceased as people have become more aware of the need to preserve the environment. The woods are now managed and used by a local pheasant shoot.

Above:
View along track towards Ley Park Woods.
Left:
Pathway through the woods.
(E. Etherington)

RICK HOUSE FARM

Further along Blaisdon Lane is Brick House Farm. At the time Blaisdon Estate was sold, it had been split into 2 dwellings and today it is again 2 semi-detached cottages.

Tom and Maggie Board and their son David moved to Brick House Farm around 1936. The house had been empty for sometime after the 1st World War as no lettings happened at that time. Their son David was about 6 or 7 years old at the time.

Mrs Board is remembered for her Whist Drives which she would hold in the Village School and when that proved too small, she moved the venue up to Blaisdon Hall. She would raise around £1000 per year for charities, particularly cancer charities. Again this was a good example of the villagers coming together as they would meet up in the School and enjoy their games of whist.

Tom died in 1965 and Maggie died aged 81 in 1988.

Top:
Brick House Farm.
Left:
Mrs Maggie Board. (A. Roberts)
Right:
Mr Tom Board. (R. Hayward)

IONA

Iona lies at the top end of the village. It is the first of the four houses on the left as you leave the village. It was built for Stan Hamblin the postmaster at Huntley.

From 1939 to 1956, Iona was the home of Mr and Mrs John Hayward and their children Bryan, Peter, Pauline, Rachel and Lesley. Three of the children were born at the Dilke Hospital so are true Foresters.

Bryan and Peter went to Zion School and then moved to Huntley where they were taught by Miss Bird, Miss Knight and Miss Lane. The girls all attended Blaisdon C. of E. School under the care of Mrs Smith and Miss Priest.

Peter Hayward has many fond memories of Blaisdon:

"I remember the fish man calling on a Friday morning and the onion man during the season. This was a man of Italian origin. There were a number of Italian Prisoners of War in the area at the time and many were employed locally. Charlie Green was the baker from Huntley who delivered his bread by horse and cart and then moved on to a Trojan Van. The bread was delivered anytime between ten in the morning and ten at night! Uncle Alfred Hayward always came annually at springtime with a bucket full of elvers.

Another caller to Iona was the local Tramp. My mother always made him a pot of custard, gave him some clothing and then sent him on his way until the next visit!

Springtime was a welcome season for daffodil picking. We children would congregate at Iona and a morning would be spent picking daffodils from a wooded area south of

Mr Board's and Mr Nelmes' farms; we children kept its location very much a secret. The area was only known to the Haywards and our neighbours, the Allen family who lived across the valley on Nottwood Hill. After picking, we would tie the daffodils in bunches with binder twine, don old clothes and, looking very poor with twine tied around our middles, proceed to Hinders Corner to sell to passing cars (one car about every twenty minutes). The daffodils were sold for one penny per bunch. If we liked the customer we would throw in an extra bunch. All this was done without the knowledge of our parents but we did give them the money.

Blackberry picking was a real family day out, and they would eventually be sold to Mr Walton at Hinders Corner. Much to our annoyance, Mr Walton would eat them as he was weighing them and he was frugal in his payment! We would also pick hips and haws and go plum picking for Mr Knight of Huntley; that was an exciting family commitment with much horseplay for the children.

Summer months were spent harvesting at Board's farm (opposite Iona). Piling stooks and loading trailers for the Fordson Tractor that had iron wheels to pull the trailers to the farm and, then, making the hayrick. At Board's farm Bryan and I learnt how to hand milk the cows. They had a farm dog black collie/labrador cross, called Sweep. We adopted him and he became the best rabbiter in the area. Most weekends Sweep would catch 3 or 4 rabbits for us, all for the table and the skins would fetch 6d each in Gloucester. Sweep would wait each day at the top of the lane for us to come home from school, much to the annoyance of the occupants of the farm. A quick whistle from us boys and the dog would turn up from nowhere!

Major Carrigan who had spent years in Africa, but then lived in the end house, gave us African spears to use when we went rabbiting. Needless to say we weren't as successful as Sweep!

The Hayward Children.
Back: Bryan & Peter.
Front: Rachel, Pauline (kneeling) & Lesley.

Another form of entertainment for us children was spent cutting up loads of newspapers and setting a paper trail across the fields, finishing with a picnic on Nottwood Hill.

Like most of the boys in the village Bryan and I took our turn at pumping the church organ. We would stand in for Norman Penny when he didn't turn up. Mr Roberts from Northwood Green was the organist at the time and to avoid the boys falling asleep during the sermon he would bring them to the front to sit in a pew and pay attention to the vicar. We were also part of the church choir and a member of the bell ringer team. I used to stand on a plum box to ring and I remember once when Norman Penny lost control and went up with the bell. Many a stay was

Top Left:
Hayward Family on Peter's 21st birthday.
Standing: Bryan, Pauline, Peter.
Sitting: Rachel, Lesley.

Above:
Bryan, Peter, Rachel, Pauline, Lesley Hayward
c1953.

Left:
Kathleen & John Hayward (1960).

broken during our time in the belfry. Mr Joe Martin was the Tower Captain and he turned out many a good ringer.

One night, after bell ringing practice, the team were invited back to Iona for supper. We set off on our bikes from the church but, on approaching Stanley Corner, an apparition appeared in the middle of the lane, at which point Bryan and I slammed on our brakes causing chaos for those following. After picking ourselves up and retrieving our bikes they returned home to Iona eager to tell what we had seen. The Rev. and Mrs Lane had also been invited to supper, but on hearing our tale the Reverend dismissed it and insisted that no such thing could have happened. However the following week Mr Pensom from Huntley also stated that he had seen a ghost in Hinders Lane and was so afraid that Mr Hayward had to take him home in his Morris 8 as he was too frightened to go alone.

Bryan and I were also handbell ringers and one snow-bound winter we were walking along the railway line from Woodgreen to Blaisdon Halt in order to get to the Flaxley Lane to ring at the Abbey when, along with Mr Martin, we all had to slide down the railway bank to avoid an approaching train. It frightened the life out of us but we made it to the Abbey and rang for Sir Lance and Lady Crawley Boevey.

One Sunday evening as we drove to Church and parked our car on the roadside, Father Dan from the Stud Farm ran into the side of it with his tractor. On seeing this Cecil Beard rang the police, unbeknown to my parents. Later that evening, the Police arrived at Iona and Mum, the driver, was later taken to Littledean Court and had to pay a fine for parking without lights. She paid the fine in three-penny pieces!

Some of the best summer events in the village were the trips to Weston-Super-Mare and Clevedon. We were always last to be picked up by Cottrells Coaches with their wooden bench seats but first off on return!

Christmas parties at Flaxley Abbey were always exciting. Sir Lance and Lady Crawley Boevey invited the village children where we were entertained with a lovely tea in the refectory and then games in the banquet room where every child was given a present from under the huge Christmas tree.

Many activities such as old time dancing and whist drives were held at the village hall. Mrs Smith the headmistress played the piano and Barry Davis played the accordion for all musical events. Sporting events were organised by the Fathers at Blaisdon Hall, cricket and football etc.

On a Sunday morning it was a common sight to see as many as fifty or more boys walk by, with many recognised as our sporting friends, they were the residents of Blaisdon Hall.

I remember the day that the plane came down in Bertie Buckett's field at the back of Stanley Farm. We saw the flames and ran across the fields, but on arrival there was nothing left except a huge black area and the smell of burnt oil. Later, when the Brabazon made its maiden flight from Bristol, the six engine aircraft flew over Iona, much to the delight of all who witnessed it."

FERNDALE

The next house is Ferndale, now known as Green Court. Before moving into Ferndale, Lewis Brooks and his parents lived next door at Oakfield. It was whilst living at Oakfield that Mrs Brooks helped dig the 60 foot well in the garden. We are told that Mrs Brooks was lowered down by her husband Fred as she dug her way through the soil. He would then pull her back to the surface along with the soil she had extracted. What an amazing thing to have done. It is understood that the bricks for lining the well were barrelled down from Mitcheldean. Peter Hayward says that all the residences in that area had their own well for drinking water.

Lewis Brooks recalls his memories of living in Blaisdon Lane:

"My Mother was Spanish, she met my Father when he was in the Army in Gibraltar. I was born in the Dilke Hospital on 23rd June 1943. A builder from Mitcheldean built the bungalow, we had no running water, gas or electricity. We had an outside toilet and used newspaper instead of toilet paper. We bred rabbits and kept pigs and chickens.

When I was about 4 years old we moved next door to the house called Ferndale. Mum used to make rugs from rabbit skins. Mr Stephens the butcher would come and kill one of our pigs and we would have two sides of bacon hanging on the stairwell. Mr and Mrs Pugh moved into Oakfield and the Regan family lived next door to them in the end bungalow, followed by Colonel Carrigan. The Colonel used to shoot rabbits on Mr Board's farm and I would sometimes go with him. I spent some time at Brickhouse Farm and on one occasion David Board sat me on a bull in the cow shed.

My mother's sister, Kathleen Malanta lived at Stanley Farm Cottage with her son Joe (Pep). Joe used to play football at the Salesian School.

My first school was Huntley. Mum would take me on a

push bike, the one in the photograph. After a short time she found it better to take me to Blaisdon School where the headmistress was Mrs Smith. On one occasion we were stopped by the Police because there was not a proper seat for me to sit on the back of the bike!

Auntie Kathleen and Joe moved to London in 1949 and we moved to Mitcheldean in 1950, where I still live. I would sometimes visit the Red Hart when Mr and Mrs Hogg & John Dunbar kept it."

3

4

2

1

6

5

1. Mr & Mrs Brooks.
2. Lewis Brooks & mum on bike.
3. Lewis Brooks & Joe Malanta.
4. Mr & Mrs Brooks with Lewis.
5. Lewis Brooks 1947.
6. Lewis with his dog, Touser.

AKFIELD

Percy and Beatrice Pugh together with their daughter Betty, came to live at Oakfield in 1946, their daughter, Joan, having already left home in her teens. Percy bought Oakfield from Mr & Mrs Brooks who then moved next door to live at Ferndale.

Betty Jones (nee Pugh) gave the following information:

"Before coming to Blaisdon, Percy had spent his working life on farms around Longhope, their former home being at No.2 Church Cottages. Percy originally worked for Mr Tom Birch at Court Farm Longhope and when he retired and sold the farm, Percy went to work at Jack Constance's farm. When Jack could no longer afford to employ Percy, he went to work at RAF Quedgeley in the Stores where he was happy even though he had worked on the land all his life.

I attended East Dean Grammar School after which I worked at W.H.Smith Wholesalers in Gloucester travelling on the bus along with fellow villagers including Rosa Bowkett, Cedric Etherington, and Peter Hayward.

In 1953 I married Cyril Jones from Popes Hill. The wedding took place in Blaisdon Church officiated by the Rev. Dennis Lane. After the wedding we set up home in Greenbottom and had three children, Susan, Alan and Stephen. Cyril worked for the Forestry Commission all his working life and Eastville in Greenbottom is still the family home.

The family were regular churchgoers and Percy was a sidesman at Blaisdon Church. Beatrice worked at Blaisdon school in the kitchen helping Mrs Doris Phelps. At that time the school dinners were actually cooked on the school premises. She was also a home help in the village, helping Mrs Goddard at the Post Office and also Mrs Tom Green at Stanley Cottages when she was very ill. I can remember the day when Edgar Green was killed on his motorbike whilst getting fish and chips from Mitcheldean.

Percy was 64 when he died in 1969 after a short illness and Beatrice went on living at Oakfield for another three years after which she sold and moved to Orchard Close in Mitcheldean in 1972. She was happy there and lived until she was 86. Percy and Beatrice are buried together in Blaisdon Churchyard."

1. Betty Pugh with her father, Percy Pugh, on her wedding day.
2. Beatrice Pugh on Betty's wedding day.
3. Coronation Day 1953:
Uncle Harry, Percy, Beatrice Pugh & Mrs Nicholls (friend).

1. Gwyn, Auntie Tot, Grampy Pugh, Percy, Beatrice Pugh,
plus Jack Constance's Tractor at Oakfield.
2. Joan Pugh 1950.
3. Percy & Beatrice Pugh with Betty & grandchildren, Susan,
Alan & Stephen Jones.
4. Rev. Lane & Betty's bridesmaid, Marion.

GLAYMAR

The last house on the left is Glaymar or, as it was known prior to William and Mary Hatch moving in, Warfield. The present owners Sue and Mark Oldham have discovered that there was no building on the plot in 1924.

After the Regan family, Colonel Carrigan lived there during the fifties. He was popular with the younger generation in view of his past war experiences and collection of African weapons. Joey Warlow remembers him cycling to the Red Hart for a drink. Whilst he was enjoying his drink she was allowed to ride on his bike up and down the lane.

In 1953, newly weds Mr and Mrs John Crompton moved into Warfield. In 1957 it was sold to William and Mary Hatch. The house got its new name when Mary Hatch's mother, Gladys bought it for her daughter Mary and her husband William Hatch. Glaymar is a combination of Mary and Gladys.

Bill Hatch kept pigs and sheep on the property and also rented land as caravan pitches. Old railway carriages were used to house the pigs etc.

The house was recently demolished and replaced by a much larger brick built house, still named Glaymar.

Top: Glaymar (M. & S. Oldham).
Centre: Aerial view showing many outbuildings.
Bottom: Lft-Rt, Lilly Hayward, Bill Hatch, Mary Hatch, Jane Board, Mrs Board. (R. Hayward)

HINDERS FARM

Hinders Farm is the final house along Blaisdon Lane, sitting at the junction with the Huntley to Longhope Road. The parish boundary is marked by the stream that runs across the lane and through its garden, putting the farmhouse in Huntley parish. However, it has always seemed to be part of Blaisdon. Mr Nelmes allowed generations of Blaisdon folk to leave their bicycles in his outbuildings while they went to school and work, knowing they would be safely there on their return.

Hinders Farm from the road.
(S. Waters)

Left: Bill Nelmes with granddaughter, Pamela at Hillview, Hinders Lane, 1957.
Above: Pamela Pensom with bike bought with plum picking money.

His granddaughter, **Pamela Weaver (nee Pensom)**, remembers her grandfather with fondness:

"My grandfather, Bill Nelmes, lived at Hinders Farm, near the top of Blaisdon Lane. Most villagers and older schoolchildren would have left their bikes in his shed alongside a hay cart while they caught the bus to school or work.

He was a true gentleman and a real dying breed even in those days. He always wore a hat; he always carried a stick and would tuck it under his arm if he were in hurry, or lighting a cigarette, which he smoked in a holder.

My grandfather always went to the livestock market on Monday. The market was then situated in the town just across the road from the railway station. He would have tea in the Cadena Café, which was in Eastgate Street and in his pocket he always had an apple, which he had shone up to give to the waitress.

Blaisdon to me was somewhere to do nice things. Like the village fete, visiting friends, going to see Brother Dan at Blaisdon Hall and tap dancing at the school with Miss Whittard. I lived up Hinders Lane (opposite Blaisdon Lane) with my two brothers and we spent a lot of our school days helping grandfather. He grew a lot of fruit trees and it was our job to pick all the plums and apples, which he sold to Mr Walton. He was a stickler for picking fruit trees clean and my brother Burton would be sent back up the ladder if he had missed a single plum.

In January, I would pick snowdrops on Sunday afternoon and tie them into little bunches with string, put them in a box and my grandfather would take them with him on Monday mornings to be sold in Mr Don Meadows' fruit and vegetable shop in Westgate Street. My grandfather lived till 1971, when he was 89.

Blaisdon and my grandfather hold very special memories for me and it is a lovely village I still love to visit."

1. William Nelmes in Gloucester on market day.
2. Pamela, Burton & Roger Pensom.
3. Ouside Hinders Farm; Pamela with her mother, Dolly, daughter, Belinda, and Granddad, Bill Nelmes.

Plum Picking in the 1950s.
Left to right: Mrs Hopkins (on ladder), Mrs Jones, children unknown, Horace Pensom (on trailer & in charge), Pam Pensom (sitting on plum box), Bell Sysum, Mr & Mrs Sysum, Doreen Jones, Mrs Hyett (lady with hat), Mrs Clifford (on ladder), Burton Pensom, Barbara & Sheila Lord, Lady up ladder ?, Boys ?, Mrs Clayson.

W. A. BRADLEY

The Shop, Little London, c1960.
Cottrells bus approaching. Sign offers plums at 2/6.
(G. Pedley)

Turning left out of Blaisdon Lane and a short distance up the hill, is the hamlet of Little London. On the left hand side is the house that was, until the 1960s, a village shop. Until the age of the motor car, many villagers depended on travelling tradesmen and the local shop for their food and household goods. Groceries for Blaisdon and Nottwood Hill families were delivered by W.A.Bradley & Sons by van every week. The order for the following week was written down in a book and handed to Ted Clayson, who drove the van. A visit to the shop meant, for most, a long walk along Blaisdon Lane and up the main road or over the top of Nottwood Hill.

Doug Allen who lived near the shop records his memories:

"I first entered the shop around 1938 as a four year old and was to use it regularly fetching and carrying groceries for mother. We, myself and other Zion schoolchildren – used to hang around there on the way home, sometimes being able to buy a sherbet dip or other sweets.

One day, having sixpence, I decided to buy a penknife from the card of knives on display, as I loved to whittle sticks. I immediately cut my left hand forefinger to the bone. The one inch scar is still with me.

The shop when I first knew it was by then owned by Mr Williams. The drapers section of the shop, the main centre and right hand side were closed at that time and only the section on the left was in use until the shop closed around 1960. Inside was a long pine counter on the left running the full length of the shop with various machines bolted to it, ie. bacon slicer, grinders etc. All loose purchases such as flour and sugar were expertly packed into brown or white paper bags by the men who served. At that time they all wore brown coats as far as I remember.

315

Every type of hardware was sold and could be delivered by Mr Bob Grabham or Mr Ted Clayson. Mr Frank Hill also served with Mr Williams. I remember him standing on top of the shop steps waiting for us children to walk by from Zion school and telling us to tell our mothers that they had bananas in stock. We were promptly sent back to the shop with sixpence for a bunch, the first since the beginning of the war."

Above:
W. A. Bradley & Sons c 1905.
Adults:
W. A. Bradley, Lizzy Bradley.
Children:
Nancy, Oswald & Bradley Armstrong.
Bradley was killed at the end of the 1st World War.
(G. Pedley).

Left:
Ted Clayson & niece, Cissie, c1950.

Nottwood Hill

The small hamlet of Nottwood Hill is part of Blaisdon Parish, the Hill overlooking the village. Its name is subject to many variations, indeed the 2 signs at the top of Chapel Lane cannot agree. To some, it is Nottwood, to others Nottswood and earlier variations include Notts Hill and Natswood. It is reached by turning into Chapel Lane just after passing Bradley's shop or by paths through the woods from Blaisdon.

Mr E. Hopkins wrote about the Hill's history in 1976:

"The first inhabitants of the Hill came from across the Severn some two hundred years ago. Small in numbers, they settled on the Hill making it their home. It must have been common land in those days, as there is record of them being driven off. After a period of time they started to build themselves cottages with stone quarried from the common, cutting timber for rafters and beams from nearby woods. They then fenced in a small piece of land and thus created their own homes. The families were mostly related to each other. The men worked in the woods timber felling or on the farms. The women also went out working on the land to help out with their meagre income. A woman's pay was about two or three pence a day and a quart of cider, which they often saved to take home to their husbands.

As time went on some of them fenced in more land enabling them to grow fruit and vegetables along with other things, which they took to Gloucester by donkey and cart to sell. Two or three of the families prospered enough to purchase a couple of horses and for many years earned a living coal hauling from the Forest of Dean or timber hauling from the nearby woods. In my own memory of these people quaint customs prevailed among them, many of the menfolk bore the name of William or Bill for short. Through inter-relationships many also had the same surnames. There were several uncles, nephews and sons besides parents bearing the same names. To make matters easier their names were prefaced with their calling, such as: Besom Bill, Butcher Bill, Roadman Bill, Hedger Bill and so on.

The Blaisdon Estate decided to take in the common land and fence it off and thus claim it as their property. There has never been any established owner of Nottwood Hill Common but doubtless the Estate thought if they used

An Aerial view of Nottwood Hill.
The road from Longhope to Huntley is at the bottom of the picture.
Chapel Lane can be seen passing up the hill from the bottom right corner.

force and social standing they would succeed. Men, horses and wagons were sent to put up the fencing but at nightfall the cottagers went out and ripped it all down again. For a time this went on until the Estate realised they would not win, conceded victory for the cottagers and withdrew. There is no doubt that if the cottagers had not persisted in their fight the common land as we know it now would have been lost for good.

Every cottage built had its own pigs-cot where it was customary for one or two pigs to be fattened for bacon. Small weaners would be purchased from a local farmer, and then fed on boiled swill from the garden along with meal from the shop at Little London. One custom was to have the meal on credit until the pigs were fit to kill, and then the shop would take half of the meat to pay for the meal. It was a very heart warming sight to see one or two sides of bacon hanging from the beams of a cottage as well as the jars of home cured lard on their shelves.

Although times were hard, as there was very little money about, the cottagers lived a contented life, making do with their lot with none of the assistance people get today. Some brought up big families of healthy children in those small cottages, which only boasted four rooms, two bedrooms and two downstairs. One small cottage accommodated a family of fourteen children who all grew up into strong healthy citizens. Spring water was a considerable distance away from most of them and they would fetch it with a yoke and two buckets.

It must be remembered there was no money paid out to families in those days or any medical treatment or assistance whatever. For childbirth, there was only the help of neighbours and in later years, a midwife from Blaisdon. If the event happened at night, the only light was a candle or a small single paraffin lamp. It was the same with weddings and funerals, the people involved had to walk to the church, usually down through woods. Four strong men would carry the deceased on their shoulders with the mourners in a long procession behind.

At one period there was religious revival in the district and a small chapel was built at the foot of Nottwood Hill. It became very popular. People from a large area attended the services. Newcomers were baptized in the brook. It soon became apparent that larger premises were needed and eventually a new chapel was built at Hopes Hill called Zion.

Of the families who first settled here, most of them have dispersed or left the district, only a handful remain. It is one of the very few places in this country that has remained unspoiled or ravaged by modern developers."

Brenda Brain writes fondly of Nottwood Hill:

"Her form was draped in mostly bracken with a few patches of grass and brightly coloured heathers, the single tracks trodden down by the sheep and the occasional fox ran like veins over her. The manmade gashes were healed by her determination, after all, she had experienced this many times, and she knew how to recover. She padded her curves and crevices with luxurious mosses, even the rocks and stones had succumbed to her velvet cloak, embracing them to her form for fear of them tumbling. From deep within her heart, she provided an ever-flowing source of fresh cool spring water.

She was a magical playground in all seasons. Springtime she would offer beautiful walks, showing off her colourful carpet of perfumed primroses, red, white and blue violets peeping through her hedgerows, her wild daffodils swaying to the rhythm of the breezes, not to forget her bluebells, her majestic foxgloves and my favourite, her harebells. These flowers that grew along her grass verges were of delicate sky blue bells suspended from feathery foliage. I believed as a child they supplied her fairies with skirts. I was convinced as a child I could never see her fairies, as they were invisible against the blue sky.

She gave wonderful panoramic views stretching out to Gloucester, Minsterworth, Westbury and the River Severn. Transforming from the death of winter now into the fresh green unfurling bracken, she was alive again.

Summer was an exciting time, she provided thrilling experiences of riding through her bracken on old bicycles, her bracken being so high not knowing where her tumps and dippies were, very often crash landing on mattresses of moss. Playing with many friends, making houses by flattening squares of bracken for each room, then going to the ash tip to collect broken pots, pans and pretty pottery, placing picked wild flowers for decoration into bright shiny tin cans. Oh, what happy memories!

Picking wild strawberries for that tasty pot of jam, it seemed shameful to disturb her white froth of flowers that spread like a blanket over those tasty red beads hanging like glistening jewels but the temptation was too great.

Her grassed area from Cherry Tree Cottage past Hillside to the very top was used in the summer as a thrilling slide. The sun would scorch her grass to a shiny carpet. That, with the combination of cardboard boxes, a gentle push and, whoosh! You had to be careful halfway down though, she housed an old ants nest which if you hit it right you would leave her shiny carpet and fly through the air - wonderful! But, there was a sting in her tail; lose your bearings and you would land in her pond, frogs, newts and all.

Autumn she would start to change colour, her bracken now tiring. Her produce for the next few months supplied blackberries for the tarts, plums for bottling and jam making, elderberries and sloes for wine, mushrooms for breakfast - yummy! A few fallen walnuts, hazel nuts and chestnuts, not to mention the wimberries hugging the banks with their delicate pink waxy flowers followed by the delicious blue fruit. These were collected for our annual tart - mm-mm-scrumptious, just enough for one precious tart!

Winter, things began to tire. She was conserving her energy for the next season. Sledging, sliding on her ice packed lane, collecting holly and mistletoe for Christmas celebrations. Oh, happy times!

Snow, ice, hail, rain and winds battered her through the winter but she would recover without fail in the spring, alive once again to give pleasure to many people. She has a special secret corner in my heart and I know one secret well; that's for you to wonder and me not to tell. Only three know still, and one of those is Nottwood Hill."

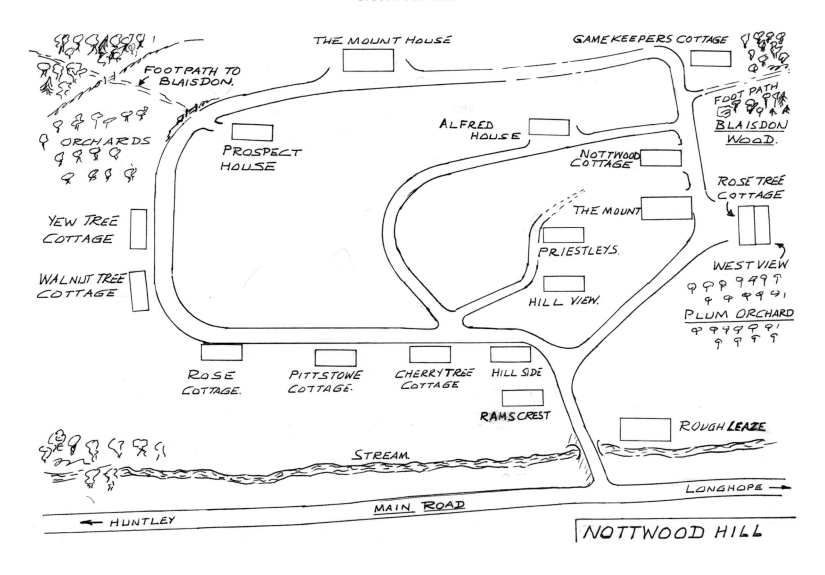

Above:
Plan of Nottwood Hill. (B. Jones)
(Not to scale)

Left: Brenda Brain & Peter Hailes on top of Nottwood Hill.

ROUGHLEAZE

Roughleaze is the first Nottwood Hill house after leaving the main road. It is situated at the bottom of the Hill, to the right of Chapel Lane and lies on the Hill side of the brook, which divides the parishes of Blaisdon and Longhope.

Many years ago it was the home of the Bradley Family, who were the Butchers in the village of Longhope. In the late forties Mr George Hopkins purchased it and since 1984 it has been the home of Mark and Ann Hopkins and their children, Rowena and Lydia. Mark is the son of the late Mr Edgar and Mrs Molly Hopkins and was brought up on Nottwood Hill.

1. Rowena Hopkins in Ron Walton's plum box.
2. Rowena & Lydia Hopkins.
3. Mark Hopkins.

RAMCREST

Ramcrest is the first house on the left of Chapel Lane. Philip Green provided the following information:

"Ramcrest was rebuilt in 1924 and the first person who came to live there had retired from the Army. He had been in the Royal Army Medical Corps so decided that he would rename the cottage RAMC then he added 'rest.'

He was followed by the son of Mr Williams who lived at Gwynfa, which is on the Longhope side of the brook. He came there around the early thirties, but didn't stay long. After that it was sold to a Mr Woolhouse who came from Yorkshire as a 'Saw Doctor' to work at the Longhope Saw Mills. He lived in the house until the fifties .

Mr Williams senior, also worked at the Saw Mills in the daytime and in the evenings and weekends he made ladders for picking Blaisdon Plums. The present owner Philip Green, remembers him digging his garden at night time with the aid of the moonlight!

I moved into Ramcrest in the 1950s and still live there now, with my wife Susan."

Above:
Ramcrest.

Left:
Philip Green in the 1950s.

323

HILLSIDE

Mr and Mrs Larner and their daughter Honor moved to Hillside in the 1940s. Mr Larner worked at the Longhope Mill and also during the war, worked at the Gloucester Aircraft Factory.

There was a barn in the garden, which contained a cider press and produced thousands of gallons of cider each year. The operator of the press and his horse lived in the barn permanently because it was a full time job. Inside this barn, the bedroom and living quarters were lined with interwoven hazel.

Top:
Hillside.

Right:
Honor Larner, top right, in the church choir alongside Ursula Howells.
In front are Norman Penny, Norma Davis & Katherine Eagles.

The family attended church each Sunday, walking through the wood along with the other residents from the hill. Honor sang in the choir and joined in the usual village activities.

When Honor left school she went to work at the Shire Hall. **_Geoff Hart_** from Northwood Green was a friend of Honor's and he remembers them attending dancing lessons together at the village school under the supervision of Miss Whittard. After Mrs Larner died in 1986 Honor went to live in Birmingham. She spent her final years in a wheelchair as she suffered from Multiple Sclerosis. Geoff remembers her as one of life's young ladies.

Mr Larner had died in 1957 at the age of 60 and Mrs Larner in 1986 at the age of 89 yrs. Honor died in June 1999. They are all buried in Blaisdon churchyard.

CHERRY TREE COTTAGE

Top Right:
Painting of Cherry Tree Cottage with Hillside beyond.
(Alan Fox)
Above:
Cherry Tree Cottage from Chapel Lane.
(E. Etherington)

Cherry Tree Cottage nestles against the hillside below the lane. It was previously known as Cherrywood Cottage and in 1935, became the home of Mr and Mrs Harold Brain. Harold met Miss May Evans from Cinderford while she was working at The Steppes, opposite the Plough Inn, Longhope. They married in the Zion Chapel at Hopes Hill and made Cherry Tree Cottage their home. Their three children, Wendy, Brenda and John were all born in the cottage.

Wendy and Brenda recall their childhood memories of life on Nottwood Hill. First, **Wendy Brain**:

"I have some lovely memories of Nottwood Hill. If you meander around the Hill the views of Gloucester and the Cotswolds beyond are so lovely, especially on a clear summer day. Right on the top of the Hill there is a huge

Mr Harold Brain (right) with Mr Luther John Richardson and Bradley's delivery van.
As a child, Luther lived in Blaisdon but when he married, he moved to Coniston, Church Road, Longhope.
Harold worked for Mr Bradley of the Little London shop, delivering bread.

Top:
Harold & May Brain on their wedding day at Zion Chapel,
Longhope.

Below:
Harold & May Brain.

dip, which had four corners. This area was big enough for us to play rounders and we used the fairly steep descent as a slide in the summer, sitting on flattened cardboard boxes. There was a small pond at the bottom but I can't remember any of us getting a dipping!

Our cottage was the last on the made up lane, but Chapel Lane was very steep and in the winter the springs in the lane iced over because the sun was nearly always the other side of the Hill. We had no running drinking water. That was fetched from around the other side of the Hill with two buckets on a yoke. Soft water was used for washday and bathing. It was saved in a huge metal water tank until Dad built one of concrete, which was a mammoth task. It had sheets of corrugated tin on top to save us from falling in.

We had chickens and two pigs, one for our table and one to sell; the money was used for feed for the following year. Mum preserved some eggs for winter use in a big pan of Isinglass. The fruit from the orchard, apples, pears, plums and currants were bottled for winter store. Mum kept a spotless black lead grate, which she had to cook on, even making toffee and welsh cakes on a griddle.

Dad's childhood home was The Plough at Longhope. It is no longer standing. When he first left school and for many more years he worked for Mr O. Bradley who had the Bakery and shop in Little London. He baked and delivered bread for many miles around, May Hill, Lea, Weston-under-Penyard and Blaisdon. He met mum as she worked for Mrs Pike who lived at The Steppes, opposite The Plough. They both went to Zion Sunday School until they married.

We didn't go to Blaisdon very often, as Longhope was more convenient. We walked through the woods most Sundays, after tea, as a family, finishing at The Plough for a packet of crisps and a bottle of pop. I spent my pocket money at Bertha Bartlett's sweet shop situated by The Turn, Longhope. They were served in white cone shaped bags; sometimes I'd have sherbet to dip my fingers in!

During the autumn, we all picked plums for Mr Frank Davis and Mr Skelton. The money was used for the upkeep and winter fuel. We also planted a long row of potatoes in a farmer's field at the Lea. These were gathered and stored in the old coalhouse, which was frost proof, for winter use. Once my little brother started school, Mum joined many other wives picking blackcurrants for Mr Knight of Huntley, and we joined in the picking after school hours.

Our toilet was at the bottom of the garden, complete with newspaper cut into squares, tied with string and hung on a nail. Christmas was a special treat when we used the tissue paper that the oranges had been wrapped in. Of course, we had our individual piece from the orange in our Christmas stocking! The mains water and electric was connected to the Hill in 1954, up until then we relied on an Aladdin lamp for light, hung from a beam in the living room. Then Dad invested in a generator for a strip light to replace the Aladdin. Happy memories but where has all the time gone?"

Left:
Wendy Brain.
Opposite from top:
John, Brenda & Wendy Brain.
Brenda Brain in the garden.
Brenda & John Brain (1952).

Brenda Brain also has memories of her days at Cherry Tree Cottage:

"I can recall dad saying that the top of the Hill that looked like a square pit was used for cock fighting, but by us in the fifties it was used for rounders. There were two water wells, one belonging to Jack Beard around the Hill on the bottom road by Gwen and Cuthbert Dowding's and the other halfway down the lane before you get to the yew tree on the left hand side, in Mr Hopkins' field. I remember walks through Blaisdon woods to a massive yew tree, climbing its stretched out branches and watching people swimming in the reservoir. I wonder if it was the monks from Blaisdon Hall? I'm not sure; but they had black/grey robes on and we would giggle at them stripping off before plunging into the water.

Cherry trees loaded with the 'white heart' cherries were looked after by dad. The birds were scared away by a contraption made of corrugated iron suspended on rope, with a rock attached to a pulley, which in turn was attached to a line that ran from the yew tree in the orchard up the washing line, finally to the bedroom window. Goodness knows what the neighbours thought at 5 o'clock in the morning when an almighty clash of the rock

smashing against the iron sheet would scare away those greedy birds, but it worked. Today, he would be accused of disturbing the peace! We sold cherries to locals and, occasionally, also sold them in little brown paper bags on the side of the road in Little London.

Dad owned a pig that we as kids used to play cowboys and Indians on. We had many chickens and bantams to provide eggs and the odd roast chicken or boiling fowl. Mum made homemade faggots, prepared from the chitterlings. The chitterlings would hang on the washing line after she had washed them. Another speciality was sheep's head broth. That was so tasty. I always knew when she cooked those delicious welsh cakes; the aroma would carry down the lane giving me the urge to get home before they were devoured by my brother. Both mum and dad were excellent cooks. She had a knack of making a little go a long way; and dad's saying was, 'There's another day tomorrow,' but tomorrow never comes, dad! Dad was quite strict but as I have grown older and have a family, I appreciate my childhood. I was brought up to accept people for what they are, not who they are and treat each one with respect. I only hope that I have passed these ideals on to my children."

HILLVIEW

Hillview c1958.

Opposite Cherry Tree Cottage, a track leads to Hillview, the home of Margaret and Claude Barnard and their daughter Christine. Margaret is the daughter of George and Rose Beard who lived at the neighbouring Priestleys. She is the only person who was born on Nottwood Hill and still living there having celebrated her 80th birthday in September 2010. **Christine Barnard** continues her family's story of life on Nottwood Hill:

Claude Barnard, aged 20, in the uniform of the Royal Engineers.

Postcard issued to the troops to send home giving minimal information!

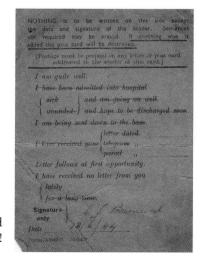

"Margaret married Claude Barnard on the 5th April 1958 on a cold snowy day in Blaisdon Church. Their wedding reception was at Latchen Room Longhope and 50 years later they celebrated their Golden wedding at the same venue and it snowed again!

Hillview was built in 1808 and has been in Margaret's family throughout that time. There was a large bread oven in the house which you could stand up in when they moved in. The bedroom walls were made of wattle and daub and one of these still remains. There was no running water so they had to carry water on yokes from the roadside.

Margaret and Claude had three children, Janice (who was stillborn and is buried in Blaisdon churchyard), Christine and Michael. Margaret went to Zion school, then had to walk to The Pound at Longhope to catch the bus to East Dean Grammar school.

1. Wedding of Claude Barnard & Margaret Beard, April 1958. Lt-Rt: Mr & Mrs Barnard Snr, The Bride & Groom, Hazel Hipwell (Bridesmaid), Rose & George Beard, John Mansell (Best Man).

2. Margaret & Claude Barnard with children, Christine & Michael.

3. Lt to Rt: Margaret Barnard holding her daughter, Christine, Claude Barnard, Cecil, Grace & daughter Gill Beard, Mabel Hipwell, George & Rose Beard.

4. Claude & Margaret Barnard cutting their wedding cake.

Margaret has grown up with plums all her life and remembers being told that she was taken plum picking for local farmers daily during the season whilst still in her pram. She followed on the tradition by taking Christine & Michael blackcurrant and apple picking for Mr Knight from 7am until 6pm before they started school and during school holidays.

After their marriage Claude and Margaret spent a lot of their time at Priestleys, her parents home, helping with the animals, gardening etc. Priestleys and Hillview both have plum orchards and so plum picking was a family event during the season and relations came to help pick in 56lbs boxes for Ron Walton. They would also make plum jam, wine etc. Claude fell out of a tree once whilst plum picking and dislocated his shoulder. Christine and Michael were keen on plum picking and from a young age were often found at the top of a ladder filling a bucket with plums.

Christine and Michael also helped out with the animals. Christine liked to help feed the hens. She used to help her Nan mash the cooked spuds, mixing them with meal and then feeding this mixture to hens that were nearly as tall as her. She was not afraid of being pecked because she volunteered to go and collect the eggs from under the laying hens, quite often having to return the china egg despite being told only to collect the warm brown eggs.

Christine and Michael loved the sheep and made 3 their favourites, Jimmy the ram, and two ewes, Rosie and Eileen. They were so tame that they could hug them and take them for walks on the Hill. The sheep could be left on the Hill all day long and they would not stray.

Margaret and Claude would take their children to Gloucester to sell their produce and in those days there were no seat belts, so they used stockings to make sure that they were safe in the back of the car.

The children used the Hill as their playground. They would make fern dens with friends and at home it was mud pie making."

1. Margaret Barnard plum picking.
2. Christine Barnard feeding the chickens.
3. & 4. Christine & Michael with Jimmy, Eileen & Rosie.

PRIESTLEYS

Sited just behind Hillview, Priestleys was the home of George and Rose Beard and their three children Mabel, Cecil and Margaret who was born at Priestleys. Around 1925, a railway carriage was hauled up the lane onto Nottwood Hill by Bill Bullock, known as Blowey and his team of horses, namely Knocker, Polly and Prince and maybe a couple more. The carriage was put into a field half way up the Hill and became the home of the Beard family. In the forties they built a bungalow around the carriage to make more room and when the building work was finished the carriage was removed from inside the bungalow and destroyed on the site.

Above & Below: Priestleys, as built over the railway carriage.

Mr and Mrs Beard were well known around the Hill and throughout the village of Blaisdon. George served for many years as a Churchwarden in Blaisdon. Among other duties, he was responsible for lighting the church candles and taking the collection. George also used to clean the graves that belonged to the Catholics buried in the churchyard and Mrs Beard did the church accounts. ***Margaret Barnard*** (nee Beard), their daughter, remembers:

"They sat in the second pew inside the church during their courting days and remained in the same pew for the rest of their lives! We were brought up to attend church every Sunday and would walk down through the wood for the services. When in 1942 George had a very bad motorbike accident in Huntley, breaking both his legs, we children had to push his wheelchair down the Blaisdon Lane in order for him to attend the services each Sunday.

333

Hill, which they used for milk, as Cecil was allergic to cow's milk. They also kept chickens and a cow was resident for a short time. Some householders on the Hill had certain rights for grazing sheep and George exercised this right and had his sheep grazing on the common land. George was able to supply not only the meat for their meals but also the vegetables from his well-kept vegetable garden. I remember that Cecil and I used to take cider apples from their orchard to hillside, put them in the cider press and manually push the handle of the press to squeeze the juice from the apples, then bring it back to George to make his cider. Priestleys still has an operating well in the orchard.

After George's accident, I was taken from school and together with Cecil took over a milk round, delivering locally. We fetched the milk in churns from the Stud Farm and delivered it by 1 pint and ½ pint measures to customers. Later on the milk round was sold and George and Rose did a vegetable round in their van through Blaisdon and Longhope. They also spent time plum picking around the local farms during the season. Mrs Beard also used to go timber-tushing in the Blaisdon wood.

George and Rose always kept pigs, killing one each year for consumption. The side of the bacon was hung in the kitchen and Rose would make brawn and faggots etc. George also supplied the pig at the village fete for people to win hence the expression 'bowling for the pig' was for real in those days. They also kept a goat tethered on the

Their son Cecil worked for Francis Blakeway and his lorry could always be seen up and down the village. In his younger days he also used to wind the church clock and like most village boys, pump the organ. Cecil was married twice, his first wife being Grace Davis and then Anita Martin, both girls from the village. It was whilst married to Anita that he tragically died in a car accident in Cornwall. He was 59 (1987) and his ashes were buried in Blaisdon churchyard near the main door.

Rose Beard died in 1974 at the age of 72. A green Altar Frontal and accessories were dedicated in her memory by the then Bishop of Tewkesbury, the Rt Reverend R. Deakin, along with sanctuary and pulpit lights in memory of William Jones, in a service of Evensong held at Blaisdon Church. George died in 1976 aged 75. They are buried in Blaisdon churchyard."

Above:
Bill Bullock (centre), known as Blowey, with horses, Knocker, Polly & Prince.

Opposite:
The Railway Carriage that was the Beards' original home on Nottwood Hill.

1. Rose Beard with her children, Mabel, Margaret & Cecil.
2. Margaret Beard, age 12.
3. Margaret & Claude Barnard.
4. Cecil Beard, age 18.

1

2

3

5

4

1. George Beard & Bruce.
2. The Beard Family, Cecil, Rose, Mabel, Margaret, George plus
dog, Bruce.
3. George Beard with sacks of sprouts.
4. George, Rose & Claude Barnard with Laddie.
5. Rose, Margaret & George Beard. Lunch during plum picking.

1

2

3

4

1. Grace Davis & Cecil Beard (daughter in law).
2. The only surviving evidence of the railway carriage that was the original home; a window complete with leather strap.
3. Rose & George Beard with granddaughter, Hazel, in the garden.
4. Blaisdon & Flaxley Churchwardens at Flaxley Abbey. From Left: ?, George Beard, Bertie Buckett, Mr Teague, Sir Lance Crawley-Boevey, ?.

PITTSTOWE COTTAGE

Back on the left side of Chapel Lane, the house beyond Cherry Tree Cottage is Pittstowe Cottage. One of the early owners of Pittstowe Cottage was a Mr Bullock known as 'Butcher Bullock.' He got the name "butcher" because most people on the Hill would call upon him to kill their pigs. There were many members of the Bullock family living locally, so most of them acquired a nick name in order to make life easier.

Mr and Mrs Meadows came to live in the house around the end of the Second World War. Mrs Meadows was Harold Brain's assistant on the bread van.

Mr and Mrs Little followed and lived in Pittstowe Cottage from around 1963 until leaving in 2003.

Top:
Pittstowe Cottage.
(Beryl Little, nee Walker)

Left:
Beryl Walker & John Little
on their wedding Day, 1962,
outside Zion Chapel.

Far Left:
Susan Little,
ouside the Red Hart.

ROSE COTTAGE

Rose Cottage: David & Ivy Marshall with a young David Tyas.

Rose Cottage, beyond Pittstowe Cottage, was the home of Sydney & Catherine Jones. They were the parents of seven children, including Mr Oscar Jones Snr, Mr Ivor Jones and Mrs Gertrude Bowkett.

Doris Bowkett, their granddaughter, remembers collecting the water from a well on the Hill. This entailed wearing a yoke around her shoulders with a bucket hanging from each end. She would set off around the Hill, going quite a distance for a young child, to reach the well. Needless to say, she managed to spill most of it before getting back to Rose Cottage!

Mrs Catherine Jones.

Next to Rose Cottage was a shed, which still exists, where Mr and Mrs Jones kept a horse and cart. In those days goods had to be brought up from the shop on the main road, including coal and fuel, so a horse and cart proved invaluable.

Mr Sydney Jones died in 1932. Around 1939 Mr and Mrs Oscar Jones and their children Oscar and Catherine, moved down from Prospect House to live with Mrs Jones at Rose Cottage. They stayed with her until around 1947 when they moved down into the village to live at 'The Cottage,' former home of Mr and Mrs Copner. Mrs Catherine Jones died in 1956 and she is buried with her husband Sydney in Blaisdon churchyard.

1

2

3

4

1. The Jones Family, left to right:
Back Row: Sydney, Laura, Sid, Gertrude.
Middle: Fred, Percy, Catherine, Ivor.
front: Ernie, Oscar.
Gertrude became Mrs Bowkett of Stanley Cottages.
Ivor married Enid & was father to Mary, Margery, Doreen & Vera.
Oscar married Barbara & was father to Oscar & Catherine.
2. The Jones family:
Laura, Gertrude, Sydney, Fred, Percy, Ernie, Ivor, Oscar.
3. & 4. Mrs Catherine Jones.

Nearest the camera are Mrs S. Jones, Mrs O. Jones & a young Catherine Jones.

1. Ivy Pithouse on her christening day, 1919.
2. Ivy 1942.
3. Ivy Pithouse.
4. Ivy & David Marshall.

After the death of Mrs Sydney Jones, Rose Cottage was sold to Mr Edgar Hopkins in 1957. After which it became the home of Mr Jim and Mrs Ivy Marshall and their son David. Jim was the son of Nellie Marshall (Nottwood Cottage) and Ivy was a daughter of Mr and Mrs Pithouse from The Mount House.

Jim served with the 5th Gloucestershire Regiment from 1939 to 1945. He was evacuated from Dunkirk and wounded at the Battle of Anzio. After the war he was employed as a sawyers' labourer, but was made redundant in 1949. He began at No.7 MU the same year and worked on Nos. 4, 2 and 5 Sites between March 1949 and April 1951, when he was transferred to the workshops. He was regraded to Labourer Skilled in 1972, assisting fitters on the more complex class of equipment. Due to ill health, he had to leave in August 1977 having served for a period of 28 years. Group Capt J.M.Allistone presented Jim with the Imperial Service Medal at 7 MU Quedgeley.

Jim died in January 1980 at the age of 60 and Ivy died in 2004 at the age of 86 years. They are buried together in Blaisdon Churchyard.

David Marshall, son of Jim and Ivy Marshall was brought up at Rose Cottage and here are his memories of life on the hill:

"I am lucky, I had a happy childhood and although my parents Ivy and Jim Marshall never had every mod con, my welfare was put first. There was always food on the table and a fire in the grate, but most important of all was that we cared not only about one another, but also our neighbours and the community as a whole. Help was always available between people without question and there was a community spirit. When you took a walk on the Hill you could usually guarantee meeting someone else where pleasantries would be exchanged. As a child I often wondered about the hill and one thing I remember is my fascination with its many footpaths which crisscrossed the hill. These paths tended to be used primarily by certain residents as they went about their business and to this day I can see in my mind these paths being used and maintained. Sadly this is no longer the case as following a recent visit there are very few left.

One of the things we looked forward to would be several visits each week by Mr Wellam who was a Mobile Grocer. As he pulled up his van which incidentally was like Dr Who's Tardis, I would try and stand at the rear of the van as he opened the doors. This was because you would be met by the most wonderful odour, a mixture of freshly baked bread and rolls, cakes and fresh fruit. If only that smell could have been captured.

Mr and Mrs Beard who lived nearby had a black painted corrugated shed and I remember going there on many occasions to buy produce mostly consisting of tinned peas, beans etc. The Shed had no signs and I concluded that it was an informal arrangement.

David Marshall 1957.

During the plum picking season of August my mother's cousins and their children would descend on the Hill to help harvest the plums at the Mount House. The Mount House was the family hub where generations of Pithouses lived. It had no electricity or sanitation until it was sold in the early 1980s. Water was provided by a well or later a plastic pipe, run from a neighbouring house. My mother cooked and cleaned for her two brothers who lived there, Albert and Ted.

The plum orchards reverberated to the sound of children's laughter as they played whilst the adults undertook the more serious task of picking the famous Blaisdon plums. At the end of a busy day the favourite reward was to enjoy a drink or two at the Red Hart Inn at Blaisdon, where Frank and Elsie Hogg would smile as the family recalled the ups and downs of the day.

During the Spring there were several areas where wild daffodils would bloom. I would take the liberty of picking many and sell them by the roadside in Little London. The trick was to bunch them up and a bunch in each hand and as a car approached, hold them up in the hope that a car driver stopped and bought some. At a shilling a bunch it seemed to work. Sadly in this politically correct world today this would probably be frowned upon."

Left to Right:
Ivy Marshall, Jim Marshall with David, Reg
Pithouse, Mary Pithouse, Harry Pithouse.

Sitting, left to right:

Jim Marshall, Albert Pithouse,
David Marshall, Jack Waite, Clive Waite,
Ivy Marshall, Ann Waite.

Standing:

John & Josephine Vick holding baby, Sharon.

Taken in the garden at The Red Hart.

Martha Ellen Marshall or Nellie, as she was known, was a much-loved member of the Nottwood Hill community. Nellie's first house on the Hill is now non-existent. However, she then moved into Nottwood Cottage, believed to be more or less next door, and spent time there until age took its toll and she moved further down the Hill to Rose Cottage to be with her son and daughter in law, Jim and Ivy Marshall and their son David. **David Marshall** gives a moving account of his Nan:

"I called her Nan. She was one of Nottwood Hill's characters. I always believed she was living in the wrong era because of her dark clothes and stern Victorian personality. Nan lived alone and I think she enjoyed her independence although she came down to us every day to eat and help wash up etc. She also walked up to the Mount each day where she would potter round, washing up and cleaning. She was a firm Christian believer and when she was able bodied, would dress up in her best clothes and walk through Blaisdon wood to Blaisdon Church on a Sunday evening, where after the service she loved to wander around the churchyard and inspect the graves and marvel at the flowers, another of nature's beauty which she adored. I always remember her delight at the thought of being buried under the fir tree against the wall just inside the entrance and she was almost looking

Nellie Marshall.

forward to it, as she had no fear because she believed there was something better at the end of this life.

Nan was also an animal lover and people often thought she preferred animals to people and this may be true as she was a strict vegetarian. During the winter months when the weather was bad I would walk up to Nottwood Cottage with her evening meal which my mother prepared and she was grateful for this, saying that I need not have bothered. She loved her open fire and I would take coal up to her and raid Blaisdon Wood for firewood. Nan enjoyed a walk down to the shop in Little London and once a week I would drive her down to Longhope Post Office where she enjoyed a chat with the locals. She also loved to attend Blaisdon, Longhope and Flaxley Fetes.

Sadly all things must come to an end and in the final part of her life she was a resident at Townsend House Residential Home at Mitcheldean where I would try and visit her once a week and she would always ask, 'How much longer have I got to stop up here?' I could not tell her the truth and so I would say that it was up to the Doctor. She would then mutter under her breath, 'Bloody Doctors.' She would then tell me that she could see Nottwood Hill from her window and because of her faith I have never doubted that she could."

1. Nellie Marshall, left, with her son, Jim, on the right.
Centre, standing, is Nellie's brother, Henry James Marshall & his wife, Rosa Adelaide, is seated.
Henry & Adelaide Lived at Hazelwood at Sutridge on Velthouse Lane. Rosa died in 1966, Henry in 1975.
2. Nellie, her son, Jim, & her mother.
3. Nellie & Jim.
4. Nellie's grave under the Yew tree, Blaisdon Churchyard.

WALNUT TREE COTTAGE

Walnut Tree and Yew Tree cottages lie next to one another on the east side of the Hill. Apart from the Mount House these two cottages enjoy the most extensive views from Nottwood Hill, taking in the whole of the city of Gloucester and the surrounding parishes. On the horizon lie the Cotswolds with the Malverns to the left and the Stroud Valleys to the right with the Severn meandering through the countryside.

Around 1936, Mr and Mrs Dowding and two of their children, Muriel and John together with Grandad Dowding and Uncle Francis moved into Walnut Tree Cottage. Their daughter Margaret went to live with her Aunt Edie at Stanley Cottage.

Cuthbert Dowding worked for the Council maintaining the roads. Gwen spent her time working for the good of the community. Every morning she would walk from the Hill and light fires in the Village school for the children when they arrived each day for their lessons. Every week she cleaned the Church for the parishioners. Every time

a cobweb is seen, older folk will still say, 'it wouldn't have happened in Gwen's time.' She would always be called upon, if someone had died on Nottwood, and she would lay him or her out. Everybody loved Gwen – a pillar of the community.

Cuthbert died in February 1982 and Gwen in February 1984. They were both aged 73 when they died. Tragically John was killed in an accident on his tractor in August 1977 when he was 41 years old. They are buried together in Minsterworth Churchyard.

Top:
Walnut Tree Cottage.

Left:
Cuthbert & Gwen Dowding,
outside Walnut Tree Cottage.

1

2

3

4

1. John, Margaret & Gwen Dowding,
on holiday.
2. Walnut Tree Cottage Aerial View
with Cuthbert outside the coal shed.
3. Muriel, John, ?, & Margaret,
on holiday.
4. Oscar Jones & John Dowding.

EW TREE COTTAGE

In the1930s, Yew Tree Cottage was the home of Mr W. Coleman, who was a Cobbler. The next occupant was Mr Archie Dowding, who was Cuthbert's Uncle, and his wife Annie. They lived there with her two children Reg and Hilda. Mr Dowding died at the cottage in 1961 at the age of 76. Annie died in 1982 aged 94 and is buried in Huntley churchyard with her son Reg.

Top:
Yew Tree Cottage.
(Buckley Family)
Right:
Annie Dowding's grave stone.

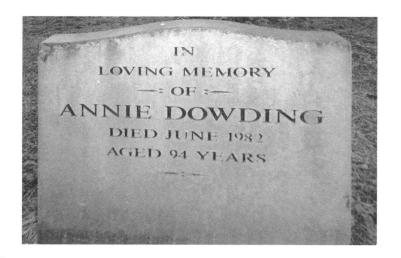

IN
LOVING MEMORY
— : OF : —
ANNIE DOWDING
DIED JUNE 1982
AGED 94 YEARS

Prospect House

Above & below: Prospect House.
(M. Burns)

Prospect House lies on the south side of the Hill overlooking the views across to Ley Park and, beyond, towards the River Severn. The path to Blaisdon leaves the Hill by this house.

Mr and Mrs Oscar Jones and their children Oscar and Catherine lived in Prospect House with Catherine being born in the house. Later, they moved down to Rose Cottage to be with Mr Jones' mother, Mrs Sydney Jones.

The Ellam Family also lived at Prospect House. They were well known for their donkey and trap. The boys also appear in the photos of the village boys' football team. The family emigrated to Australia.

In 1953, Mr and Mrs Pymont and their young family arrived from Cumberland. Mr Pymont had been appointed as Head of Horticulture at Hartpury College and thought Prospect House an ideal spot to live. The house itself was also a challenge as little had been done to it since it was built. **Mrs Pymont** describes their house and their life in it over the next ten years:

"Prospect House was a white washed period building with beams and set into a sloping site, so the rooms were on

various levels. It was possibly built in the 18th century, but this has not been confirmed. When we arrived in 1953 it was crying out for love and repair! There was a lounge and dining room with kitchen leading off. Next, down the slope, was another room, which we eventually turned into an entrance hall with oak door. Then, down two steps, was a stable, which we converted to a garage. The lounge was beamed and had a modern tiled fireplace. This was replaced with a low long fireplace that Eric, my husband, built with small bricks. Leading from the kitchen at the back was a cellar, which we plastered and this became Eric's workshop for DIY etc. We put in a bathroom also leading from the kitchen, not ideal but better than the loo in the garden. Above the cellar from the outside was a tool shed, which was very useful and on the other side of the bathroom area, a woodshed.

There was no water or electricity, but we bought the house knowing they were on the way. It was a great shock to me to go back to paraffin lamps, flat irons, primus stoves and cooking on a range in our dining room. It was anybodies guess when lunch would be ready. It depended on which way the wind was blowing! I struggled for five months until the power came. Oh joy! We had massive water tanks by the woodshed and with power we were able to pipe that in for baths etc. until the mains water arrived.

Upstairs there were three bedrooms, but the floor of the third was level with the window, not a good idea with 10-month-old twins, so we were able to lower this over the entrance hall and still have ample headroom below. We turned the stairs round to the entrance hall and also had a separate staircase from the hall to the new fourth bedroom built over the garage.

The garden was tamed and was very productive and the orchard also being mainly Blaisdon plums and apples. Outhouses in the orchard allowed us to keep poultry.

We thoroughly enjoyed our time on Nottwood Hill with our young family. They had the freedom needed, and for them at that time it was ideal."

1. Mrs Pymont with Stephen, Rachel, Laura & Fiona.
2. Fiona & snowman.
3. Rachel in the garden.
4. Rachel, Fiona, Stephen & Laura.

CYRIL BAGGOT'S HUT

At one time Cyril was married and lived at Flaxley. He worked with his father on the Hall Estate, doing maintenance jobs around the place. He moved to Nottwood Hill alone, living in a hut, which was brought up from Flaxley on a horse and trolley and put into Mr Ellam's field. When Mr Ellam sold up it was moved into Mr Pithouse's field with the help of some locals; Albert Pithouse, Ted Walker, Sam Bullock and Jim Marshall.

Cyril spent his time as an odd jobber and did work at Gaulett Farm and around the village, including digging the graves.

The young children were, for some reason or other, quite fearful of this old man. He would appear in the village with his dog and stick. Even worse was to meet him in the woods on the way up to Nottwood. Perhaps too many fairy stories were being read?

Mrs Pymont and her family lived in Prospect House, which was next door to the field where Cyril had his home and she writes the following memories about Cyril:

"Cyril lived in the most appalling conditions. Each morning smoke would come out of the chimney, followed by smoke from the eaves of his shed. After that Cyril

Cyril Baggot's Hut can be seen in the background. Laura Pymont is on the swing in the garden of Prospect House.

appeared out of the door coughing and spluttering. He was a dour man, yet very kind. Always wanting to give the children sweets, so filthy they were immediately whipped away by Mum. He was rather the butt of humanity. I recall one Christmas when the 'lads of the village' decorated his hut with holly and candles. He was later taken ill and sent to home/hospital at Westbury for some time.

Sometime later a man appeared on the Hill, clean with snowy white hair, whom nobody recognised. It was the new Cyril, but sadly despite Social Service care workers, it did not last. How could it, living in his hut? No water, no sanitation, nothing."

Cyril was last seen leaning over the churchyard wall watching the funeral of Mrs Daniell of Velt House Farm on the 18th February 1960. He was found the next day outside his hut – dead.

1. Cyril Baggot & his dog.
2. Cyril with horses and ?
3. Cyril with ?,?
Possibly at Gaulett Farm.

 **LFRED HOUSE**

Alfred House lies near the top of the Hill on the north side with lovely views of the Slad. It was the home of Oscar and Joyce Jones and their children Richard and Sandra.

Oscar had been brought up on the Hill before the family moved down into Blaisdon village in 1947. As a young child on Nottwood Hill, he lived with his parents in Prospect House and, later, Rose Cottage.

Following his school days in Blaisdon and then East Dean Grammar School he went to work with Mr Young, who lived next door at Western View and who worked as a mechanic at Cottrells. Oscar learnt the trade with Mr Young, but at the age of 18 he joined the RAF with his friend Barry Davis, spending 5 years in the Service. Oscar's time in the forces took him to many places abroad, including Egypt and Aden.

Joyce started school at Huntley and moved on to Abenhall. After leaving school she worked as a waitress upstairs in the Cadena Café in Gloucester.

Joyce sang in the choir at Huntley and Oscar rang the bells

Alfred House.
(E. Etherington)

there. Love blossomed and they were married in Huntley Church in 1960.

They lived at Alfred House throughout their married life, having two children, Sandra and Richard. Oscar died in April 2006 and Joyce in March 2009. They are together again in Blaisdon churchyard.

2

1

3

4

Oscar Jones at Prospect House.
Oscar lived in Prospect House, then moved with his parents to
Rose Cottage.
1. Oscar with his mother, Barbara Jones & her mother, Mrs Stanley.
2. Oscar Jones with his parents, Oscar & Barbara Jones.
3. Oscar & Catherine Jones.
4. Oscar & Catherine with their father.

1

2

3

Oscar Jones in the RAF.
1. John Keating, Oscar Jones, Joe Milanta.
Egypt, early 1950s.
2. & 3. Oscar Jones in RAF uniform.
4. & 5. Oscar with aeroplanes.
6. Oscar Jones & Joe Milanta.

4

5

6

Oscar and Joyce were so proud of their children. **Sandra Jones** shares her lovely memories of her life on the Hill with her Mum and Dad and brother Richard, not forgetting Rex:

"Dens, mud pies and tadpoles all spring to mind when I think of Nottwood Hill, but I'll start with the bits I have been told. I think all children are delighted to hear what panic they've given their parents and can now laugh about!

My first adventure was in the plum fields with Dad up the ladder, me in my pram and my brother Richard, who was about three and a half at the time. Richard decided to break my boredom and took me for a little ride. Dad looked down through the leaves only to see the pram picking up speed with Richard in tow. Dad jumped to my rescue, only too late. My carriage had hit a molehill and overturned. Thinking the worse Dad turned the pram over only to find that I was laughing my head off!

One late Saturday afternoon Mum returned home on the 5.20pm Cottrells bus from Gloucester. She had gone to town to buy some fish for tea and some cakes and other stuff. Mum would always bring Dad sprats and kippers from the market, even in later years. However, Dad and I were up the top of the garden when Mum shouted for him to give her a hand. Dad left me with my trowel and my faithful companion Rex, for only a few minutes. When he returned panic set in, where was Sandra? Where could a toddler have gone in such a short time? They checked the house, the garden, the orchard, but nothing. Dad went a bit further as we lived on the edge of Blaisdon Woods. There I was, halfway along the main path with my bouncer, Rex, there to protect me.

Mud pies are every child's favourite pastime. My first batch were made in my overturned rainwater tank, which was in the walls of an old fallen down pigs cot in our orchard. I kept my house spick and span and later moved to a larger property under a tree behind the garden shed where I made coffee from the mud and water to go with my cakes. It had more space for entertaining when my friends came to play. Rose petal perfume was fun, except when Mum asked why there were no heads on her beautiful bushes!

How many people can fit into an Austin Riley? It was a green one, Dad at the wheel, Grampy beside him and Mum, Nanny, Richard in the back with me on Mum's lap. 'Whatever you do don't let her go to sleep. Keep her awake,' Grampy kept saying. Most children go off to sleep when travelling and I was one of those. Dad put his foot down, 'Won't be long now, just keep her awake.' You see I had stuck a button right up my nose and no matter how much pepper I inhaled or nose blowing it just would not budge. We pulled up outside A & E, everyone piled out, just going through the doors when 'Aitchoo' out flew the button. I just don't know what all the fuss was about.

I remember Mum used to wash our hair in rainwater with all those squiggly things in it. Yuk!

As I got a bit older, Mum would let me go to the shop in Little London, usually a Saturday morning for a bag of flour and some lard etc. so we could do some baking. Mrs Gibbs would weigh me out some aniseed balls for my 2 pence. I'm sure she put in extra as a treat.

Cleaning the chickens and geese out was not a pleasant job, but it had to be done as, like many, we relied on the eggs and at Christmas ate one of the old birds. Dad would cut the bracken down off the Hill and we would put it in for the geese's bedding.

As the parents could be quite neglectful and clumsy with the recently hatched, we would often bring in chicks or goslings, to keep warm, and hatch eggs on newspaper under the fireguard in front of the open fire. Sometimes Mum would put the goslings inside a warm oven but not to cook. Once they had dried out and warmed up they would go back in the nest. I wanted to keep them all.

Fruit picking was a frequent event. We would take a packed lunch and walk through the wood to Gerald Ackerman's currant fields up behind Blaisdon church. We would pick a bucket, weigh it in, get paid and then go off and make friends, leaving Mum to earn some holiday money. Richard once found some beehives by accident. Well, he didn't sit on those again!

We would pick our own fruit as well. Dad would make wine and Mum would make jam and puddings. All our food was home grown. Dad would share our crops of plenty with family, friends or neighbours.

Top:
Oscar & son, Richard, feeding the geese.
Bottom:
Oscar & Daughter, Sandra, with the Austin Riley.

Our home was always an open house and everyone was made to feel welcome with cups of tea, slice of mum's cake, the tipple of home made wine. 'Sip it,' they would say to me, 'It's not pop.' Then it would be 'only a drop more.' It made me glow. I remember different wines bubbling away by the bathroom heater, on full, ready to be bottled. Uncle Bernard would bring out his bottles to sample. 'Too sweet,' Dad would say. He preferred a dry plum or a medium elderberry but I liked it all.

Christmas time was always exciting. We would go for a walk in the wood and gather pinecones and pretty bits and pieces. We would sit in the warm kitchen, table covered with newspaper and spray and glitter to our hearts content. Carol singers would pop in annually for mince pies, biscuits and a glass of sherry, oh, and sing. Mum's old tights would be filled with presents and placed at the bottom of our beds. I loved trying to pull them out, as some could be quite resistant in that nylon weave.

One Christmas, Dad invited Mrs Larner from Hillside Cottage to dinner as no one should be on their own at Christmas and I'm sure she was on her own a lot. Tape recorders were first out and Richard had one from Mum and Dad. He was chuffed to bits recording all morning and replaying it. We were on Christmas pud and Dad asked, 'more cream Mrs Larner?' in quite a broad accent. 'No thank you, Mr Jones,' she replied. Well she was so surprised when Richard played it back, she just couldn't grasp how she got in that little black box! We all laughed.

One year, it was very cold and it had snowed very heavily. It was so deep it touched my pony's belly. We were snowed in and had to dig our way out of the drift. Dad heated some baked beans, put them in a flask and traipsed his way to Mrs Larner's cottage. There was no chance of any vehicles getting in or out, so that's what Dad would do, make sure everyone else was OK

As we got older family and friends would meet at Alfred House on Boxing Day. Dad would lead the troop through the woods and fields. The Red Hart would welcome us with our annual ploughman's. Then when we got to our teens we would go further a-field and walk over Huntley Hill, then May Hill and end up at the Glass House. Everyone would then end up at ours for cold turkey, pickles and a piece of Christmas cake for tea.

Top:
Joyce, Sandra & Richard at Alfred House.
Bottom:
Oscar at work in the garden.

Blaisdon wood was an adventure for any child. We would have spent many hours at the 'Rezzer' (reservoir) catching tadpoles in our jam jars. Often getting our wellies stuck in the mud and walking home with wet muddy socks. They, the tadpoles, would live in an old enamel bath of rainwater until they finally hopped away. On the way back from the 'Rezzer' we would swing on the old yew tree, then head home for tea.

Albert and Ted Pithouse lived on top of the Hill and owned the orchard outside our kitchen window, with an ancient Morris van in it. We loved taking it in turns driving the firmly planted vehicle in our imaginations.

We would occasionally all sneak over to Yew Tree Cottage, home to the Buckley family for many years now, but before that it was dusty, exciting with old bottles and bits of furniture. 'Don't go upstairs,' Mum said as it was not safe, but the boys always did.

Many a den we made in the fern. Birthdays were great playing hide and seek with Dad seeking us out. We would pick Daffodils and sell bunches of them in the lay-by, as well as bags of plums, making us a bit of pocket money.

I used to love our family nights in by the open fire. We'd probably watch the Two Ronnies or Dick Emery on a Saturday evening. Dad would put some homegrown onions into the hot ashes, turning them occasionally so they were cooked evenly. Mum would bring in big wedges of fresh bread and butter and chunks of cheese. Dad would take off the burnt outer skin of the onions and there was the soft fleshy middle, absolutely yummy and washed down with a tipple of homemade elderberry wine. Other times we'd play cards to be followed by crackers, cheese and homemade pickled onions. Oh! and crumpets on the toasting fork.

Alfred House will be home forever, even though mum and dad have passed. I've still got good vivid memories and so have my children, Georgia and Jamie. I hope Sam and Amanda, the new owners, have the happiness we had and a wonderful future. I would have loved to have stayed on Nottwood Hill forever. My kids have had a good start. They have enjoyed much fun and love from Alfred House. I'm sure Oscar and Joyce Jones were known to many people, they were part of the community. Dad was a very kind person and a couple of years before he died he received Maundy money, presented to him at the Cathedral by the Queen. We were so proud. There are too many things to write about my parents apart from they were loved and appreciated by many and missed very much."

Oscar & Joyce At Gloucester Cathedral.

Below Left: Maundy Money.

Oscar Jones was selected as a recipient of the Maundy Money. The occasion took place at Gloucester Cathedral on Thursday 17th April 2003 in the presence of Her Majesty the Queen, who presented the recipients with their purses of Maundy money.

It is an annual ceremony that has its origins in Christ's washing of the disciples' feet at the Last Supper. The Royal Maundy service is intended as a show of humility by the monarch towards her subjects, but the last sovereign to wield the soap and towels was James II in 1685!

The Queen distributed the Maundy money to 77 men and 77 women, each receiving 77 pence in specially minted Maundy coins. The number of recipients and the amount, is determined by the Queen's age. Recipients are chosen for their church and community work. Oscar spent many years making money for the local churches particularly by his sponsored cycle rides around the parishes each year.

1.Oscar with his nephew, Paul.
2. Oscar & Joyce's nephew & niece, Paul & Carol.
3. Joyce with nephew, Paul, outside Alfred House.
4. Oscar Jones (2004).

362

GAMEKEEPER'S COTTAGE

A small Stone farmhouse tucked into a nook of Blaisdon Wood, high on Nottwood Hill, Gamekeeper's Cottage was probably privately built around 1780. It was later acquired by the wealthy iron master Henry Crawshay along with much of the fragmented ownerships of Blaisdon in the 1860s, when his son Edwin built Blaisdon Hall. Possibly before, but certainly after, it became the Gamekeeper's Cottage for the estate. The last Gamekeeper to live in the Cottage was George Rutter from 1897 till about 1910 when the cottage became redundant when the new Stanley Lodge took over in that role. ***Martin Webb***, the present owner, writes about one of his predecessors and the rumours that persist about his death:

"There is local gossip about one of George Rutter's predecessors. In 1893 Jehu James Dawe had become the new Head Gamekeeper. He and his wife Sarah originally came from Dorset. They had married in 1887 and had five children. By 1895 Sarah was again pregnant but on February 19th Jehu died, officially of influenza after a very short illness, but the rumour is that he may have been murdered after dallying with the squire's daughter.

Job Rudge who lived 150 yards away at the Mount House, definitely arrived at the scene as he is mentioned on the death certificate, but the rumour is that he came only after hearing Jehu's screams as he died in agony from strychnine poisoning and so indicating a murder possibly with collusion from the doctor who signed the certificate.

On March 1st 1895 the Blaisdon Village School log book shows that Jehu's children left the school, 'because it was necessary as the family had to leave their home' and Sarah and the family returned to Dorset.

All this could easily be discounted as nothing more than a local myth, but what some find curious is the inscription on Jehu's gravestone, located immediately inside the church gate and taken from John VI. Vs. 37, which reads:

'Him that cometh to me I will in no wise cast out'

Who erected the stone? The wife or the squire? Are these the kind words of a bereft and loving wife, or maybe of a betrayed wife glad her husband had died of flu and who may have baked a cake with a little extra ingredient? Were they the thoughts of a benevolent employer lamenting a much-valued servant, or those of an employer who felt betrayed and was glad Jehu had died of flu, or had he helped him on his way? Years later did the rumour of the romance find its way to D.H.Lawrence's 'Lady Chatterley's Lover'?

Above:
Death certificate of Jehu James Dawe,
stating influenza & pneumonia as cause of death.
Below:
Jehu's gravestone.
Left:
Gamekeeper's Cottage from the rear.

Nottwood Cottage

Nottwood Cottage. (Carpenter family)

Ernest William Carpenter served in the First World War as a Driver with the Royal Field Artillery. Mr Carpenter was a wartime enlistee who joined the Royal Field Artillery in 1916. After training and service at home he was posted overseas in 1917 and served abroad until the end of the war, being demobilised in 1919.

Together with his wife, Mary Elizabeth Carpenter (nee Fairless), and their children they moved into Nottwood Cottage in 1939. They had a large family with around 14 children and lived happily on the Hill until the late fifties when they moved to Longhope Village. Mr Carpenter died in 1973 at the age of 74 and Mrs Carpenter died in 1998 at the age of 90. They are buried in Longhope churchyard.

Two of their children, Arthur and Ron, have written about their time on Nottwood Hill. First, **Arthur K. Carpenter** writes:

I was born 1 September 1936 at Stroud Workhouse. We moved to Nottwood Hill in 1939 with my 2 sisters, Rose and Muriel who had been born in January and October 1938. Life was very basic compared to today. We had a toilet in the backyard with old papers as wipes. When the toilet bucket was full, we had to dig a large hole in the garden to empty it into. Bath time was in a big tin bath, taking turns with the other children. Water was collected from Nellie Marshall's well.

We would fetch bread from the bakers in Little London, Monday to Saturday every morning at 6.30 a.m. so my father had sandwiches for work. Sunday tea was bread and dripping. Coal was carried from the point of delivery, half a mile away and firewood from the local wood. I would borrow a donkey and cart from the Elham family to get wood and blocks from the sawmills in Longhope. This family kept bees and supplied honey to the locals. They emigrated to Australia in 1949; they had two boys, Richard and Robert. Robert was deaf and dumb.

1

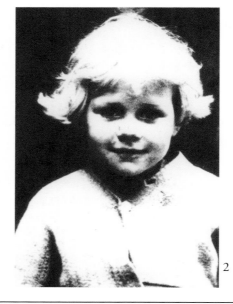

2

4

3

5

See from the earth the fading lily rise
It springs, it grows, it flowers and dies
So this fair flower - but blossomed for a day
Short was the bloom and speedy the decay.
Anon.

1.Driver Ernest William Carpenter,
Royal Field Artillery, 1916-1919.
2. Muriel Carpenter who died in 1945, aged 7, & is buried in
an unmarked grave in Blaisdon Churchyard.
3. Inscription from the tombstone of a child who died in
Blaisdon in1756, aged 7.
4. Mary Carpenter, on the left, with Mrs Guy.
At the seaside in the 1960s.
5. Ernest Carpenter in Longhope.

Some of the boys and girls were friendly with the Father and boys of the school at Blaisdon. We would play them at football; they would put on plays and concerts and would invite us to them. I would take my sister, Rose and they would always put us in the front row. Another highlight was hearing Dick Barton, Special Agent on the radio.

To get pocket money, I had a paper round (the Citizen) 6 days a week, Monday to Saturday, and would deliver all over the Hill, The Slad, Little London, Hopes Hill and Longhope.

I would go carol singing every Christmas in the local area. I helped my father with digging the garden at The Red Hart, Blaisdon every Saturday and Sunday. The landlord, Mr Price, was OK and would slip me a shilling on Sunday afternoon so I could go to the pictures in Gloucester.

Bonfire night was another highlight. We boys would cut the bracken and then we would gather and try to make the biggest bonfire ever. Everybody would help us with old trees, tyres, etc. so our bonfire was bigger than the one on The Slad. Come bonfire night, all the families on the Hill would come and let off their fireworks.

1945 was a bad year as my sister Muriel died of pneumonia aged 7 years. She was buried in Blaisdon churchyard. Everyone at Zion School went to the funeral. We all walked through the wood to church.

1947 was a very cold winter and everything was frozen up. To get our meat ration from the butchers, Mr Ackerman at Huntley, my sister, Rose, and I took our sledge and collected the meat. It took us hours as it is about 5 miles round trip. If ever we heard a pig squealing, we knew there was a pig being killed and that we could have a game of football with its bladder.

Every year the whole family would go plum picking for Mr E. Hopkins, who I believe was our landlord. Also, we picked plums for Mr Knight in the orchard at the back of Blaisdon Church. At that time, there were apple and pear trees in the same orchard.

There was a reservoir in the wood where we boys would go to try and catch fish and to swim. I remember while playing on the Hill we saw an aircraft on fire and watched it go down on the other side of the wood. We ran along the road and near the gateway to Mr Buckett's field, looking up from the road we could see the plane on fire. The Police arrived and told us to go away.

We lived at Nottwood Cottage from 1939 until 1959 when we moved to Longhope. Another seven children were born during our time at Nottwood Cottage, 3 girls and 4 boys. One boy died in 1940 aged 10 months.

I passed my 11 plus in 1947 for East Dean Grammar School in Cinderford. After a year, I was moved to Abenhall Secondary School, not due to a lack of intelligence, probably more to do with the numerous patches on my trousers. I stayed there until I left school in 1950.

I moved from Gloucester in 1983 for work reasons. I bought a detached bungalow in North Wales with views of the River Dee and Liverpool in the distance. Looking left outside my back door, I see sandy beaches and the Irish Sea."

Ron Carpenter continues:

"I was born on the 25th April 1947 at Westbury-on-Severn workhouse. My mother often talked about how dad had to dig his way through the snowdrifts to get Mum to the workhouse when I was born. It was a particularly hard winter in 1947 and as we had no transport, Mum and Dad had to walk all the way to Westbury whilst Mum was about to give birth.

One of my earliest memories was going down to the bottom of Nottwood Hill with my Mum who would pick up a sack of coal and carry it on her back up to the cottage. Back then this was a normal way of life.

Mum would send my elder sister and me to the butchers at Huntley, which was a round trip of 5 miles. I also remember going to the shop at Little London, mainly for sugar and tea. I liked the trip to the shop, as we would have pennies for sweets. I was always first in the queue.

I can recall going out with Mum to the garden to fetch some water and a great big rat came out of the pump. It frightened both of us to death.

Mum and Dad always sent us to Sunday School at Zion Chapel, Hopes Hill, walking through the woods there and back.

Bath time was on a Sunday and it was always a terrible time for me, carbolic soap and all. I could never get out of it. All my brothers and sisters washed before me and I was always the last one in the tin bath. I'm sure I was dirtier when I got out than when I went in. The finale was yet to come having washed my hair with carbolic soap I then had to go outside and bend over and Mum would tip a bucket of cold rainwater over my head to rinse off the soap.

It was a very sad time for me when we left Nottwood Hill. I didn't want to leave the cottage and Nottwood, the place I loved so much. My Dad didn't want to go either, but Mum had been offered a new council house with inside toilet, water and electricity. Although Dad had been offered a bigger cottage on the other side of the Hill, alas Mum won the day and we moved to Longhope during the fifties. My love for Nottwood has never left me and I still yearn to be back there to this day."

Ron Carpenter,
at his school desk.

WEST VIEW

West View is tucked away on the Hill opposite The Mount. It is adjacent to Rose Tree Cottage.

In the thirties it was the home of Mr Alfred and Mrs Gertrude Green. Before Gertrude Green (nee Hopkins) was married, during the First World War, she worked at the Munitions Factory at Quedgeley supplying, among other things, shells for the guns.

Philip Green, their son, remembers growing up on the Hill:

" Like all children then, I was made to go to church on a Sunday and we would walk down through the woods to attend our church. I remember the Rev. McNamara when he was the Rector there. My mother had a good singing voice and would always wear a large hat to church.

West View.
(1976)

Philip Green,
Age 10.

A child in those days had to obey, I remember very well being taken down to church with an unwilling heart. All the children on Nottwood would attend school at Zion School at the top of Hopes Hill rather than Blaisdon School, even though Nottwood was in the Parish of Blaisdon. On leaving Zion School, I then travelled to Sir Thomas Rich's in Gloucester to continue my education. After which, during the Second World War, I served with the Palestine Police Force.

I will never forget the day when I was eligible to buy my first cigarettes, which were 'Woodbines' at the price of two pence ha'penny!"

Alfred Green died at the age of 80 in 1948 and Gertrude died aged 77 in 1969. Their grave is in Blaisdon churchyard.

1. Gertrude & Alfred Green.
2. Gertrude & her son, Philip Green.
3. Philip on his tricycle.
4. Philip in the uniform of Sir Thomas Rich's School, Gloucester.
5. Miss Gertrude Hopkins, while at the munitions Factory during the 1st World War.

1

2

3

4

1. Police Training College, Bristol.
Philip Green, 2nd right, back row.
2. Philip Green in Home Guard uniform, age 17.
3. Philip & Colleague in Jerusalem, 1940s.
4. Philip in London.

ROSE TREE COTTAGE

Rose Tree Cottage, now known as Freedom Cottage.

During the 2nd World War, the Rickett family moved to Rose Tree Cottage. Elsie and Joe were originally from London and had 2 daughters, Alice and Doreen. Joe was a bridge building overseer and was sent to Quedgeley, to work on the RAF site. After a bomb hit Quedgeley, Joe asked if anyone knew of a property to rent where his family would be safer. Joe Stock from Little London, said that his girlfriend and future wife, Dolly Hopkins' family had a cottage on Nottwood Hill, which had become vacant. They promptly re-located to Rose Tree Cottage. Although lacking the modern conveniences that London had to offer such as electricity and running hot water, they settled happily in their new surroundings. Alice was later to be bridesmaid to Joe and Dolly.

Alice Hyett (nee Rickett) remembers:

"My Parents, Joe and Elsie, organised the Blaisdon Friday night Social at the School. This was a thoroughly enjoyable event attended by most of the village. My Dad would play the piano and people would sing. People would dance and refreshments brought to share and everyone had a jolly good time. We would go back to Nottwood through the woods, with only the moon, a lantern or a candle in a jam jar for light. My father would also play the piano in the Red Hart and when Gideon called 'time,' Dad would play a hymn such as, 'Lead kindly light' and Gideon would stand in the doorway and sing along." An Italian Prisoner of War living in Ley Lane in Huntley by the name of Tony English, loved to come along and join in the fun."

Elsie and Joe remained in the area they had grown to love, living out their latter years in Huntley.

Joe & Elsie Rickett.

THE OUNT

The Mount lies below the summit on the north facing side of Nottwood Hill. It is one of the most attractive decorative buildings on the Hill. The history of The Mount goes back some two hundred years. The original dwelling was one of the cottages built by the early settlers. The owner, a widow, got into a dispute with a neighbour. She went to law and engaged a solicitor from Gloucester to fight her case. She had no money but offered her cottage and land as a security, which was accepted. She lost her case and the Solicitor, whose name was Herberts, took her property for his services.

He was much taken up with the position and view and decided to demolish it and build a house of his own design on the site. This he did and even employed the unfortunate widow to help haul stone with her donkey and cart for the new building. He lived at The Mount for a number of years and was much sought after by the locals for legal advice and otherwise. He was known locally as 'Lawyer Herberts.'

In 1917 George and Rebecca Hopkins came to live at The Mount. George was a travelling Railways Inspector. They had eleven children namely: George, Charlotte, Gertrude, Beatrice, Philip, Alfred, Ida, Ernest, Frank, Marjorie and Edgar, but not all the children lived at The Mount.

Their son, Edgar, married Lily Mary Green (Molly) at Blaisdon Church on the 30th November 1940. On the death of his father in 1941 Edgar and Molly moved into The Mount. They lived there with Molly's daughter, June, and their son, Mark. Edgar and Lily lived at the Mount until they died, Edgar in 1991, aged 83, and Molly on the 15th September 2010. She was buried with her husband Edgar and alongside his parents in Blaisdon churchyard.

1. & Opposite. The Mount.
2. George & Rebecca Hopkins c1940.
3. A young Edgar Hopkins with a scythe.
4. The Summer House at The Mount.
5. George Hopkins and his son, Edgar, at The Mount.

Reminiscences of the late **Edgar Hopkins**, kindly provided by his family:

"When a boy, George Hopkins, my elder brother, was playing on a loading crane in the railway sidings at Severn Tunnel and his hand was drawn in and badly crushed by the gear wheel cogs. His father managed to free him and rushed him to the doctor who wanted to amputate. His father refused to consent and he made a remarkable recovery. This meant he could later join the army where he was killed at Gallipoli in the First World War. His name is on the war memorial in Blaisdon.

When approaching 60 my father George Hopkins senior decided to look for a cottage for his retirement. The Mount came up for auction and Father and Mother travelled by train to Longhope to inspect it. Father was much taken with it, no doubt it reminded him of his childhood home in Llandogo with the hills and woods. He eventually bought The Mount, Nottwood Cottage, Rose Tree Cottage and West View (formerly Fletcher's Cottage) plus 3-4 acres of land in 1917.

Edgar & Molly Hopkins,
on their wedding day.

The big day arrived when we were due to move. Staites of Barton Street, Furniture Removers were engaged; their transport was a steam engine with a van body and large trailer. We loaded up and set off to Little London. I rode on the last tailboard with my brother Frank and my little black and tan terrier 'Trix,' who every now and then would jump down and try to bite the big rear wheels of the engine. At that time the road was completely empty of other mechanical traffic, there was only an occasional pony trap or wagon.

We eventually arrived at the turn into Chapel Lane and the driver completely refused to venture down the steep pitch. Father appeared, having travelled by train, and tried to persuade the driver to go down the lane but he remained unmoved. A crowd of local people had gathered at the unusual sight of a steam engine and trailer and someone suggested a wagon and horses to move the stuff. 'Besom Bill,' the timber haulier was visited and agreed to do the job. That meant hauling the wagon up around the Hill and down 'The Steep.' Looking back it was fantastic the way the local people rallied round to help. Carrie Bullock, 'Besom Bill's' daughter worked very hard carrying smaller things, some of them not so small. Fred Dowding and his wife lived in Hillside and Mrs Dowding brought out tray loads of refreshments, which were most welcome. Others readily gave help.

We settled in at The Mount, the family then being myself, my parents, Marjorie and Frank, and the two young girls, Dolly and Becky. The other boys stopped in Gloucester and the girls were all in different jobs. Father kept on his

1

2

3

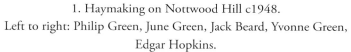

1. Haymaking on Nottwood Hill c1948.
Left to right: Philip Green, June Green, Jack Beard, Yvonne Green,
Edgar Hopkins.
2. Edgar feeding the cow in the orchard above Roughleaze (1948).
3. Mark Hopkins feeding a lamb.
4. Mark Hopkins & June Green (Molly's daughter) c1957.
5. Molly & Edgar harvesting plums (1948).

5

4

work as travelling railway inspector, often being away for several days, but if possible he would slip back and get off the train at Grange Court then make his way home through the woods. He retired aged 63, having worked for 45 years with the GWR.

During the depression my Uncle Frank came to live with us for a while. He was a miner but became a victim of the General Strike when all the pits shut down for a long period. He did a lot to help tidy up the place as it was very overgrown and with the help of a friend he sank the well in the orchard at Hillview when others backed out after hitting solid rock. I used to help wind him up out of the well when he lit the fuses for the explosives and was scared to death every time. We would take cover and after several seconds there would be an almighty bang and rock would fly up into the air. The well was then full of fumes and would have to be left until the following day.

Unknown to Father this area was noted for the Blaisdon plum and he was agreeably surprised when he was told we could sell all we had at £5 per ton. The entire crop in those days was no more than 3-4 tons but it was a useful addition to our income. A jam works was set up in Longhope but unfortunately was short-lived and Joe Walton from Liverpool took it over and used it for many years as a depot to receive the plums before sending them up north.

While Uncle Frank was with us, he helped to make West View habitable, fixing up the matchboard ceilings in the bedrooms and concreting the floor in the kitchen. He also helped with the other cottages, which were then tenanted at 4 shillings a week. Father also started pig breeding and kept half a dozen sows, selling the young for meat. Often, when working in the orchards he would look at Roughleaze and think how he would like to get hold of the land. Fred Bradley then used it for store cattle and Bill Bullock and family occupied the house. He finally managed to buy both the house and land when the Blaisdon Estate sold off various small lots. Father had managed to pay off the mortgage on The Mount with the fruit money so was in a position to take up another for Roughleaze. We planted up The Ruffet and Roughleaze bank with plum trees but used the rest of the land for grazing for some years. Father eventually became ill with heart trouble but wouldn't give up the work on the land and finally died at the age of 79.

I married Molly in 1940 and the property passed to me on the understanding we looked after my mother, Rebecca for the rest of her days. We had several poor plum crops then I heard about the new sprays available for killing the blight, which affected the trees. We used stirrup pumps to spray the trees. The second World War was now on with controlled prices imposed on all the fruit and plums were £2 per ton which was quite good. After the war prices fell as imports started again; in the meantime I planted up Breezes orchard and The Meadows so our crops were getting bigger and our turnover likewise, although wages for picking took a large slice of the profits. I was still relying on the horse for haulage but knew it would never cope with heavy crops so I bought a Ferguson tractor from Harold Green, who was giving up his land. I then bought an Allen scythe, followed by an Allen spray pump and these machines cut down a lot of physical labour. Soon after I bought a small Lister stationary engine and a saw bench.

Pymonts, the small orchard near Prospect House, came up for sale for £75 followed by Herberts Patch at £150 and Rose Cottage at £875. My last purchase was Fir Piece.

The Mount is built onto the original cottage, which was taken after being put up as security in a lawsuit in 1875. It took some years to build and Lawyer Herberts who owned it laid out the grounds with shrubs and had the summer house built, the decorative rustic work being done by a skilled craftsman from Blaisdon. There used to be statues placed at intervals up the drive. He gradually bought up pieces of land nearby so that he was nearly surrounded by his own property, including cottages, now called Nottwood and West View. He built Rose Tree cottage on the back of West View in the same style as The Mount and used it to house his staff. He and his family lived there till 1897 then the house was sold to a Mr Sims, whose grave is in Blaisdon Churchyard. He made more improvements and lived there till he died in 1916. He had become more and more of a recluse after his daughter died, shutting himself away and turning the tenants out of the cottages. He allowed the trees and shrubs to grow wild and every gate and building was locked, the keys hung up in order over the fireplace in the kitchen in V formation so any missing would be quickly noticed. My father bought the house in 1917.

Nottwood Cottage was empty for some years, the first tenants I remember were a Mr and Mrs Fox. He was a charcoal burner working close by in Blaisdon woods and previously living in a horse drawn caravan. The next tenant was Mr Clayson and his 3 sons, Harry, Cyril and Ted and daughter May. He was a baker at Bradleys bake house. After a while he asked if they could move down to

Rose Tree Cottage and he married his housekeeper. Then there was Mr and Mrs Goodyear, Ivy and Jim Marshall, followed by Nellie Marshall. At one time Ivor Jones, uncle to Oscar Jones, and his wife lived there."

Molly Hopkins, who lived to be 97.
A wonderful lady, full of fun and always with a smile.

MOUNT HOUSE

The Mount House is a stone farmhouse perched atop Nottwood Hill, built around 1780 and then extended in 1807 according to its date stone. Long before Henry Crawshay's time it had been owned by Blaisdon Manor and leased out. In the 1930s when the Blaisdon Estate was being sold, The Mount House was bought by the Pithouse family and remained in their ownership until it was sold following Albert's death in 1981.

Above & below: Mount House showing the later extension.

The Pithouse family lived there from the latter part of the 19th century. William Harry Pithouse was an employee of the Blaisdon Estate for over 40 years. He died, aged 77, in 1938 and is buried in Blaisdon churchyard. He and his wife, Jane, had 13 children, Annie, Harry, Fred, Dorothy, Judy, Olive, Reg, Wyburn, Ivor, Ruth, Albert, Edward (Ted), and Ivy.

Stone inscribed:
J A
//
1807.

Harry & Jane Pithouse with 9 of their children.
L-R back row: Ruth, Ivor, Annie, Reg, Dorothy.
L-R middle row; Olive, Harry, Jane, Dolly Dowding.
L-R front row: Albert, Ted, Ivy.
(J. Reid)

1

2

3

1. William Pithouse (Harry).
2. Mr & Mrs Bullock, parents of Jane Pithouse.
3. Jane Pithouse.
4. Mary & Jane Pithouse (sisters).
5. Jane & Ted Pithouse, outside Mount House.

4

5

1

3

Albert Pithouse:
1 & 2. In The Grenadier Guards.
3. In his youth.
4. With 3 nieces, Bridget Morley (R) & Joan Wyman giving
Margaret Pithouse a piggy-back.(J. Reid)

2

4

On 3rd February 1899 tragedy struck the family when the clothes of 15 month old Fred caught fire. He had been left in the charge of his 5 year old sister, Annie, whilst their mother was in the orchard gathering firewood. A cry for help brought both parents back to the house together, the burnt clothes were removed, and William Harry Pithouse walked, carrying his young child wrapped in a shawl, to Mitcheldean where the burns were dressed by Dr Searanche. Sadly, the child died from his burns 5 days later.

Ivy, the youngest child, married Jim Marshall and they lived in Rose Cottage on Nottwood Hill. Albert and Ted remained bachelors and lived together at the Mount until Ted died. The other siblings married, some staying in and around the area, others moved further afield. Albert, who was the owner of the Mount House, continued to live there until 3 years prior to his death, apart from the time he spent in the Grenadier Guards.

Three years before he died, Albert was involved in a road accident. The vehicle he was travelling in rolled over and he banged his head. A month later he was in The Red Hart at Blaisdon when he happened to say to Iris, who was landlady at that time, that the previous night he had seen all the spectrum of the rainbow in his eye and then it went black and he couldn't see out of it. He refused her offer to take him to see the doctor and went off home. Later that day, Iris drove up to the Mount House, having first spoken to the Doctor herself. She found Albert lying on the sofa, and said she had come to take him to the hospital and relayed what the Doctor had said. It took much persuading to get him into her car to go to the hospital, but get him there she did. As suspected, the diagnosis was a detached retina which, if left untreated, would almost certainly have left him blind in one eye. Following a delicate operation and 14 stitches in his eye, the authorities would not allow him to go back home, as he lived alone; they would find him a place where he would be taken care of. Over the many years that Albert had been coming to the Red Hart he had become more like an extended family member and the thought of him going into a home was unthinkable. It was therefore decreed by John and Iris Dunbar that there was 'a room at the Inn' and he would be taken care of there.

This arrangement carried on after he had fully recovered from his operation. He slept at the pub and ate his main meal there. During the day he returned to Nottwood Hill to attend to his animals and go about whatever business he had to do, returning each night to the pub to eat and sleep until one night in September 1981 this arrangement came to an end. Albert had come 'home'. He had eaten his meal and was ready for bed. He usually sang as he walked the length of the landing to his room at the far end, this night was no different. He shouted 'night John, night I,' as he called Iris, and went along the landing singing as usual. As he got to his door he had just reached the words, 'And I shan't see me darlin' any more.'

Albert died during the night in the place where years before he had said he would like to be when his time came, at The Red Hart Inn at Blaisdon.

Albert was a much loved local character, who left all who knew him with many fond and amusing memories. There follows a selection of writing about Albert.

The following tribute was written by **Humphrey Phelps** following the death of Albert and is reproduced here with his permission. When it was written, he entitled it:

A Tribute to the Forest Falstaff.

"Without any intimation that he was leaving us, Albert Pithouse died on Thursday, 10th September, 1981, in his seventieth year, and our world became a poorer and drabber place.

Albert was, as we all knew and had said many times, 'a character.' How little, and yet how much, that meant; all of us are characters, big or small, but he was the best and greatest we have ever known or will ever know. There will never be another like Albert, yet he is timeless; Shakespeare called him Falstaff, Dickens called him Sam Weller. We called him Albert, always Albert, never Bert, or Mr Pithouse.

He had the gift to turn the world around him to merriment. His quick wit brought forth an apt reply in any situation and laughter. His humour was the cause of humour in others, and men, women and children loved him; the man was fascinating, we could not help but love him, and if there was any who did not, it was a sign that they had some serious defect, and were best avoided.

Albert lived in the house on the top of Nottwood Hill in the parish of Blaisdon, and on his few acres he grew Blaisdon plums and kept sheep. Before, and during, the war he had been in the Guards, and when the fighting was over he decided, as he once told me, 'to live by my wits and call no man master.'

He would give a hand with haymaking or harvesting, or lay a hedge in the winter, but he was still his own master. In this, he was in the old tradition of a bold peasantry; he worked when he wanted to, not when someone ordered him. And if he had a good year with his plums and sheep, well, why work at all, when he had sufficient to see him through the winter?

Albert loved cider, and a pub he found the most congenial of places; there can be few in Gloucestershire he has not visited. 'For abstinent virtues I care not a damn.' How well that poem of F. W. Harvey's fitted him. He will be sorely missed by his many friends throughout the county, but he will not be forgotten, and death cannot quench his personality

He was a big, strong, handsome man, but my faltering pen cannot do justice to his personality, that gusto and charm we all found so invigorating and endearing, or the delight we found in his company. A boon companion, friend and philosopher, a man of compassion and courage: that was Albert, and his death leaves me with a deep sense of loss; a loss tempered, though, with the merriment he gave, and will give me, until I, too, am dust."

The following 'In Memoriam' was sent to Albert's family shortly after he died by **Mrs Anne Waites** of Bradford:

"For forty years I had known dear and loveable Albert Pithouse, through a wartime friendship with my brother Gordon, who died in 1943, serving in the same regiment of Guards together. Albert was a constant friend to all members of our family, and now your loss is our loss too. My prayers for the repose of Albert's soul, now safe in

God's tender keeping. My love and sincere regards to Ivy and family."

David Kibble wrote in 2001 of a cricket match between his team, Flaxley, and local farmers:

" I happened to be bowling when one Albert Pithouse strode to the wicket, an imposing figure wearing a single pad. He detoured to the bowler's end and demanded, 'Yer, ol butt, doesn't thee get bowlin' fast mind.' I found this rather amusing, as my deliveries were slow spin.

In the spirit of the game, I bowled him a full toss. His hearty swing, however, did not result in the majestic sound of leather on willow and his middle stump went back. 'You young b*****,' echoed round the ground. However, local rules were that farmers could not be out first ball and the sport continued.

About 10 years later, some friends and I visited the Red Hart Pub in Blaisdon, which was Albert's local. We were viewed with great suspicion by the locals, but not by Albert. He smiled wryly and winked at his mate and I knew what he was thinking. After a while, he nudged up to me and whispered, 'Yer, I da know thee don't I? You're the young b***** who bowled me out at that cricket match.'

1

Jane Pithouse:
1. With Reg Pithouse & Bimbo, the dog.
2. With Rosemary O'Hara & David Marshall.
3. In her garden.

2

3

Behind Mount House.
Back Row: Ted Pithouse, Jim Marshall, Albert Pithouse, Sam Bullock, Jane Pithouse.
Front Row: ?, ?, ?, Ivy Pithouse.
(J. Reid)

NOTTWOOD FOLK

2

3

1

1. L-R: ?, Oscar Jones Snr, Tom Green. (S. Jones)
2. Young Ladies on Nottwood Hill, occasion unknown:
Majorie Westley (6th fm right), Becky & Dolly (2nd, 3rd fm left).
(C. Jones)
3. Lady & children on horse, possibly members of Catherine Jones
family. (C. Jones)

1

2

3

4

5

1. Blowey Bullock.

2. L-R: Tommy Davis (Roughleaze)
Sarah Angove (Rose Tree Cottage)
Mark Hopkins (The Mount).

3. Mark Pitt enjoying a game.

4. Blowey Bullock with horse & cart at railway
sidings. (M. Beard)

5. Lawrence Stanton, Christopher Green and
Mark Pitt,
on the summit of Nottwood Hill.
(L Stanton)

FETES

Fetes were and continue to be a major event in the village. They are an opportunity for everybody to get together, have fun and raise much-needed funds for the upkeep of the church and village hall. The photos on these pages reflect that element of fun and show various fetes held in the village during the 1950s.

Top: Fancy Dress prizewinners: Maureen Blake, Barbara Watts, Susan Evans.

Left: Opening the fete is Mrs Gowthorpe (?). Others present include:

Bertie Buckett, Rev. Dennis Lane, Vera Jones, Marjorie Jones, Mrs Etherington, Susan Young, Mr Pickering with Judith, Elizabeth Etherington, Susan Cox, Mrs Board, Joe Martin, Mrs Bobbie Young, Mr & Mrs Angove, Janet Hayward.

Right: Susan Evans (obscured), Anita Martin, Elizabeth Etherington, Susan Young, Barbara Watts, Heather Martin, Jane Martin, Maureen Blake, Margaret Hogg.

1

2

3

4

5

1. Rev. Dennis Lane bowling for a pig.
Mr George Beard on the right.

2. Biddy Keating, Mark Hopkins, Judith Pickering, Patricia Angove, Rev. Dennis Lane.

3. Photo includes: Mrs Martin, Mary King, Brenda Davis, Norman Penny, Mrs Hopkins.
Headmistress, Mrs Smith, at the piano.
Carnival boy, Mark Hopkins.

4. Photo includes: Diane Smith, Heather Martin, Maureen Blake, Anne Daysh, Valerie
Keyse, Graham Keyse, Mrs Watts, Ronald Martin, Honor Larner.

5. Dancers: Sylvia Price, Anne Daysh, Margaret Hogg, Doreen Jones, Valerie Keyse,
Susan Young, Elizabeth Etherington.

CORONATION DAY 1953

1. Elizabeth Etherington as 'Cover Girl.'
2. Iris Hogg & Doris Bowkett as Dutch Boy & Girl.
3. Coronation Day 1953 at Flaxley Abbey.
Scotland: Sylvia Price.   England: Elizabeth Etherington.
Britannia: Susan Young.
Wales: Margaret Green.   Ireland: Susan Cox.
4. Procession of Queens & Maids.
5. & 6. In the grounds of Flaxley Abbey.

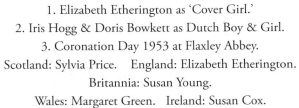

MOTHERS' UNION

The Mothers' Union is an International Christian Society that seeks to support families worldwide. It challenges root causes of injustice and works for better conditions in society for children and families. A diverse range of programmes meets the needs of people within local communities, from training and health education to gifts for children.

The Blaisdon Branch of The Mothers' Union opened on 18th January 1950 at Iona, the home of Mrs E. Hayward. When numbers dwindled, the ladies would get on their bikes and join in with the Flaxley Branch. It is not certain when the Blaisdon Branch closed but the banner still sits in the Chancel of St Michael's Church.

Top:
MU members at Flaxley, including:
Mrs Young, Nellie Watts, Phyllis Coopey & child,
Barbara Griffiths, Nancy Young, Elsie Hogg, Dinah
Etherington, Rose Young, Mrs Willie, Mrs Beryl Keyse
& Sheila.
(July 1965)
Left: MU Banner.
Right: Dinah Etherington's membership certificate,
signed by Mary Lane.

392

WOMEN'S INSTITUTE

North Deanery MU Rally at Westbury-on-Severn, 2nd June 1960.
Mrs Jayne, Mrs Warren, Mrs Elsie Hogg, Mrs W. Jones, Mrs O. Jones.

An extract from the speech given by **Mrs Patricia Manners** at the 40th birthday celebration of the Blaisdon Women's Institute, held on 26th April 2003:

'I never dreamt 40 years ago when I was involved in setting up this W.I. that we would still be living in this village now. We came here temporarily! It is a great honour to be asked to be with you and I am so glad that I can be here. I read from the Minutes of 27th March 1963 that a resolution was proposed by Patricia Manners and seconded by Alice Hyett, that a W.I. should be formed in Blaisdon.

Committee members were: Isobel Back, President, Sheila Daniell, Mrs Day, Mrs Humphries, Mrs Janes, Mrs Billie Jones, Mrs Ivor Jones, Mrs Keating, Ada Keyse, Mrs Martin, Mrs Phelps, Margaret Pickering, Mrs Redpath, Miss Rees, Mrs Smith, Mrs Townsend and Mrs Warren. All very familiar names to this village though sadly only 4 of us are still here.

The first meeting was on 6th May 1963; annual subs were 5/- (25p). And so, Blaisdon W.I. was born. With the closure of the village school and its purchase to use as a village hall, there was now a permanent home for the W.I.

and for many other village activities - Fetes, Dancing and Music classes, Harvest Supper etc.

It is interesting to note that the first W.I. was started in Ontario, Canada in 1897 to provide 'an opportunity for isolated women to meet together to learn about home economics, childcare, jobs on the farm,' and in September 1915 the first one was formed in this country, actually in Llanfawpwll, in Wales.

It is worth remembering that even in 1963 the women in this village hardly left the village, except for one trip a week to Gloucester. Life revolved around their families and the village. The W.I. provided a useful opportunity to learn new skills, to promote community spirit and perhaps most importantly, to broaden our horizons.

I have been fascinated to read in the Minutes books of

the vast diversity of subjects you have had talks on, cooking, cake icing, gardens, countryside matters, travel talks, but also social topics, drug abuse, community health, crime prevention, osteoporosis, Sue Ryder Home, Local History, British Council and also Laughing at Life, a talk on Fish and Decorating goose eggs! I remember well the slight stir caused when I suggested we should have a talk on mental health and another on cancer in the days before it was a mentionable subject. As well as all the interesting talks there have been a variety of excellent outings and theatre visits and obviously all enjoyed sharing these moments.

So you see, it is no longer Jam and Jerusalem and there are great opportunities to indulge in a huge diversity of interests and abilities involving the modern, articulate, educated and independent woman, as well as to promote the traditional skills of women.

It is so good to note that the membership of Blaisdon W.I. has been extraordinarily consistent over the 40 years and this surely says much for the organization and astuteness of your Committee and Presidents.

And so it is with the greatest pleasure that I congratulate you on not only surviving but flourishing over the last 40 years and I hope you will all join me in drinking the health of Blaisdon W.I. and wishing it every possible success in the years to come."

In 2009, due to falling numbers it was no longer viable to keep Blaisdon W.I. going and the remaining members have now joined forces with Longhope W.I.

Blaisdon Women's Institute Banner, Hanging in St Michael's Church.

DOCTORS & NURSES

Various Doctors served Blaisdon during the 1940s and 1950s. There was Dr Searanche from either Huntley or Mitcheldean, Dr Selby from Newnham, Dr Wright from Westbury, and from Mitcheldean we had Dr Pauli and the much loved Dr Parsons.

The County was divided up into small Regional Nursing Associations. The Blaisdon, Flaxley and Longhope Association of Nurses and Midwives was based in Blaisdon. Nurse Gilbert lived in an extension built on the side of Home Farm (Spout Farm) and later, after the sale of the Estate her successor, Nurse Coney, lived opposite The Gardens (Blaisdon Nurseries).

Dr Parsons has written his memories of life as a Doctor in and around Blaisdon:

"I became Dr Pauli's partner on 1st July 1955, in place of Dr Tommy Hope, who went to Hong Kong in the hope of becoming a consultant, and one of the conditions of my partnership was that I would undertake all the Obstetric work, which Dr Pauli did not much like, and in which I had a good grounding. However, he was quite ready to come out and give an open Chloroform anaesthetic if I wanted to do a forceps delivery!

Dr K. C. Parsons.
General Practitioner to Blaisdon area, based at Mitcheldean Surgery, from 1955 to 1987.

In those days Blaisdon folk had the choice of Dr Wright's practice in Westbury or ours in Mitcheldean, both practices holding branch surgeries in Huntley Cottages. In those days the railways were still running, and it was possible to catch a train to Longhope, where we also held a branch surgery next-door to Bonnie's Café and then catch a train back to Blaisdon afterwards. We used to leave prescribed medicines at the branch surgeries, or sometimes at the post office to be delivered by a willing postman.

The Salesian school at Blaisdon Hall was still active, and it fell to me, the Junior Partner to examine all the boys in the Autumn term on behalf of the local authorities who had placed them there. The 'pro forma' I had to complete, asked specifically, amongst other things, to examine each for the presence of a hernia. This required asking each boy to cough while palpating his groin. I cannot remember ever finding a hernia, but it earned me the name of 'Dr Cough,' and on other occasions when I visited to attend the sick or injured, if the boys were out and about in the grounds, they all began to cough!

I remember visiting various people in Blaisdon. There was Mrs Brown at Vectis and I saw her dishing out stew to her large family of healthy looking children around the large dining table. I often went to see Mr and Mrs Keyse at the nursery and admired his magnificent Dahlias. I also oversaw the delivery of their son, Aubrey. I visited Mr. Cedric Etherington, and hearing all about Blaisdon Conqueror's horseshoes, which were as big as dinner plates! Visiting Mrs Buckett and her son at Keeper's Cottage involved a lengthy walk over a couple of fields. I visited Mrs Board at Brickhouse Farm regularly, and remember her lovely old Labrador in his final illness, when he expired

at the foot of the stairs gazing upwards. I remember Mr and Mrs Magee too, and was saddened by the tragic loss of their son.

There was a near tragedy in the Mill stream once: I did a mad dash down from May Hill where we were living then; it was a Sunday, I believe, but by the time I got there the small child had been rescued from the stream and resuscitated.

I have been retired for 22 years, and can hardly believe it. Medicine had always been my main ambition until I witnessed the bombing of Newport and volunteered for flying duties in the RAF After demob in 1946 I applied for entry to Cardiff Medical School, and qualified in 1952. We were welcomed by a fourth year student who was the vice chairman of the Medical Students club who made a special mention of returning ex-servicemen. I married her three years later."

In the days before antibiotics, children who contracted contagious diseases were sent to isolation hospitals at either the Wilderness Hospital above Plump Hill, Mitcheldean, Over Hospital, at Over, or to Standish Hospital near Stonehouse. This was a traumatic and very frightening experience for a young child to be taken away from their home and family.

Josephine Warlow remembers being sent to the Wilderness Isolation Hospital when she contracted scarlet fever and says she was terrified being left there alone and not knowing when or if she would return home. She was aged 8 and living at Blaisdon Nurseries at the time of her illness. She says she spent 6 to 8 weeks in hospital. She remembers lying in her hospital bed and the sun by day and moon by night shining through the trees making patterns on the walls, which at night often frightened her. She was visited regularly by her family and recalls in particular being given a pair of pink slipper boots. She also remembers having to drink half a mug of liquorice from a white mug as part of her treatment.

Six of the Brown children from Vectis were taken ill at the same time with yellow jaundice and were all sent to Over Hospital. This was something of a phenomenon for six members of one family to all be in hospital at the same time with the same illness. Colin Brown recalls they were in hospital for 4 weeks and because of that he lost a whole term of his schooling due to the illness.

Heather Martin was sent to Standish Hospital after contracting tuberculosis possibly caught from drinking the milk from cows belonging to her grandmother, Mrs Godwin. She was 6 or 7 years old at the time and spent 6 months in hospital. She, together with other children who were hospitalised there, received school lessons at the hospital school. The bus to Standish ran twice weekly and because of this she was only able to see her family twice a week. These visits were very traumatic and unsettling for Heather. Her sister Anita recalls that when they had to leave her, Heather had to be held down to prevent her from running after them. Indeed, on several occasions Heather and another child she became friends with hid on one of the buses in an attempt to get away from the hospital but were found and returned to the ward before they could make good their escape!

Dr K. Pauli,
GP from 1945 to 1972.

HARVEY'S ACRE

Harvey's Acre is situated in the field behind The Old Rectory and Spout farm. It was the playing field for the village and was frequently used to play all sorts of sports. In the days of Blaisdon Estate, tennis courts were laid out and also a bowling green. Blaisdon Cricket Team played there, as did the village football team. The pavilion they used still survives. After the 2nd World War, Blaisdon no longer had its own cricket team, though some, such as Cedric Etherington, played for neighbouring Flaxley. The Salesians also used it for their sports, including their Sports Days.

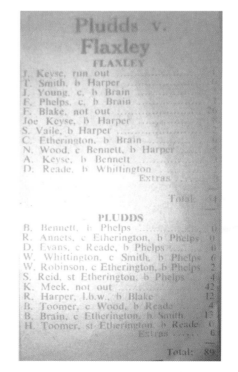

Top: The Pavilion.
Left:
Cedric Etherington on a bench from
Lord's Cricket Ground.
Right:
Scorecard of a match involving
Cedric.

Pludds v. Flaxley

FLAXLEY
J. Keyse, run out
T. Smith, b Harper
J. Young, c b Brain
F. Phelps, c, b Brain
F. Blake, not out
Joe Keyse, b Harper
S. Vaile, b Harper
C. Etherington, b Brain
N. Wood, c Bennett, b Harper
A. Keyse, b Bennett
D. Reade, b Whittington
Extras

Total

PLUDDS
B. Bennett, b Phelps
R. Annets, c Etherington, b Phelps 0
D. Evans, c Reade, b Phelps 0
W. Whittington, c Smith, b Phelps 6
W. Robinson, c Etherington, b Phelps
S. Reid, st Etherington, b Phelps 4
K. Meek, not out 42
R. Harper, l.b.w., b Blake 12
B. Toomer, c Wood, b Reade 4
B. Brain, c Etherington, b Smith 13
H. Toomer, st Etherington, b Reade
Extras 6

Total: 89

Michael Jones recalls playing on Harvey's Acre:

"I especially remember the football and cricket matches there, either watching or, when I was older, playing. From about 1943 to 1950, the main football matches were the Salesian Brothers versus the Italian POWs from Newent. The POWs brought busloads to watch the matches. The other games were The Salesians versus The Rest, which comprised Old Hall Boys with a few villagers, such as my father, Percy Jones. Later a few games were played against Popes Hill.

Cricket matches were between the Brothers versus The Rest. Cedric Etherington played in several games, as did my dad. Occasionally, there were games against Grange Court or Longhope.

Matches were played on a Sunday, which caused a few eyebrows to be raised at first. There were even a few objections. Those feelings, however, were gradually overcome and locals accepted and even looked forward to the games."

Top:
Blaisdon Tennis Club members.
L-R. Mr Moss, Mary Harvey, Jack West, Marjorie Bullet, Sue Harvey, Harold Harvey, W. West, Frances Knight, ?.

Left:
Salesian School Sports Day.
Fr Rector Wrangham presenting prizes with Fr Rogers behind.
(T. Brady)

399

Oratory Football Teams. c1950s.

Above:
Back Row; Bro. Pat McGrath, Gerald Wyman, John Dowding, ?, ?, ?, Bro. John Booth.
Front Row: Andrew Ashcroft, Michael Keyse, 'Dongo' Marshall, Jimmy Grace, Roger Etherington, Don Marshall.

Right:
Back Row: Bro. Frank Treanor, ?, ?, Fr T Hall, Joe Milanta, John Keating, Fr Maguire.
Front Row: Tony Kibble, Kevin Keating, Phillip Jones, Owen Kibble, Michael Jones, P. Wyman, Eric Weeks.

Above Right:
Boys away at camp (1947).

Above:
Back Row: ?, John Keating, Oscar Jones, Mr Percy Jones, Phillip Jones, Pep Milanta.
Middle row: Jimmy Grace, John Dowding, Tony Kibble, Michael Jones, Kevin Keating.
Front Row: Peter Grace, Michael Keyse, Freddy Grace, Roger Etherington, Anthony Jones.

Left:
Back Row: Oscar Jones, Richard Ashcroft, ?, John Dowding, Tony Kibble. Standing: Michael Keating.
Front Row: John Keating, Kevin Keating, Michael Jones, ?, Phillip Jones.
Brothers thought to be John Connolly, Martin Daley & Michael Brazel.

Above Left:
Kevin Keating, Ashcroft, Tony Kibble & 'Digger' Ellam (1947).

BLAISDON GIRLS & BOYS

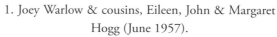

1. Joey Warlow & cousins, Eileen, John & Margaret Hogg (June 1957).
2. Margaret Hogg bathing her dolls (August 1949).
3. Susan Young & Joey Warlow.
4. L-R: Iris Daniell, Pep Malanta, Ursula Howells, Eric Weeks, Sheila Daniell.
   In Front: Betty Howells & Doris Bowkett.
5. Elizabeth Etherington & Judy the dog.
6. Iris Hogg off to catch the train.
7. Elizabeth Etherington, waiting for Margaret.
8. Margaret setting off to catch the bus to school.

PLAYS & A QUEEN

27th January, 1951

THE BLAISDON PLAYERS
will present

Uncle John from Yorkshire
and

Too Many Brides

Including Popular Songs

BLAISDON SCHOOLROOM

Commencing at 7.30 p.m.

TICKETS 1/6. (Children half price)

As well as the Social Evenings at the village school, 'Blaisdon Players' was formed in the 1950s. The more adventurous members of the community were keen to show off their acting skills, while others joined under pressure. A local newspaper thought one such occasion, in 1951, merited a report:

Queen Mary.

'Too Many Brides' at Blaisdon.

The newly formed Blaisdon Players presented two sketches at a concert given in the schoolroom. They were entitled 'Too Many Brides' and 'Uncle John from Yorkshire.'

The Producer was Mr J. Chiswell and those taking part were Mr and Mrs John Hayward, Mr C. Etherington, Mr H. J. Buckett, Mr Phillip Jones, Mrs J. Smith and Miss Ursula Howells.

The Rector, the Rev. D. C. Lane sang during the interval accompanied by Mrs M. Lane at the piano.

There is a village legend that Queen Mary, wife of George V, passed through Blaisdon and one or two people have mentioned seeing Her Majesty as the car passed down Blaisdon Lane. It is known that she stayed at Highnam Court and also paid visits to the Newent Land Settlement, dined at Flaxley Abbey with the Honourable Crawley-Boeveys, and also went to the Dilke Memorial Hospital in the Forest. It can be concluded therefore that Queen Mary did in fact drive through Blaisdon and, hopefully, enjoyed its pleasant lanes as, hopefully, you have enjoyed these memories of Blaisdon's bygone years.

FINALLY

This is, hopefully, just the start of the story of Blaisdon. There are almost another 50 years of memories waiting to be told, to bring the story up to date, as well as of the centuries before.

If you have memories, documents or photographs relating to Blaisdon and would be willing to share them, please contact us. The address and email is on page iv at the front of the book.

Thank you, in anticipation.

Stephen Waters

INDEX